PRECARIOUS PARTNERS

ANIMAL LIVES

Jane C. Desmond, Series Editor; Barbara J. King, Associate Editor for Science; Kim Marra, Associate Editor

BOOKS IN THE SERIES

Displaying Death and Animating Life: Human-Animal Relations in Art, Science, and Everyday Life
by Jane C. Desmond

Voracious Science and Vulnerable Animals: A Primate Scientist's Ethical Journey
by John P. Gluck

The Great Cat and Dog Massacre: The Real Story of World War Two's Unknown Tragedy
by Hilda Kean

Animal Intimacies: Interspecies Relatedness in India's Central Himalayas
by Radhika Govindrajan

Minor Creatures: Persons, Animals, and the Victorian Novel
by Ivan Kreilkamp

Equestrian Cultures: Horses, Human Society, and the Discourse of Modernity
by Kristen Guest and Monica Mattfeld

PRECARIOUS PARTNERS

Horses and Their Humans in Nineteenth-Century France

KARI WEIL

THE UNIVERSITY OF CHICAGO PRESS
CHICAGO AND LONDON

The University of Chicago Press, Chicago 60637
The University of Chicago Press, Ltd., London

Published 2020
Printed in the United States of America

29 28 27 26 25 24 23 22 21 20   1 2 3 4 5

ISBN-13: 978-0-226-68623-3 (cloth)
ISBN-13: 978-0-226-68637-0 (paper)
ISBN-13: 978-0-226-68640-0 (e-book)
DOI: https://doi.org/10.7208/chicago/9780226686400.001.0001

Library of Congress Cataloging-in-Publication Data

Names: Weil, Kari, author.
Title: Precarious partners : horses and their humans in nineteenth-century France / Kari Weil.
Other titles: Animal lives (University of Chicago Press)
Description: Chicago : The University of Chicago Press, 2020. | Series: Animal lives | Includes bibliographical references and index.
Identifiers: LCCN 2019031493 | ISBN 9780226686233 (cloth) | ISBN 9780226686370 (paperback) | ISBN 9780226686400 (ebook)
Subjects: LCSH: Horses—France—History—19th century. | Horses—Social aspects—France. | Human-animal relationships—France—History—19th century. | Animals and civilization—France.
Classification: LCC SF284.F7 W45 2020 | DDC 636.10944—dc23
LC record available at https://lccn.loc.gov/2019031493

♾ This paper meets the requirements of ANSI/NISO Z39.48-1992 (Permanence of Paper).

In memory of Holly

CONTENTS

PREFACE

I started work on this book over twenty years ago. It grew out of research for my first book, which dealt with notions of androgyny and representations of changing or ambiguous gender in French, German, and British literary works of the nineteenth and early twentieth centuries. I was struck by French women who were described as "cross-dressing" in order to work with horses and ride astride—much to the shock of their contemporaries. Horses, I understood, offered one perspective into the massive changes in gender relations, but also in class and race relations, that were taking place during the nineteenth century. Or that was how my more established colleagues encouraged me to see the value of my research. But for me there was more in it. As a rider and lifelong lover of horses, I was also interested in them for their own sake. I wanted to understand the kinds of relations people had with horses, whether on the ground or in the saddle. I feared, however, that studying animals in this way not only was unconventional but also risked being dismissed as sentimental and unworthy of an academic. The field of animal studies did not yet exist. Its emergence and growth over the past fifteen years or so have had an enormous influence on this work, not only by making me believe in the importance and relevance of my topic, but also by bringing me to consider emerging debates about animal agency and consciousness, about the politics and ethics surrounding "companion species," and about the significance of our joint bonds—then and now.[1] Indeed, I had hoped to catch some glimpse or insight into what might have been a horse's own point of view two centuries ago, but in this effort I was stymied by a dearth of source materials, by fear of my own projections, and by my ignorance of how to locate the traces of that viewpoint other than in the effects reported by a horse's human.

When I first presented some of my work at an animal studies conference (not the French and comparative literature conferences I had mostly attended), another presenter, a political philosopher, asked how I could in good conscience ride horses. Isn't it comparable to slaveholding, he asked, the horse's bit another kind of shackles? I understood where the question was coming from, having familiarized myself with animal abolitionist arguments, but I felt unprepared to answer. I could have said I believed some horses (not all) like being ridden and enjoy the partnership they experience with a rider. Riding is also one way we humans can get to know the personality and individuality of a particular horse (and vice versa). At the same time, a statement of Jean-Jacques Rousseau's came to mind. "It is neither for slaves nor for tamed horses to reason about freedom," for they know only their "broken" state. "The untamed steed bristles its mane, stamps the ground with its hoof, and struggles impetuously at the sight of the bit."[2] Although horses or other domestic animals may not choose it, I believe that some form of training (or education) can give them a means of communicating with humans and in some instances may protect them from far worse fates like slaughter. This, of course, is not always the case, but as I have argued elsewhere, if "abolitionism" in the animal rights movement means simply allowing all domestic animals to perish, we can and must find better alternatives.[3]

Sometime after that conference I put aside my horse book to pursue different and often more theoretical questions raised by my readings and collaborations in animal studies. This pursuit was aided by my move from French departments to programs that promoted more interdisciplinary study, first at the California College of Art and then at Wesleyan University. In my classes and my research for my previous book, *Thinking Animals: Why Animal Studies Now?*, I turned to twentieth- and twenty-first-century literature, art, and theory that zeroed in on knotty issues of animal ethics but also looked deeply into problems of language and representation and the dangers of anthropomorphism and anthropocentrism. When I returned to research on horses in nineteenth-century France, these issues presented themselves in new and often unforeseen ways, even as my focus was contained within a more specific historical and geographical context that was largely absent from *Thinking Animals*. Nevertheless, as I was finishing the manuscript I was surprised to find how relevant many of the issues continue to be.

To be sure, horses are no longer central to daily life as they were in the nineteenth century, but the contest over who or what they are and who and what they and their image serve continues to be waged in ways that reflect ongoing social, sexual, political, and ethical issues. Just last summer the University of Wyoming released its new marketing campaign with the slogan "the world needs more cowboys." Faculty protested because of the cowboy's "white, macho" image, and Native Americans on campus joined in, saying that for them "'cowboys' holds a negative connotation."[4] Race was also at issue last summer, when the town of Charlottesville, Virginia, witnessed one of the largest protests in its history in reaction to the potential removal of the statue of a "man on horseback," Robert E. Lee, the Confederacy's top general.[5] Those who favored removal saw the statue as a monument to white supremacy. Those who opposed removal accused the other side of wanting to erase history—a history, we can assume, of white men riding high on their horses to rule over those able (or authorized) to move only on foot. In the aftermath of several such protests, Roy Moore, the Republican Senate candidate from Alabama, rode his horse to the voting booth in a clear attempt to prove that the good old southern cowboy of yesteryear was alive and well. Moore's Senate run was foiled not only because of his racism, but also because he sexually assaulted underage girls. Social media turned this into satire as Moore's horse, Sassy, claimed #MeToo on her own Twitter feed.

Although he is no horseman himself, President Trump's character and legal standing have been visibly shaken by a young equestrienne and porn star known as Stormy Daniels, with whom he allegedly had a sexual encounter. As Daniels continues to contest a restraining order that forbids her to speak publicly about the affair, she also takes pride in her growing visibility and especially her appearance in X-rated films with her new Irish stud.[6] In this, she may remind us of the strong-willed and crafty nineteenth-century actress Adah Menken, who became famous for riding onstage in a sheer costume and attracting the gaze of a line of suitors. Adah was a new breed of woman rider who contributed to the slow demise of the European image of the "man on horseback," one that depended on associations not only of gender, but also of aristocracy and hence of race. Adah was American, barely middle class, and Jewish.

The popularity of equestriennes like Stormy and Adah, however, has done little to soften the association of horse ownership with the upper classes, if not with the dangerous carelessness attributed to excessive privilege. In our previous presidential election, stories circulated about a certain "stunningly elegant" $100,000 dressage mare owned by Mitt Romney's wife, the potential first lady. Connecting her and her husband with the "blue-blooded sport often associated with kings," the mare furthered what comedian Stephen Colbert called Romney's "privileged princeling image."[7] More troubling was the news that the mare was to be ridden in the Olympics by a trainer who had been sued for fraud after selling a horse without disclosing its severe foot problem. Stunning elegance was a cover for sleazy abuse.

Government attention to animal abuse dates back to the nineteenth century, but government agencies in the United States today seem to be doing their best to obscure their responsibility for the animals in their care. Under the Trump administration, the Department of Agriculture has removed reports of abuse from its website. Wild horses in particular are viewed much like immigrants who have overrun, if not infested, American land and need to be controlled. In April the Bureau of Land Management released its plan for the "management" of wild horses, which can include not only removing them from the range but also killing up to 100,000 of them or selling them for slaughter.[8] Largely because of their symbolic value (and for reasons that were debated in nineteenth-century France), Americans have traditionally resisted slaughtering horses for food, but this has not stopped the government from lifting restrictions preventing the sale of American mustangs to horsemeat dealers who sell to Canada and Mexico.[9] Although Americans won't eat horsemeat, we believe it's good enough for our neighbors.

On stage and in films, audiences have been introduced to the noble horse as comrade and companion, brave if also suffering. Of the three deaths in Joe Wright's 2012 film version of *Anna Karenina*, only that of the horse features a drawn-out shot of a body writhing in pain. The other two deaths are instantaneous. In Nick Stafford's magnificent stage adaption of *War Horse*, where life-size, Deborah Butterfield–style puppets perform with the elegance and sensitivity of the real thing, and in Steven Spielberg's epic film of the same title, the focus is less on the systematic wrongs of the horse world than on the wrongs that have resulted from the entanglement of horse life and human life. We send horses to do our bidding, riding them into violent combat where they are often left to die alone on the battlefield. *War Horse* is also the story of a boy's love for his horse and of whatever might be the horse's equivalent of love for the boy. Our media and our society have surely traveled a long distance from the Cartesian tradition of the animal as a machine that feels no pain and cannot suffer because it has no consciousness. Horses make news or entertainment because they do suffer, and it is their suffering that is meant to move readers and viewers to sympathize, if not to prevent their abuse. Similar campaigns to raise awareness of the abuses inflicted on horses, not only on the battlefield but also on the street, led to the establishment of the first SPCAs and to anticruelty laws in England, France, and the United States. But just as the Romney family was criticized for giving its horse better health care than many Americans could afford, in the nineteenth century the cause of animal protection would stir class envy and provoke animosity toward the horsey set, who were said to treat their animals better than their workers.

Then as now, horses reveal our intimate, if conflicted, relationships with other animals, including other humans. For some, horses inspire an even greater need to prove our mastery and power and conceal our animal inadequacies. For others, horses remind us of our shared vulnerability and suffering—our need for compassion, to be sure, but also our need for the joyful exuberance we can share with another creature. This is a learned joy, one that develops along with restrictions on freedom for horse and human alike. It entails what we might regard as ethical obligations: I won't try to teach you something you won't like, but you mustn't buck me off. Moreover, because the riding relationship depends on the very senses of touch and feel that have been most disparaged by humanist prejudice, it can challenge the grounds of the human-animal hierarchy and reveal our shortcomings, both physical and intellectual. The bit is evidence of our human dependence on a prosthetic to communicate and to control. We should be grateful to horses for accepting it and our shortcomings.

Is riding merely a form of domination? It certainly can be, but as I hope these essays make clear, it can be much more. Most important, riding is a "becoming with," a way to know another, particular animal and to make oneself vulnerable to being known in return. It is a way that both horse and rider become something and someone new and discover a new joy in partnership.

INTRODUCTION

The Most Beautiful Conquest of Man?

In the middle of the eighteenth century natural historian Georges-Louis Leclerc, Comte de Buffon, declared the horse "the most beautiful conquest man has ever made."[1] By the nineteenth century this description had become so "classic and proverbial" that it was impossible to pronounce the word horse "without immediately inciting, vocally and mentally, the inevitable response of 'the most beautiful conquest.'" Or so claimed Albert Cler, the contemporary chronicler of the horse world.[2] Though the phrase is often understood and translated as "the most *noble* conquest," readers would note a certain irony in Cler's words, which come from his 1842 satirical look at the French horsey set, *The Comedy on Horseback: Fads and Follies of the Equestrian World*. With chapters on the Jockey Club, the races, and the latest mode in carriages, not to mention the new "Sunday riders," Cler's book presents a not so subtle mockery of the nineteenth-century equestrian world, which for him had lost its prerevolutionary associations with grace and nobility. Nostalgic for the aristocratic equestrian sphere and the studied training that had once prepared horses and men together for war, Cler describes the contemporary horseman as a boorish, bourgeois man of fashion who has turned the horse into a moneymaking spectacle for an increasingly crass consumer.

Not everyone agreed with Cler's perspective. Some twenty years later Thomas Couture, painter and teacher of such luminaries as Édouard Manet, offers a very different picture of the public promenade on horseback, one he claims could "equal the merit portraits of the greatest masters, even as it would have a completely new physiognomy."

> On this public promenade, I see a cavalier accompanying a young girl: they are very distinguished. . . . Look at the pretty *costume d'amazone*,

> how it chastely outlines the shape of the upper body. . . . This thoroughbred horse, how he seems proud to carry his mistress. The cavalier's outfit is elegant and simple. . . . I can't help comparing what I see to the portraits left by our masters . . . but I would not hesitate to show my preference for what I see here to admire.[3]

Édouard Manet agreed with Couture, and that very year he included the woman rider or amazon in the middle of his painting of the Universal Exhibition. Indeed, many artists and writers of the time would make men and women on horseback the subject of their paintings and writings, although the "new physiognomy" Couture mentions would be ambiguous in its implications and change greatly during the century.

Horses, I argue in the chapters that follow, came to represent the social and cultural changes taking place during the century following the Revolution. As boundaries between classes and genders became increasingly fluid, the omnipresent horse could represent both what was lost and what was gained. Indeed, men of all classes were confronted with a new and sometimes threatening relationship between women and horses, one hinted at in Couture's reference to the horse's "pride" in carrying "his mistress." Writers and painters turned to horses to illuminate these changes and offer their varied reactions to them. But horses were more than symbolic objects. They were partners and agents in these transformations: prideful, perhaps, but certainly feeling and revealing the effects of change to those who would take time to look at them. Horses in the countryside and in the city, in private and in public life were everyday evidence against Descartes's notion of animals as machines, undermining the supposedly clear boundaries between human and nonhuman. Horses were sensitive, feeling creatures—all the more apparently when they were seen as victims of the very "progress" they made possible. As their labor (and eventually meat) would be regarded as essential for the growth of French industry and culture, so would their "misery" become increasingly evident. But as the suffering of horses seemed comparable to that of the workers who most depended on them for their livelihood, there arose a competition for redress, for justice. Over the course of the century workers would achieve solidarity and make their demands heard, but who would or could speak for the horse?

The question hovers over the very birth of the Republic, when we find horses connected to the expression of new political and moral sentiments that link animal suffering to the suffering of workers and also, as historian Pierre Serna demonstrates, to women's agency and rights of ownership. This becomes evident in a scene reported in *La décade*, the quasi-official journal of the Directory from 1798, that offers an aspect and physiognomy of the horse rather different from the glitzy spectacles described by Cler or the elegance pronounced by Couture. The report describes three horses struggling to pull a loaded wagon until one collapses on the road. At that the driver gets down from his seat and begins violently beating the horses before a critical but passive crowd. Only one woman, a vegetable vendor, takes it upon herself to try to stop the driver. She threatens him with a rock, shouting, "Go on, beat him, I dare you to beat him, you inhuman monster!" While some of the onlookers applaud the woman, one emphatically scolds her, saying she should mind her own business. Since the horse "belongs to the driver," this well-dressed man insists, "the driver has the right to do what he wishes, even to kill him if that is his pleasure."[4]

The actors in the scene are not the glossy thoroughbreds and social climbers Cler described but members of the working class, humans and horses alike. It is a scene of suffering rather than show, and it takes a woman to stop the abuse. "Could there be a silent, unspeakable complicity between the beaten horse and the beating woman? One submissive, the other refusing her submission?" asks Serna.[5] One might remember that early modern marriage manuals compared the obedient wife to a well-broken horse. Not for this woman. Serna notes that the author of the article, who witnessed the scene, was a member of a nascent Republican school of medicine—the veterinary school of Maisons-Alfort—and he questions why it was the woman and not he who intervened. The combination of compassionate witnessing and nonintervention illustrates how the subject of animal suffering or animal sensibility gained traction in conjunction with the idea of a Republic and universal human rights, but it also shows that the path could be conflicted—that the way forward was fraught. Did one have a right to inflict suffering? If so, upon whom and for what cause? How was one to weigh the unspoken, if unspeakable (in human terms), suffering of animals against the rights of workers, whose needs were just beginning to be voiced. How might women finally express their affinity with the beaten horse?

Equestrian culture with its evidence of the "continuity . . . of former aristocratic visions," historian Daniel Roche writes, was only one part of the horse world of the nineteenth century. It was also, he adds, "one of the theaters for the democratic transformation of such representations and manners of seeing and being seen."[6] This theater would increasingly include such scenes of abuse and suffering, leading to the rise of legal protections for horses, but also to methods of hiding infractions from public sight or even turning horse slaughter into a new form of spectacle. Cler ends his own book with a chapter on Montfaucon, the Paris slaughter yards that closed in

1842, which he describes as a theater of another sort. Distinctions between breeds or owners mattered little in this final act, and Cler's contemporary, Théophile Gautier, would paint its colorful repertoire of flesh, blood, and fat into something of a surrealist literary tableau (discussed in more detail in chapter 4). Indeed, one wonders what "regimes" of emotion or affection allowed for a horse's companionship, talent, and affection to sink into oblivion or onto the plate.[7]

Moving between literature, painting, natural philosophy, popular cartoons, sport manuals, and tracts of public hygiene, the essays collected here take readers to this era when horses were an inescapable part of daily life, when owning horses became an increasingly realizable dream even for middle-class (bourgeois) boys and girls, and when the lives and deaths of horses were determined by the complex material circumstances and changing personal and political relations of the humans they depended on. Objects of affection for some (most apparently women), for others they were mere tools of social mobility and expression. When Gustave Flaubert's Emma Bovary dreams of Paris, her hazy vision includes a tableau of men who, "their abilities unappreciated beneath their frivolous exteriors, rode their horses to death for the enjoyment of it."[8]

Once regarded as the privilege of the aristocracy, in the nineteenth century riding was increasingly democratized. People wanted more horses in daily life, and at the same time they felt pressure to display the right horse and the correct riding style. "Fashion wants everybody to learn to ride," wrote the historian of equitation Étienne Saurel. And the popularity of riding led to a rise in equestrian rhetoric, its sexual, class, and racial inflections influenced both by Anglomania and by colonialist attraction to the traffic in the "hot-blooded" horses of the Middle East and North Africa.[9] The novelist Honoré de Balzac frequently noted the attention and prestige an Arabian horse could bring to a man on the move.[10] Although not restricted to men, riding was nevertheless a gendered activity because of its associations with a form of virile mastery and military mobility that was denied to women and because women were required to ride sidesaddle, the position of *amazones*. Men often compared their horses to their women, whether in number or in terms of "breed" or reputation.[11] Horse breeding itself became of national concern during the century, whether for the army or the racetrack or because it informed eugenic practices. Efforts to improve native breeds by importing purebreds from England or Africa would eventually be implicated in a contemporary race discourse that raised fears over the degeneration of the French "race" and concerns about how to ensure the potency and moral standing of its progeny. By the end of the century, the "herd instinct" of humans would be perceived as more threatening to society than its manifestation in any other group of animals. Updating Plato's charioteer in the *Phaedrus*, painted and written representations of horses and their riders expressed anxiety about what breeding and education would produce the noble horse and the correctly embodied mind that would allow the charioteer to guide him properly. The ever-present image and reality of the horse, in other words, would bring new pressure to understand the nature of the human and discover the ways both horses and humans might be better bred and better trained.

The contexts for such changes will be the focus of this introduction, but the essays that follow are not meant to constitute a history of equestrian life or of horses in nineteenth-century France. Instead, through close readings of a range of visual and literary works and practical guides, I will attempt to show how our relations with horses became a focus for articulating changing ideas and manifestations of gender, race, and class and changing attitudes toward nonhuman animals more generally. If Paris became the "capital of the nineteenth century" by virtue of its cultural production and industrial invention, much of this production was assisted by the ever present if mostly unacknowledged strength, intelligence, and compliance of horses. Horses were crucial to humans for their daily chores, their leisure activities, and their self-identities. Many bestowed an image of "nobility" on their owners or offered a new sense of freedom, and most offered a combination of hard labor and devotion even to those who were reluctant to acknowledge it. And if the swept forelock and soft eyes represented in Théodore Géricault's *Head of a White Horse* (plate 1; discussed in chapter 1) are any indication, some horses were there simply to be admired and loved.

CONQUEST FOR WHOM? CLASS, GENDER, AND THE MAN (OR WOMAN) ON HORSEBACK

By all accounts, the nineteenth century and in particular the Second Empire could be called the era of the horse. This was especially true in Paris, the century's capital. Whether on the streets, in the parks, or in the circus, harnessed to a carriage or under saddle, horses were omnipresent in the city both as beasts of burden and as the focus of a dandified public lifestyle that brought the *grand monde* together with the world of entertainment. Horse dung littered the streets, its scent filling the air, a reminder that horses were no longer the exclusive domain of the aristocracy and the military.[12] Napoleon III was a great admirer of horses, and with his encouragement the city of Paris annexed the Bois de Boulogne as a place for riders to exercise and to show off both their athletic talents and their mounts. This democratizing of equestrianism would change the image and meaning of riding and lead to a new understanding of the horse as partner, laborer, and object of admiration and affection. This is not to say that horses' associations with nobility were forgotten. On the contrary, such associations fueled the aspirations of the middle class and inspired the bourgeoisie and even the "demimonde" to imitate the aristocracy. As Rastignac learns in Balzac's *Père Goriot* (1832), in Paris success equaled power, and success for a man required both a woman's attention and travel on horseback or by horse-drawn carriage. How one rode mattered too, as Flaubert reveals in *L'éducation sentimentale*, where Frédéric touts the English manner of riding promoted by the Comte d'Aure while his wealthy friend and rival, the Marquis de Cisy, defends the French methods of dressage advanced by the riding master François Baucher.[13] Toward the end of the Second Empire, as seen in Zola's *La curée*, the inspection of horse-drawn carriages and their accoutrements by curious or jealous onlookers often caused frustrating traffic jams on the city streets.[14] According to the *Almanach illustré du sport*, nobility could be acquired in two ways: "by admission to the Jockey Club" (founded in 1834 in France) "and by the purchase of a carriage made by Ehrler, Thomas Baptiste, or Keller."[15] For this group nobility was less a matter of blood than of money, and its successful appearance could be crowned by owning a *pur-sang*: a "pureblood" or thoroughbred horse. The cost alone made such a horse the privilege of the wealthy, but the significance of the breed was undeniable. According to the popular *Les Français peints par eux-mêmes* (The French according to themselves), "The superstition of the pureblood . . . is more than an axiom; an incontestable theorem, it is a religion, a fanaticism, a fetishism."[16] Well into the nineteenth century, to purchase a thoroughbred was to buy "noble blood."

In the 1753 entry "Le cheval" (The horse) in his *Histoire naturelle* (Natural history), Buffon writes not only of the horse's "natural proportion and elegance" and his "courage in combat," but also of the horse's ability to "repress his movements" and his desires. It is an image that, according to Jacques Roger, mimics the one Buffon holds of himself as an aristocrat.[17] His concept of the horse draws firmly and singularly upon the white horse of Plato's *Phaedrus*, that "noble horse of good breed," "lover of honor with modesty and self-control; companion to true glory" who, partnering with the charioteer, is likened to the soul.[18] Buffon's charioteer must guide his white horse and his own passions toward the ideals of truth and beauty, but his horse shares in this effort. The horse's agency is visible as he willingly cedes his being to the "will of another." A century later, according to Cler, these qualities of character and good breeding have been lost in the age of republicanism when riders know as little about governing either themselves or others as they do about controlling a horse's unpredictable temperament: "After the revolution of '89, the popular classes seized the reins of the state with a strong hand, but they didn't know how to hold the reins of a horse."[19] Cler's antirepublicanism outweighs his knowledge of the horse world, but his words emphasize how the image of the nation itself was intertwined with the image of the man on horseback. The democratizing of this image so that more and more men could see themselves in it was a sign for some of national glory, for others of national decline.

Fier et fougueux—proud and fiery—is how Buffon describes the horse, and it is this second adjective that Napoleon I borrowed when he asked that his portrait depict him "calm on a fiery [*fougueux*] horse."[20] Indeed, the long tradition of equestrian sculpture and portraiture was founded on the notions of nobility, military might, and glory conferred upon the man on horseback who, like Plato's charioteer, could guide his people to victory. Despite Napoleon's wishes, however, after the French Revolution official equestrian portraits seemed less able to convey power.[21] The image of the man on horseback would come face-to-face with its demoted, if not ignoble, counterparts during the course of the century, beginning with Napoleon's defeat, continuing through to his nephew Napoleon III's promotion of pleasure riding, and coming to a climax with the defeat and ignoble retreat of General Georges Boulanger in 1889. Called the "man on horseback," Boulanger came to fame with the message of avenging French losses in the Franco-Prussian War of 1870–71, revitalizing the image of the noble horseman. His political failure was foreshadowed by Emmanuel Frémiet's equestrian sculpture, erected in 1874. The first of its kind, it figured an equestrienne, Joan of Arc. Bearing little relation to the recent war or the men who fought in it, the sculpture figures woman as an allegory—a symbol of courage and victory yet to come.[22]

Joan of Arc is the exceptional woman, as shown by her masculine armor and her riding astride. Women were not allowed in combat roles in France (and still aren't), and they needed legal permission to wear clothing that would allow them to straddle their horses (the law, which was amended in 1892 and 1909 to allow women to ride horses and bicycles, was revoked only in 2013).[23] In Greek mythology the Amazons were women warriors. In nineteenth-century France, *amazone* was the name given to a woman's riding habit and to the woman rider—usually of the upper classes—who rode sidesaddle, a position clearly less suitable for war. Whereas aristocratic women of the eighteenth century were permitted to ride astride, the growing bourgeoisie imposed new gender distinctions, even in the saddle. "Few things, without doubt, better symbolize the extreme concern for sexual difference than the sexed practice of equitation, and this concern carries the mark of the bourgeoisie," writes French historian Gabrielle Houbre.[24] As more and more women took up riding, trainers and health professionals questioned how it might affect a woman's health, her ability to have children, and of course her femininity. Fears regarding just how far riding might produce a "virilization of woman" were countered by strict counsel on her attire, her horse, and the kinds of outings she should engage in. Women must never ride unaccompanied, and they should ride only calm and well-trained horses, "because it is not in the character of the timid and graceful sex to expose herself to wage battle with her horse."[25] So wrote François Baucher, the celebrated riding master and advocate of haute école dressage in his 1833 treatise on equitation. His words were echoed and amplified at the very end of the century in the Baron De Vaux's 1885 book *Les femmes de sport* (Sportswomen) and in the writings of Jules Pellier, chief trainer of the Royal Riding School. Pellier derided the "villainous practice" of women's riding astride under Louis XV and chastised contemporary British women who joined the hunt. "French manners condemn absolutely the usurpation of the masculine role and will not accept that a husband expose his wife to rolling on the ground with her horse like a steeplechase jockey."[26] If men on horseback hoped to achieve or hold on to a certain nobility, women on horseback were expected to maintain their natural *pudeur*, or modesty, and not compete with their men.

Despite such admonitions, the increasing numbers of women riders would change what was regarded as "natural" for woman more generally. Théophile Gautier's novel *Mademoiselle de Maupin* tells of a woman who presents to the narrator as a man on horseback, and the book helped to incite fear about the "virilization" of women who ride. To be sure, Gautier's preface to the novel speaks with a decidedly masculine "we" to whom God gave "strong thighs for gripping the sides of stallions," and his male protagonist d'Albert looks for a mistress as beautiful as his horse.[27] But in this novel dedicated to beauty for beauty's sake, d'Albert will learn that beauty transcends gender, as he also learns to question his assumptions about women through his encounters with the gender-fluid Maupin. No horse is too *fougueuse* (spirited) for her/him (significantly, the feminine form of the adjective is used with the French word for mount), and in male attire s/he rides with a skill and speed that leaves men amazed. For her part (to the extent that she accepts an assigned gender), Maupin looks to riding as the ultimate means of acquiring the secrets and privileges known to men and forbidden to women.

Maupin's sense of power and freedom on horseback will be repeated in the work of such renowned women as George Sand and Rosa Bonheur. Despite or in defiance of the fact that her father died from in a fall from his horse, Sand transgressed the principles of feminine equitation by wearing male attire, and she sought to develop the strength and ardor that come from a hard ride. While there is some question whether Sand ever rode astride rather than *en amazone* like her transvestite protagonist Gabriel(le), the artist Rosa Bonheur spoke freely of the pleasure and sense of freedom that riding *en califourchon* (astride) offered her and her partner, Nathalie Micas. Both were authorized to wear men's clothes. "It was thus not as amazons, with the classic veil and hat, that we traveled these steep slopes, but rather as real cavaliers, straddling our mounts" and sometimes even riding double to economize.[28]

As women on horseback became a regular feature of the city streets and parks, they also triumphed on horseback as new stars of the circus. It was the British cavalry sergeant Philip Astley who created the circus in London in 1770 to highlight equestrian spectacles.[29] In 1782 Astley brought the circus to Paris, where in 1807 the Italian émigré Antonio Franconi transformed it into the equestrian Cirque Olympique, which would be called a "temple of equitation."[30] The popularity of the circus continued to grow over the century, and from 1845 to 1877 Paris saw the construction of three "hippodromes": vast arenas for staging chariot races, pantomimes with mounted fairies, and military battles in historical costume. All were performed by professionals who often rode "naked" horses, without bridle or saddle. It was also at this time that the professional woman rider, or *écuyère*, became a particular attraction for audiences, whether in the saddle or posing on top of it. Her feats moved the circus even further from the military maneuvers of haute école dressage that had been its original raison d'être, and she was distinguished from her military forebears not only by her acrobatics but also by her revealing attire, popularized in the posters of Henri de Toulouse-Lautrec and James Tissot. Admired for her skill, the professional *écuyère* was to be distinguished from the *amazone*, who was considered a woman of good breeding. The *amazone* was also distinguished from the *lorette*—a kept women or courtesan. Despite these distinctions, *lorettes* could be found renting horses to test their merit (or their appeal), whether on the Paris streets or in the Bois de Boulogne, and they were frequently taken for women of the upper classes. Revealing once again his aristocratic prejudice, Cler distinguishes the *amazone* and *lorette* not only by details of dress (the *lorette* preferring showy colors) but also by their visible pleasure in riding. In contrast to the *lorette*, the *amazone* would own, not lease, her horse, and her pleasure was calm and contained, keeping her "a respectable woman" (*une femme comme il faut*) whose pleasure from horses did not compete with her pleasure from her man.[31] The *lorette*'s pleasure, we can assume, constituted a threat.

CONQUEST AT WHOSE EXPENSE?

It had become something of a topos of nineteenth-century literature that Paris was "hell for horses." As Ulrich Raulff explains, the topos derives from an axiom coined in the sixteenth century and changed slightly to become the adage "Paris is paradise for women, purgatory for men, and hell for horses." It was made popular by Louis-Sébastien Mercier in his *Tableaux de Paris*, published toward the end of the eighteenth century.[32] The adage even makes its way into the impressions of the French capital published by the Egyptian writer, teacher, and Muslim intellectual Rifa'a al-Tahtawi, who traveled to Paris in the 1830s, although the adage was often cited as much for what it said about the licentious freedoms of Parisian women as for the suffering of its horses.[33] In the nineteenth century, Parisians were no longer able to turn their eyes from the common sight of their mistreatment. Some horses, of course, fared better than others, and some humans were held more accountable than others when abuse occurred. This was especially true for those "ill-bred" workers who depended on horses for their livelihood. Breeding and class thus distinguished horses and humans alike. The beautiful purebred horse would increasingly be a pampered pet and have little in common with the workhorses that drew heavy carriages through the city streets or descended deep into mines, rarely seeing daylight.[34] Even for the most well-bred horses, however, "conquest" could be far from beautiful. In the eighteenth century, Buffon acknowledged the severe impact of domestication on the horse's body. Comparing the horse's servitude to slavery (*esclavage*), he writes that "it is through a loss of freedom that its education begins," and he details the marks of that enslavement and the "cruel imprint of work and suffering": "The mouth is deformed by wrinkles caused by the bit, the flanks are slashed with wounds or furrowed with scars made by spurs; the hoof is covered with nails, the bodily comportment continues to be hampered by the persistent impression of habitual constraints."[35]

Buffon hesitates between accepting this "education" as a necessary and moral part of human dominance over the natural world (a dominance justified by that of spirit over matter) and his aristocratic, or perhaps Platonic, belief that the original order of nature was an ideal form.[36] Domestication might occur, in other words, as a variation of what Buffon understood to be the natural process of species' "degeneration" resulting from changes in climate or environment.

Such views of domestication would change greatly through the century, inspired by new conceptions of nature and a growing imperative to shape and control the animals within it. Historical progress and France's civilizing mission required and justified the labor that domestication made possible. According to Pierre Leroux's *Encyclopédie nouvelle* of 1836, the horse's natural "intelligence and instinct for association . . . predisposed him in the most happy manner toward domesticity."[37] At the same time, increasing attention to animal sensibility (and objections to Descartes's notions of "animal machines") raised questions about the line between legitimate use and unacceptable abuse. Animal abuse and animal suffering would become an important theme for authors such as Alphonse de Lamartine, Eugène Sue, Victor Hugo, and Jules Michelet, motivated especially by the violent whipping and beating of horses that were daily occurrences on the streets of Paris. Such abuse would furnish the major rationale behind the founding of the French Society for the Protection of Animals in 1845, itself inspired by the Royal Society for the Prevention of Cruelty to Animals founded in England in 1824. "Mistreatment, whipping, negligence only inspire fear and hatred, dulling and ruining" horses, write the authors of the entry "The Horse" in the 1836 *Encyclopédie*, adding that one must deplore the revolting heartlessness that *les misérables* unleash upon these unhappy creatures who deserve the opposite treatment.[38] But as Maurice Agulhon has claimed, the SPA did less to bring awareness to animal suffering or to raise questions concerning the ethical parameters of animal labor itself than it did to condemn the "dangerous class" of workers who were most frequently accused of unjust behavior. The intent was to protect innocent but susceptible others from witnessing or being influenced by their misbehavior.[39] Inhumane behavior was unsightly and bad for business. Humane treatment of horses consequently was not always proposed in the horse's interest, a fact made especially apparent when it was claimed as a rationale behind the midcentury effort to legalize human consumption of horsemeat. Health officials and zoologists argued that eating horses would reduce their abuse because they would be brought to market in better condition and better health so as to reap more cash per pound.

In a different register, arguments against the abuse of animals complicated the "zoological grounds" on which some sought to justify slavery.[40] Whereas antislavery campaigns depended on the wrong of reducing humans to beasts of burden, animal protection proponents questioned the grounds on which one could justify enslaving animals and thereby accentuated the uncertain line of human/animal difference that had been the focus of eighteenth-century natural historians. As Jeremy Bentham argued,

> The French have already discovered that the blackness of the skin is no reason why a human being should be abandoned without redress to the caprice of a tormentor. It may come one day to be recognized that the number of legs, the villosity of the skin, or the termination of the *os sacrum* are reasons equally insufficient for abandoning a sensitive being to the same fate. What else is it that should trace the insuperable line? Is it the faculty of reason, or perhaps the faculty of discourse? But a full-grown horse or dog is beyond comparison a more rational, as well as a more conversable animal, than an infant of a day, or a week, or even a month old. But suppose they were otherwise, what would it avail? The question is not, Can they *reason*? nor, Can they *talk*? But, Can they *suffer*?[41]

Karl Marx feared that sympathy for animals could interfere with anti-slavery campaigns, and he insisted on a firm distinction between domestication and slavery, the former being control over material objects, the latter control over subject-persons.[42] Although sympathy for horses and for animals in general would eventually be regarded as a necessary component of human sensibility and humane behavior, legislation moved primarily toward removing mistreatment of animals from sight and confining it either to designated slaughter yards beyond the walls of the city or to the laboratory, where sentient creatures could be deposited for experimentation.

THE INSUPERABLE LINE: RACE, SPECIES, AND PUREBRED FANTASIES

"What is it that should trace the insuperable line?" Bentham asked, between those beings that are worthy of our care and those that (or who) are not? Calling attention to that line's variability, he illuminated its political significance for those who should be granted rights. The line separating species and race, however, was itself at issue. In France the definition of race was necessarily intertwined with the notion of breed, and the understanding of breed was especially endorsed by the breeding of horses. According to Leo Spitzer, the word "race" derives from the Italian *razza*, which was first used to describe a horse in a poem of the fourteenth century. The later practice of horse breeding, with its emphasis on blood and purity, would come to have implications for eugenics more generally.[43] Describing both lineage and family descent, race was an important component of aristocratic thought. It was also the idea behind the studbook that was established in England in the 1790s to ensure the pedigree of thoroughbred horses by registering the names of purebred sires and their descendants. To say that a horse was of a "good race" often meant it was of a good family, but it also came to mean being good for a specific task such as hauling or farming or racing. According to Charles Du Haÿs, the breed's historian and enthusiast, the French Percheron was prized for its beauty, which could "rival the English horse," and was also considered the "highest rung of truly useful breeds [*races*]." As Du Haÿs writes in *Le cheval percheron* of 1866, however, the future of the race was already in jeopardy owing to his century's pursuit of "luxury," its fancy for (improper) crossbreeding, and the absence of a studbook to trace genealogies.[44] Du Haÿs calls specific attention to the dangers of degeneration, a term that, as we will see, also came to have relevance for France as a nation and for the French as a people. Theories of breeding figured prominently in attempts to understand and manipulate what blood and race meant for horses and citizens alike.

The very nature of a breed or a species was the subject of significant debate during the eighteenth century when, as Michel Foucault asserts, "Western societies took on board the fundamental biological fact that human beings are a species."[45] For Buffon, that all races or breeds were said to derive from the same original model and have a "unity of composition" argued against a hierarchy of species or races, since all were said to participate in the original "grace of creation." "The supreme being wanted to use only one idea and to simultaneously vary it in every way possible. . . . Not only the donkey and the horse, but even man, the monkey, the quadrupeds, and all animals are to be seen as making up one family."[46] "Species," Buffon wrote, is only an "abstract and general term" that we construct by comparing past and present individuals. Families are our "construction," since nature "contains only individuals."[47] Species can legitimately be determined only over time and by their reproductive capacities, a point he underscores in a telling comparison of (human) race and (equine) species. "If the Negro and the white couldn't reproduce together, if their offspring remained infertile, if the mulatto was really a mule, there would be two distinct species; the Negro would be to man what the donkey is to the horse."[48] Buffon instead believed that races or breeds were essentially the result of differences of environment and of "education," which included everything from feeding and grooming to training and even naming. In this regard, the fineness of Arabian horses was to be attributed not to a separate origin, but to the close watch kept over all aspects of their upkeep and breeding by the Arabs themselves—a cultural difference that is also telling with regard to al-Tahtawi's view of the state of horses in France.

The entry on the horse in Leroux's *Encyclopédie nouvelle* illustrates how the understanding of a breed was changing during the century. Leroux praises Arabian "blood," whether North African or Turkish, for its ability to improve other horse breeds.[49] Indeed, blood would come to define the purity of a breed and so constitute an essential currency within the increasing traffic in horses during the century, especially those bred for the races or for show. This is the animal equivalent of Gayle Rubin's "sex/gender system," those arrangements by which society transforms biological sexuality into products of human activity.[50] In the studbook, breed and patronym confirm the importance of the stallion's "prepotency," or ability to impress his characteristics on his progeny. The three original sires of the thoroughbred, the Byerley Turk, the Darley Arabian, and the Godolphin Arabian, moreover, are known not only by the name of the breed but also by the names of their British breeders—whose "knowledge" was crucial for the breed's formation.

Whereas Buffon attributed the fineness of Arabian horses to the care given by their Arab owners, the 1836 encyclopedia entry makes no mention of such care as influencing the breed. The article does call attention to a "true intimacy" and "sentiment of recognition" that exists between horse and Arab, whose own race is described as *demi-sauvage*—half-wild, or perhaps half-animal. Indeed, the affinity between the race of Arabs and that of their horses would become a popular subject for writers and artists and, as I discuss in chapter 2, contributed to the admiration of the horse even as it also promoted a certain animalization of the Arab. As a consequence, influenced by the growth of colonialism and an orientalist ideology, Arab ways of caring for their horses were not regarded as knowledge.[51]

What threatened the idea of the pureblood was the idea of "degeneration." As noted above, Buffon regarded degeneration as a natural phenomenon that occurs as varieties became more distant from the original model. He also believed it to be reversible. As the term was medicalized during the next century, however, it would become associated with racial and ethnic characteristics that could not be erased. Monogenists like Buffon—or those who upheld the (often religious) belief in the unity of creation and the common descent of all human races from Adam and Eve—would find themselves losing ground to polygenists who claimed the existence of distinct races of humans with distinct origins almost on the order of species. It was the French naturalist Georges Cuvier who identified three distinct "races" of man (Caucasian or white, Mongolian or yellow, and Ethiopian or black) and suggested that their differences could be the effect of the same kind of catastrophic events that were responsible for extinction.[52] In the absence of a theory of evolution, Cuvier was the first to point out the possibility of extinction and of the creation of new species. The important point for Cuvier was that races were permanently defined and that their fixed biological or anatomical qualities were ineradicable. Degeneration was the sign of a racial or inherited weakness that had always existed and could not be reversed.

Cuvier's ideas about "fixity" would eventually lose out to Lamarckian adaptation and Darwinian evolution, but his views mark an important shift toward the nineteenth-century understanding of the essential "inequality of human races" (as the Comte de Gobineau would underscore in his 1853 essay of that title) and thus to explaining the social divisions that continued to plague the nation despite its claims of equality. The entry on "Race" in the Larousse *Grand dictionnaire universel du XIXe siècle*, published from 1866 to 1876, states that "polygenism asserts itself more and more" and that races do not disappear into one another as easily as the monogenists claim. In addition to the influence of climate, the essay asserts, one must acknowledge the enormous differences races present in "intelligence" and "social standing": "One is necessarily savage or half-savage, the other has an advanced political organization, powerful weapons, and agricultural procedures that permit it to conquer the soil." One cannot deny, the author concludes, "the persistence of race."[53]

As the dictionary entry turns to the meaning of race (as breed) within the context of natural history and zoology, the author admits that its meaning is more "general" and that breeds and species are often difficult to distinguish. At the same time, the important "persistence of race," he writes, can also be "applied to animals." It is especially visible among domestic animals, where the vast majority of "races" exist owing to the "hand of man." Indeed, it is with regard to domestic animals that Lamarck's views of inherited traits become most apparent, underscoring the evidence that breeders can manipulate those physical and mental traits that are most desirable and that those traits will be passed down to offspring to create a new "race" of animal.

The author does not mention the thoroughbred horse in this regard, but it constituted one of the most important and visible proofs of a newly created "pure" race. First sired sometime in the early eighteenth century in England but documented only with the publication of the studbook in 1791, the origins of the thoroughbred, as Donna Landry writes, are both "ideologically loaded and scientifically contested."[54] Landry and Richard Nash each give insight into the story of the British conquest and appropriation of "oriental blood" (including Arab, Turk, and Barb) to create a new, idealized breed that transcended (or perhaps suppressed) its crossbred origins to become the epitome of beauty and nobility.[55] Known in France originally as the *pur-sang anglais* or English pureblood, the thoroughbred was to become simply the "pureblood," produced through France's own traffic in Eastern and English horses both through gift giving and as capital exchange. After the establishment of the French Jockey Club and studbook in 1833, "pureblood" entered popular discourse to refer not only to the horse but also to a born lawyer or businessman or to a woman of good breeding. What is especially revealing about the thoroughbred as both cultural metaphor and real, if idealized, horse is the effect it had on the nineteenth-century imaginary to reinforce the importance of race (as blood) for horses and humans alike. This was the case both for those aspects of race that were understood to persist and for those that could be changed or corrected.

Over the course of the century, degeneration would be understood less as a natural function of milieu (as Buffon claimed) and more as a pathology of inherited deficiencies caused by social and cultural influence and behaviors. First noted in an 1857 treatise titled *The Degeneration of the Human Species*, published by the French doctor and alienist Bénédict Augustin Morel and increasingly studied in the aftermath of France's demoralizing defeat in the 1870–71 war with Prussia, the pathology of degeneration was said to afflict the French "race" in particular, with symptoms ranging from impotence to hysteria.[56] This decline was thematized in naturalist and decadent novels by writers such as Émile Zola and Joris-Karl Huysmans, which attributed it to heredity and assumed that the harmful behaviors would be passed on to offspring. Race and even class played into such theories, which identified certain groups as more susceptible to particular degenerate or brutish behaviors and moral illness.

In 1753 Buffon had proposed crossbreeding to guard against degeneration, advancing the idea that reproduction among individuals from different climes would reduce the effects of their particular environments on their offspring.[57] One hundred years later crossbreeding, or intermarriage between races, classes, and ethnicities, would be regarded less as a cure than as an underlying cause for the infection and weakening of the French race. And as polygenism became the reigning theory of the time, so too did the belief that degeneration was biological and irreversible. Nevertheless, as the creation and training of the thoroughbred showed, polygenism could also offer a potential cure—at least as metaphor if not in fact. Such was the thinking behind the pamphlet titled *The Art of Creating a Thoroughbred Human* (*pur-sang humain*), published in 1908 by Professors Georges Rouhet and Edmond Desbonnet. These "doctors" advised their readers that just as the English had succeeded in creating new pureblood horses whose offspring continued to show their qualities and talents, so should the French be able to create a new race of "thoroughbred humans." The key was in creating strong men who could be the "stallions of the future race."[58]

At the century's close, when the French were beginning to wax nostalgic about the "end of the horse" and to witness its replacement by bicycles, cars, and new forms of spectacle, thoughts of a beautiful conquest were thus transferred in a more direct manner from the equine body to the human body, and to the means by which a pure race of human thoroughbreds might counteract the effects of degeneracy for generations to come. Horse training and breeding became the model by which the French took being a species as "the object of a political strategy" and their "basic biological features" as the necessary forces of what Foucault called biopower.[59]

THE ESSAYS

In his recent vast history of the decline of the horse, Ulrich Raulff emphatically claims that "every single great idea that fueled the driving force of the nineteenth century—freedom, human greatness, compassion, but also the sub-currents of history uncovered by contemporaries such as libido, the unconscious, and the uncanny—can be traced one way or another back to the horse."[60] My essays here make more modest claims as they seek to expose and understand horses' actual, physical, and figurative significance to the social, sexual, and political developments of nineteenth-century France and to the men and women who had their own experiences, if not conquests, on horseback. Whether in life or in literature and art, the horse was "the animal" most familiar to nineteenth-century thought. Horses inspired fundamental changes in human-animal relations, and representations of horses revealed changing notions of what constituted animality itself: how to nourish it, when and how to train and contain it, and when humans could be more bestial than any beast. Emphasizing these changes, the essays are organized in a loose chronological fashion, even as the focus of each is thematic and determined by the relevant texts and artworks.

Chapter 1 opens by considering the horse's importance in natural history and in the academic traditions of history painting that celebrated military conquest. It contrasts this tradition to the early military portraits of men and horses by Théodore Géricault, which offer, I argue, a different idea of history, one that paints a new physical and psychological companionship between soldier and mount. Turning to Géricault's later Rome paintings, the chapter charts the representation of new and queer intimacies between horses and the men who run beside them rather than ride astride. Representative of changes in the aftermath of the Revolution and the Empire, these horsemen appear to have gained in muscle but have lost the power over nature and history that Hegel saw as exemplified by Napoleon on horseback.

Chapter 2 begins with a horse beating in the streets of Paris depicted in Eugène Sue's fictional horse biography, *Godolphin Arabian* (1838), about the first thoroughbred sire. The chapter was inspired by Jacques Derrida's reference to an ongoing "war on pity" that had its origins about the time of the French Revolution and examines what role sympathy for animals and the recognition of animal suffering might have had in the eventual founding of the French SPA in 1845. Asking whether we can compare pity to the empathy that is so lauded today, I examine the political value of pity in a range of poems and essays from 1803 through Charles Baudelaire's ironic consideration of pity in his prose poem "*Les faux monnayeurs*" (The counterfeiters), published posthumously in 1869. Like empathy, we learn, pity can be good for business.

Sue's story of the thoroughbred is cited as the inspiration for one of the last works by the painter Rosa Bonheur, *The Duel* of 1897, showing the story's lasting influence. Whereas Bonheur's crossdressing and lesbian commitments have made her an icon for queer readings over the past two decades, I suggest in chapter 3 that such readings have overlooked the important status of horses in her work. Arguing that her mission was to reveal their intelligence, their work ethic, and consequently their important role in world history, I read her paintings *Horse Fair* and *Ploughing in the Nivernais* in the context of the prioritizing of talent and industry in the Saint-Simonian commune. Bonheur came of age at this moment (her father was a member of the commune), and she was well aware of contemporary debates in natural philosophy concerning a human-animal continuum and the function of domestication as a kind of "rehabilitation of the flesh"—the phrase the commune's leader, Father Barthélemy Prosper Enfantin, used to describe his own mission. That mission, I argue, was also influenced by the Cuvier-Geoffroy debates in zoology and comparative anatomy. As a friend of the Saint-Hilaire family, Rosa Bonheur took it upon herself to translate the truths of science into a visual medium.

At the center of the book, chapter 4 raises what might otherwise seem an anomalous issue: eating horsemeat. Why and how in the middle of the Second Empire, when the popularity and presence of the horse as worker, prized possession, and even pampered pet were at their height, was human consumption of horsemeat legalized in France? I explore this question with reference to Derrida's notion of what it means to "eat well" and through an analysis of contemporary debates surrounding slaughter, hygiene, gastronomy, and once again the role of domestication. Indeed, the zoologist Isidore Geoffroy Saint-Hilaire, who wrote the entry on domestication for the *Encyclopédie nouvelle*, was the primary voice behind the crusade to eat horses, and he saw no contradiction between their service as fellow laborers and as food.

Chapters 5 and 6 focus on questions of gender, but gender as inflected by race and class and by "becoming with" horses. Donna Haraway emphasizes the idea of "becoming with" to remind us how we become who/what we are through our engagements with others, including other animals. At the core of these chapters is a performative becoming with horses on stage or at the circus.[61] After a discussion of the rise and reputation of the woman rider or *amazone* in life, in the literature of Sand, Balzac, Gautier, and Zola, and in Manet's painting *Universal Exhibition of 1867*, chapter 5 turns to Adah Menken, a woman in Second Empire Paris who became the star of the theater in 1866 (the same year hippophagy was legalized). Menken played the male role of Mazeppa in the hippodrama *Mazeppa*, and reactions to her performance and especially to her riding across the stage in only a sheer bodysuit reveal the fantasies and fears provoked by a woman and a horse together. In Menken's case, moreover, the bestial nature of their relationship is accentuated by perceptions about and reception of her Jewish breeding.

Chapter 6 takes readers to a new kind of circus that was founded during the 1880s, "the aristocratic circus," where notable men mounted horses and trapezes in a show of bodily strength and agility. The subject of paintings by Tissot and a novel by Daniel Lesueur (pen name for Jeanne Loiseau), this particular circus, I argue, represents an attempt to take back the meaning of the "man on horseback," whose demise can be traced from the novels of Stendhal through to the Third Republic. With attention to new manuals of sports medicine, I situate this circus within a larger effort to promote the idea of sports for the nobility, making it acceptable if not advisable for an aristocratic male to show off his physical and, by extension, moral capacities. Performers and sports enthusiasts alike called on horses to virilize and rejuvenate the nation at a time when the biological sciences warned of the degeneration of the French race, confirmed by the army's defeat in the Franco-Prussian War of 1870.

In the final chapter I pick up a materialist thread that runs through many parts of the book, linking affect, animals, and moral behavior. This materialism finds its roots in Jean-Jacques Rousseau's account of pity as a natural, animal, and therefore moral sentiment, as discussed in chapter 2. It reappears in those connections between animal bodies and mental health that are evoked by the looming structure of the Salpêtrière mental hospital in Rosa Bonheur's *The Horse Fair*, discussed in chapter 3, linking humane treatment of horses and of the insane. And it is present in theories of degeneration that link physical to psychic and moral weakness in the writings of fin-de-siècle sports enthusiasts in chapter 6. This questioning of a material or animal morality finds its culmination in the image of the unruly masses or crowds in Émile Zola and Gustave Le Bon, the French social psychologist Freud turned to for his understanding of the "herd theory." Noting the contrast between the "brutish" behavior of Zola's human workers in *Germinal* and the dignity of his workhorses, I question what is "the animal" in his novel and where is it to be found. More important, I ask what distinguishes the destructive contagion of Le Bon's crowd from what twentieth-century theorist Gilles Deleuze regards as the creative, liberatory potential of the pack. Le Bon believed that the crowd, like animals and women, was to be controlled rather than let loose, and he turned to the training of horses and the "psychology of dressage" as an unconscious, affective method for inculcating moral behavior. In this, moreover, his methods recall eighteenth-century practices of animal magnetism or mesmerism. But whereas animal magnetism originally lent itself to a radical, democratic politics, its practice at the end of the nineteenth century, I argue, served a protofascist effort to reveal the moral weaknesses not only of animals but also of certain races and sexes of humans. All require a strong leader—preferably one on horseback—to control them. Charting a rising and significant interest in the field of animal psychology, the chapter offers a cautionary tale about the dangers of the search for human/horse or human/animal likenesses and a plea to attend to also to their differences. In so doing I want to acknowledge and emphasize our limitations for knowing and representing those differences.

CHAPTER ONE

Heads or Tails? Painting History with a Horse

The horse may be the only nonhuman animal deemed worthy of visual representation throughout history. Equines were the most numerous of the animals depicted on the walls of the Lascaux Cave in France during the Paleolithic era. Throughout Greek history horses were painted and carved with or without chariots to emphasize their importance in battle and for travel. The tradition of equestrian portraiture depicting emperors and noblemen on horseback began in antiquity and flourished in Europe during the Renaissance and early modern period. In visual records of heroic action or royal governance, horses appear both as literal support and as symbolic embodiment of the defiant forces of nature that a figure of authority, usually male, has harnessed. This is why Buffon described the horse as the "most beautiful conquest of man," beauty and utility being inseparable in eighteenth-century aesthetics.[1] Significant events in human history depended on horses, a fact many written histories, unlike visual accounts, ignored. But what about the horse as a subject in his (or her) own right? Might the horse also be a subject of history so that, as Daniel Roche suggests, we might reverse Buffon's adage and say, "Man is the horse's finest conquest"?[2]

"Does history need animals?" This question was posed by a special issue of the journal *History and Theory*, and the answer depends both on what we mean by history and on what we mean by animals.[3] If we accept that we humans are animals, certainly there would be no history without us. The notion of an animal history, however, takes us beyond regarding animals as worthy historical objects of our world so we can see how such objects must also be regarded as historical subjects and thus as themselves agents of history—ours and theirs. Horses are our partners on the battlefield as in the streets, but it is a precarious partnership that can be threatened on both sides, whether by resistance, by miscommunication, or by a breach of trust.

This notion of animal partnership and hence agency becomes especially visible in horse paintings of the nineteenth century, which also constitute a significant challenge to any lingering acceptance of the Cartesian idea of the animal machine, subject only to "management" by its owner.[4]

In many regards the eighteenth century was transitional for horsemanship and for visual representations of horses and riders. Donna Landry argues that the increasingly popular importing of "Eastern" horses into Europe and especially into England at this time changed methods of training and handling because of their different physical and mental capacities.[5] The particular intelligence of Arabian horses influenced British horsemanship, Landry writes, and made them into lauded subjects of equine portraiture, if not also critical viewers of those portraits. Legend has it that the famous racehorse Whistlejacket reared in reaction to the portrait George Stubbs painted of him in 1762.[6] Art historian Walter Leidtke writes that the eighteenth century marked the culmination of the tradition of royal equestrian portraiture, but it was also a period of "unintended parody," as in Goya's "dismounted equestrian portraits."[7] With the rise of aristocratic and bourgeois riders, equestrian portraiture was no longer reserved for royalty; in the works of George Stubbs (1724–1806), it could indicate nostalgia for the pleasures of nature and the countryside.[8] The growth of natural history during the century also contributed to notions of animal agency, even as its organization and taxonomy emphasized an animal's subservience to human history and human use. Buffon, for example, appeared to recognize a certain agency on the horse's part insofar as the horse accepted not only his domestication but also his participation in a history made by his master.[9] "The horse shares the fatigue of war and the glory of combat; as intrepid as his master, the horse sees peril and confronts it."[10]

Artistic representations of horses, and of nonhuman animals more generally, informed the new field of natural history by confirming human dominance over nature and regarding domestication as divinely ordained. In taxonomies such as Buffon's *Natural History* (published in thirty-six volumes from 1749 to 1789) or Thomas Bewick's *General History of Quadrupeds* (1790), horses were placed at the top of the animal kingdom, closest to man through their service to him or their ability to reflect his power and nobility, though assuredly distanced from him as part of the natural world. This closeness was also regarded as moral insofar as obedience and will become the same thing. Thus Buffon ascribes agency to the horse who denies his own will and represses his desires in order to obey his human master. "It is a creature who renounces his being in order to exist only by the volition

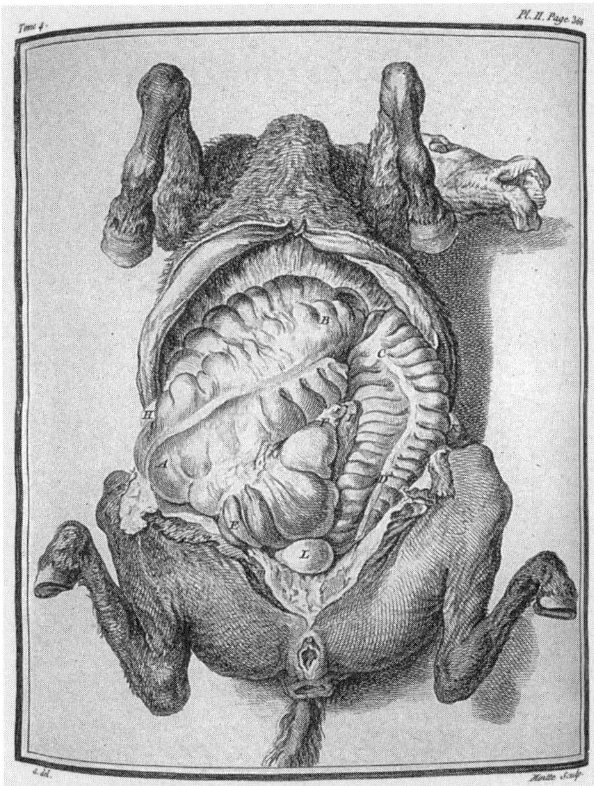

Figure 1.1. Abdomen of a horse, published in Georges-Louis Leclerc, Comte de Buffon's *Histoire naturelle, générale et particulière, avec la description du cabinet du roi*, published in several volumes, 1749–1804. Image courtesy of the Wellcome Library at the University of London.

of another," he writes, adding, moreover, that the horse "will even exhaust himself and die in order to obey."[11]

That horses could will their own death out of obedience is visually confirmed by the illustrations in Buffon's *Histoire naturelle* (fig. 1.1), where the horse's prostrate and fully exposed position (shared by many of the mammals represented) suggests that he died not only for his master but also for his master's science and need to know. It is in this regard that eighteenth-century representations of the horse confirm a particular Enlightenment ideology regarding the natural order and man's place within it. The conventions of natural history and art history in England, as in France, were mutually influential in depicting the animal order and man's place above it. The long tradition of history and equestrian painting lends support to Buffon's pronouncement that the horse is a conquest of man, evidence and symbol of his (and I use the masculine deliberately) power over nature, as over history. But the work of Théodore Géricault paints a different picture of the horse and of history—one that defies human separation from nature as it confuses hierarchies of human and horse as conqueror and conquered.

At the end of his book Walter Leidtke looks ahead to the works of Géricault and Rosa Bonheur and to a shift whereby the horse's rearing is attributed to "the power and, one might add, the nobility of the animal, and not of his master."[12] This shift in the locus of agency from human to horse is echoed by Karen Raber and Treva Tucker, who describe a new "Romantic version of the horse in art," often riderless or "free," as in Géricault's Rome paintings. They argue that this changed role of the horse in visual representation echoes a shift in contemporary manuals of horsemanship, such that in the early modern period "we move from an irrational horse that must be restrained and contained by the rational (and, if necessary, forceful) control of its rider, to a rational horse that must be persuaded by its rational rider to form a cooperative, yet still highly disciplined partnership."[13] Intelligence, will, and agency are also vital to Géricault's horses, who are indeed partners of their riders. But that partnership loses its rational balance and, as a result, newly illustrates the animal or bodily passions shared by horse and human as each negotiates the entangled worlds of nature and culture.

Géricault's equestrian paintings are emblematic of shifting and conflicting attitudes toward the natural world in France in the early nineteenth century and toward the place and nature of human-animal relations within it. Visible in his work is the shift from the homosocial horse world of the *Ancien régime*, where riding offered privilege and prestige to aristocratic and military men, to the bourgeois horse culture of the more modern world that would increasingly be dominated by women riders and by the sports of racing and hunting. Equestrian portraits of bourgeois men and *amazones* would grow more and more popular, and whereas Buffon, like his contemporaries, would celebrate the horse for sharing in the "fatigue of war," by the middle of the nineteenth century the painter Gustave Courbet would depict horse and rider sharing the fatigue of the hunt (fig. 1.2). Beauty and nobility are not part of the image. Caught within this shift, however, Géricault's particular way of painting the horse, and especially of painting horses and humans together, defies easy identification of personage, activity, or class, because his horses are neither mere accessories to historic (and virile) conquest nor aestheticized possessions. Until the final stages of his shortened career, Géricault paints the horse as a subject and other who can be neither

Figure 1.2. Gustave Courbet, *Hunter on Horseback*, ca. 1864. Image courtesy of the Yale University Art Gallery.

conquered nor fully controlled. His paintings of horses and of history, I argue, contest the certainties established in Enlightenment and historical picturing and thus contest the status of the knowing human subject. Turning the animal gaze upon the paintings' viewers, Géricault's horses reveal the limits of man's knowledge and dominance in the world.

If I call Géricault's horse an other, I do so not in the sense of Simone de Beauvoir's descriptions of woman as man's other, defined through and against the priority of the masculine/human. To be sure, critics such as Linda Nochlin have suggested that horses might stand in for women in his paintings,[14] but I suggest that his horse is what could be called a queer other who challenges both anthropocentric and gender norms. This sense of queer draws on understandings of "queer ecology" (or ecologies) that merge ecological criticism and queer studies in order to contest accepted notions of a "*natural* order" that excludes nonnormative sexual relations on the grounds that they are somehow against nature. Queer ecology is a necessary corrective to accepted notions of the "natural" in both environmental and sexuality studies that would frame nonnormative sexual activity (within or between species) as outside or against nature.[15] Indeed, any such separation of human and natural worlds that valorizes nature as "normative" goes against the very meaning of ecology, which, Timothy Morton writes, "demands intimacies with other beings that queer theory also demands." Such intimacies, Morton argues, prove the antiessentialism of evolution itself, insofar as it is a process that "abolishes rigid boundaries between and within species."[16] Géricault was deeply intimate with horses. He painted them attentively throughout his career and kept a horse-head sculpture in his studio. He also rode with what has been called a "suicidal passion" and died from a fall off his horse. What or who were his horses to him?[17]

ANIMAL PICTURING: FROM ENLIGHTENMENT IDEALS TO ROMANTIC ALIVENESS

Géricault began painting before the theory of evolution promoted a view of the animal order as "nature red in tooth and claw," nature whose brute savagery needed to be separated from humans and tamed before entering their households. His view of natural fertility and reproduction also precedes the scientific understanding of sexual selection (pitting male against male for access to the female) and follows from Enlightenment conventions that pictured animals as either objects of anatomical knowledge or extensions of the human world. Animal picturing was integral to natural history, and as Alex Potts argues, its prominence coincided with an "idea of picturing [that] functioned in Enlightenment science as an important general model for the systematic observation and representation of natural phenomena. The aesthetic dimension was seen as integral to its scientific function as a clear and coherent display of knowledge."[18] To picture was to know; Potts's use of "picturing" has echoes of what Martin Heidegger has called the "world picture" or "the world conceived and grasped as picture."[19] In his essay "The Age of the World Picture" Heidegger links the growth of modern Western science to a new objectification of the world by and before a viewer who frames what is to be seen, a viewer who is made subject through this view. As the picture renders the world knowable and calculable in relation to the viewing subject standing outside it, no allowance is made for the possibility that the world—or more specifically for my purposes, the animals within that world—might return the gaze or have a viewpoint of their own. In this way, moreover, Enlightenment conventions painted animals as part of a natural order that is continuous with the perceived social order: the animal body was clearly distinct, but it enabled the human mind and body to perform its work.

Heidegger's "world picture" describes the very organizing principles of both Buffon's *Histoire naturelle* (published from 1749 to 1804) and Thomas Bewick's *A General History of Quadrupeds* (1790). In Buffon's gigantic thirty-six-volume project, animals are organized in terms of their proximity or usefulness to man. Similarly, Bewick categorized animals in terms of their impact on human experience and thus, according to Harriet Ritvo, "presented the animal kingdom as rationally ordered and easily comprehensible."[20] An illustrator by trade, Bewick understood picturing animals as integral to knowing them and, like Buffon, relied on illustrations to reveal an animal's essence or "totality." Both used the convention of narrative vignettes to place the representative of a species within a particular social setting that would indicate its function and its owners' social and sometimes moral status: working dogs and horses would thus make reference to the work ethic of their owners while a saddle horse would imply a certain aristocratic idleness. More generally, the very notion of picturing was central to Buffon's understanding of what it is to know an animal through a comparison of resemblances to and differences from other animals. The important distinctions and likenesses are those that stem not from a description of individual aspects, but from an understanding of the animal's essence, what Buffon calls the "totality" of the animal.[21] The link with neoclassical aesthetics is most clear, moreover, in Buffon's contention that such "totality" could only be "distorted" "by the movements to which [the animal] naturally inclines when it is excited by needs or agitated by passions."[22] In natural history as in neoclassical painting, all observations must be synthesized into a composite ideal that is undisturbed by any emotions on the part of the animal (and perhaps of the artist as well) in order to picture "true" being.

This same synthetic and static ideal is evident in the early anatomical drawings of the horse that George Stubbs produced in the 1760s. In his later works, however, movement will become an essential feature and be especially important for the comparative function of his anatomical studies of 1817. Not surprisingly, these studies found disfavor with the scientific community because of their potentially unsettling effects. By filling each page of his work with the figure of either a human, a bird, or a quadruped, Stubbs presents species as analogical and thus, Potts writes, raises the question of "the legitimacy of envisaging the human figure . . . as a mere bodily thing," an animal (28). The legitimacy of regarding the human as animal was integral to eighteenth-century materialist views that understood the brain as an organ of thought rather than the receptor of divine intervention. If humans moved like horses and other animals, that could suggest that all movement was the result of what Descartes would describe as mechanical "reaction" and not rational intention. Conversely, it could also mean that all creatures, human and nonhuman, moved by intention and will.

Stubbs gives almost equal weight to the portraits of horses and of humans and so marks his departure from Enlightenment conventions. On the one hand, horses are important as reflections of their owners' social standing. But the impression one receives from Stubbs's comparative framework is that the figure of an animal stands in what Potts calls "an uncanny relation of literal equivalence to the figure of a human being."[23] In Géricault this relation of "uncanny equivalence" between human and horse will be exaggerated to even more unsettling effect. And whereas for Stubbs equivalence is largely a matter of physical or anatomical likeness, for Géricault equivalence between human and horse is physical and emotional, and analogical possibility is extended even to the matter of expression. In his equestrian portraits and military paintings, horses are depicted less as steeds who have been tamed to carry men into honorable battles than as physical and emotional partners in combat and in fear. Caught in events of unknown proportions and unknown outcomes, his horses and riders often move in opposed directions, sharing expressions and sometimes physical stances but rarely purpose or act.

Whereas Enlightenment paradigms sought to tame otherwise unruly relations between humans and animals, Géricault offers a new paradigm that challenges the Enlightenment picture of the natural order in two ways. At a first level, he unbridles the horse's gaze to allow him (or her) to look back and defy the viewer's objectification of the natural world. At a second level he implies a shared corporeal, if sometimes erotic, bond between the artist/viewer and the unknowable (and indomitable) animal bodies within the picture. Géricault turns the question of the picture back onto its picturing subject, thereby raising doubts about the very possibility of a world picture made from an outside, objective position.

Moving excitedly if awkwardly through a range of passions, Géricault's horses reveal a growing Romantic effort to capture a certain aliveness of the animal, whether in illustration or in painting, and to move away from the "static objectification" that was so important to earlier natural histories. His departure from his neoclassical predecessors is especially visible in his attention to those emotions and passions that make one alive and that are witnessed in horses. Such concern with emotional aliveness signals the end of what Stefan Germer has called "artistic practice as active enlightenment"[24] and the beginning of an art of sentience. It establishes the possibility for a psychological comparison between humans and horses, if not for an emotional or even erotic relationship. Indeed, what is singular in Géricault's horses is not the way they look but that they do look, and look in a way that seems to defy our capacity to develop a singular world picture. This becomes especially apparent with respect to the traditions of history painting and equestrian portraiture into which Géricault inserted himself early on, and where the melding of paradigms of classical and natural history is especially evident. Within these traditions, the power to paint an accurate narrative of history derives from an Enlightenment view of man's place at the top of the world order, looking out over the events he commands and brings to a coherent close. The soldier on horseback is a classic example, reaffirming man's power over nature as over history. Such was Hegel's description of Napoleon as a world-historical hero who, "sitting on a horse, reaches out over the world and dominates it."[25] In Géricault's paintings, however, historical domination is put into doubt; in scenes where the outcomes are anything but certain, the burden of historical action appears to fall not on man, but on the horse. Indeed, in many of his paintings we might say that the matter of history itself shifts from a depiction of past events to an uncharted exploration of intersubjective relations in which men are thrown from dominance to land in a position where horses are their primary interlocutors.

HISTORY, HORSES, AND HUMANS: PARTNERS IN PASSION

While Géricault's most famous painting may be his huge *The Raft of the Medusa* (1819), which depicts the starving survivors of a shipwreck, equines dominate the rest of his oeuvre. His first teacher was the popular horse painter Carle Vernet, but his own horses differ both from those of Vernet, for whom they functioned primarily as a nod to English fashion, and from those found in the French tradition of equestrian portraiture that still flourished at the turn of the century. In that tradition, a horse could signal the virility and power of the man who controlled him, which is one reason Napoleon informed his court painter, Jacques-Louis David, that he wanted to be painted "calm on a spirited horse."[26] The result, David's *Bonaparte Crossing the Alps at Mount St. Bernard* (plate 2) is a composite of historical narrative and equestrian portraiture that renders event and animal together as a fixed, idealized image before the viewer. Despite his reputation as a poor horseman, visible in his awkward leg position, the consul is pictured in complete control, and he and the horse function together as a union of opposites: calm and frenzy, mind and body. More important, the frenzy is reined into a classical dressage levade, or rise on the haunches that, in traditional paintings of noble and royal figures, signaled control over the horse as over oneself.[27] It is with such control that the future emperor will be expected to lead his horse and his people to victory.

When we compare David's painting with Géricault's *Charging Chasseur, or Officer of the Imperial Guard on Horseback* of 1812 (plate 3), the first of his paintings to be admitted into the Salon, we find a very different relation between man and horse, if not also between man and power. The work is said to have originated not as a historical painting but from a street scene of a horse rearing as it tried to free itself of its harness.[28] Whereas in David's painting we are dazzled by the bright red of Napoleon's cape that flows forward to envelop both horse and rider, in Géricault's canvas that color, signaling empire and monarchy alike, becomes fragmented, dispersed onto less clearly articulated (and thus ambiguous) bits of clothing.[29] One might try to read an opposition of animal body or instinct and human mind into the painting, but given that horse and rider appear to be moving in different directions, one cannot say that one dominates the other or that they function as a unit like Napoleon and his horse. As a portrait, it is Janus-faced—horse and rider looking left and right, their eyes registering equally, if differently, the destruction around them. There is no indication here that the officer's contemplative gaze is a match for the horse's energetic vitality, or that he is even able to support the bearskin hat and plume that seem on the verge of engulfing his head. Whereas Napoleon points his right hand forward to the future, this officer, perhaps to correct the imbalance of his twisted body and outflung leg, points his sword toward the horse's genitals, inadvertently gesturing toward the material sign of the power he lacks. With the man wrapped in and surrounded by animal furs that are nevertheless unable to compensate for the human body's weakness, agency falls to the horse.[30] Géricault merges the single focus of equestrian portraiture with the huge scale of historical narrative so that both the subject of the portrait and the historical event are unknown. The idea behind the heroic event itself and the possibility of knowing and representing that event are both in question.[31] "A War effigy? Certainly!" writes Régis Michel, "But charge or retreat? Victory or defeat? Realism or propaganda? Allegory or Portrait? For or against the Empire? . . . We don't know."[32]

This uncertainty over the meaning of the event subverts the status of the viewing subject as one who knows, as we see in Géricault's *Officier de la garde* and to an even greater degree in *The Wounded Cuirassier* of 1814 (fig. 1.3)—a painting intended to act as an antithesis to the first.[33] Here Napo-

Figure 1.3. Théodore Géricault, *The Wounded Cuirassier*, 1814. Image courtesy of Erich Lessing/Art Resource, New York.

leon's reversal of fortune is signaled by the fallen officer, whose body simulates the startled recoil of his horse, and once again Géricault merges genres of portrait and historical narrative to subvert our recognition of either: Who is the soldier, what and where is the situation, which way are they moving?

Between horse and rider, who is leading and supporting whom? Much has been written about the strange foreshortening and occlusion of the horse's hindquarters and of the "failure to articulate the key areas of muscular exertion necessary to complete the action."[34] The result is that horse and rider are brought into a status of "uncanny equivalence" like that Potts describes with regard to Stubbs. Physically, their bodies mimic one another in that the horse's front legs—one bent and raised, the other straight to the ground—are repeated in the soldier's. It is a precarious stance for both horse and human

Figure 1.4. Théodore Géricault, *Carabinier with His Horse*, ca. 1814. Image courtesy of the Musée des Beaux Arts and the Réunion des Museés Métropolitains Rouen Normandie.

and only temporarily supported by the counterparts of the horse's barely visible (or useful) hind leg and perhaps the soldier's sword (now used as a cane). Emotionally their eyes register a similar state of fear and apprehension, even as they too look in different directions. Indeed, one could say that the focus of the painting is not the specific event (which is unclear) but the intersubjective relations established between two beings caught in a history that both physically experience but neither can recognize. That the horse may be the soldier's primary interlocutor and not just his means of transportation is made apparent in the 1814 *Carabinier with His Horse* (fig. 1.4). Here, even though the officer meets our gaze, his defiant stare and inflated armor appear to guard against or compensate for the knowing and vulnerable look of the horse that is barely visible in his shadow.

This brings us back to Géricault's transgressions of the genre of equestrian portraiture, if not of the portrait itself. What is the function, and who is the subject of these portraits? Henri Zerner remarks that while Romantic portraiture took on new importance as a "document of human psychology" under the influence of the Swiss physiognomist Johann Kaspar Lavater, Géricault himself was never much of a physiognomist. Indeed, his work often appears to deliberately contest physiognomy's efforts to read identity or character in a face or to give proof, as in the work of Pieter Camper, of the great chain of being through the angle of the face. A follower of Lavater and an anatomical illustrator, Camper insisted that the more vertical the angle from forehead to chin, the more human the face is, and the more horizontal, the more animal—a belief that placed white Europeans at the pinnacle of being.[35] What then are we to make of Géricault's *Head of a White Horse* (1815) (plate 1), a painting that is as striking for the verticality of the horse's face as it is compelling for its insistent, if inscrutable, subjectivity? This head appears to express what the *Carabinier* portrait only hints at—it avows what philosophy, and animal picturing, has disavowed: that the animal can look at me. "It has," as Derrida writes, "its point of view regarding me."[36]

This is not the look of the symbolic animal; it is the singular look of this or that cat, dog, or horse who has been a particular companion. To be the object of this horse's gaze changes the status of the representing, viewing subject. Indeed, even though this horse looks at the viewer with a directness that is rare in Géricault's oeuvre, that we cannot focus on his/her two eyes simultaneously reminds us of the limitations of our vision. Neither the expressive vacancy nor the averted gaze found in many of Géricault's human portraits, this alert but melancholic look lingers and beckons to me. This is the face described by Emmanuel Levinas: "In its expression, in its mortality, the face before me summons me, calls for me, begs for me, as if the invisible death that must be faced by the Other . . . were my business."[37] This may be due to a certain nakedness in the horse's expression—what we might call its antitheatricality—that, as in the *Carabinier with His Horse*, contrasts sharply with the man's defensive glare and armor.[38] We don't believe that horses can pose, but the Napoleonic Wars showed, pace Levinas, that they were certainly capable of bravery and sacrifice.[39]

In these early equestrian works, horses turn the picturing lens back onto the artist himself to check the representation of history and its presumed agents. Unlike the symbolic animals of natural history and neoclassical painting, Géricault's horses do not confirm man's "conquest" but instead reveal the limits of that conquest. Judged, beckoned, and seduced, Géricault's subject is thrown from his established position above or before the animal into a confused and conflicted situation of passionate connection with animals. In this rejection of the Enlightenment tradition of animal

Figure 1.5. Théodore Géricault, *The Wild Horse Race at Rome*, ca. 1817. Image courtesy of RMN-Grand Palais/Art Resource, New York. Photo by Philippe Bernard.

picturing, horses are figured not as machines but as conscious, emotive subjects. The possibility of measuring their distance from us all but disappears.

INTERSPECIES INTIMACIES IN ITALY

Whereas in Géricault's early works the passionate connection between men and horses is elicited primarily by the face and expression, in the works produced in Italy during 1816–17 that connection is increasingly located outside the conscious or emotive, outside the self-aware and theatrical, and in a more physical, bodily aliveness. This physical aliveness is at its height in what was known as Géricault's Italian project. His later studies of severed limbs or of the vacant, passive stares of monomaniacs evoke a subjectivity that is between or outside both mind and body, human and nonhuman animal.[40] But in the unfinished Rome project, titled *Course de chevaux libres*, or *The Wild Horse Race at Rome*, the inseparability of being alive and being animal (if not being childlike) is the product of a hypermasculine, heroic fantasy where differences of sex and of species are elided through violent erotic contact (fig. 1.5).

In a disregard for neoclassical codes, aliveness here is above all a function of movement, and movement whose heroic quality is inseparable from its animal and sexualized status. Men and horses are stripped of clothing and tack, their muscles gleaming as they run in uncharted directions and are thrown into an "uncanny equivalence" not by their expressions, but by the entangled thrusts of their bodies. As a physical, if not psychosexual, connection is graphically displayed, the ethics of companionship give way to a bestial erotics; knowledge of the other is sought not in the face, but beneath the tail.

One might call these displays homoerotic given the interplay of man and equine, but queer is a better term given that I want to argue for both a sexual and a species uncertainty or fluidity. The race of riderless or free horses was a local event in Rome, but Géricault's plan to represent the race in a monumental mode had no precedent, and its genre has perplexed art historians. Abigail Solomon-Godeau writes that Géricault's subversion of the laws of genre is related to a "disturbance in the field of gender . . . [and] has certain consequences for the representational stability of sexual difference."[41] The breach of genre, I would add, has consequences for the representation of species difference as well. Linda Nochlin has argued that Géricault's horses are a "displacement of the feminine" and, more important, a means to surreptitiously represent women with the corporeal and erotic power and presence they were otherwise denied in painting. "What we have here is 'femininity without women,'" Nochlin writes, as she moves on to discuss the central place occupied by the equine body that is lovingly explored throughout Géricault's career—from forelock to fetlock as it were. She cites an anecdote where Géricault patted a friend on the back saying, "We two X . . . we like big a__s."[42] But whose ass is he referring to? Must we say that the horse's ass stands in for the feminine?

Indeed, Géricault's interest in the horse's rear is an idée fixe in his work, from his *The Charging Chasseur* (plate 3), where the sword of the otherwise distracted officer directs the viewer's eyes to the horse's hindquarters at the center of the painting, to his 1813–14 studies of horses' rumps (fig. 1.6)—with variously coiffed and fetishized tails to highlight the different coats—to his painting of horses led to market (fig. 1.7), and to his later (1821) lithographs of workhorses entering the Adelphi Wharf (fig. 1.8). While there may be "blood horses" among them, it is neither race nor intelligence that makes them of interest; it is the physical power of their massive haunches (*croupes* or *fesses*) that constitutes their attraction.[43]

The *Race* series thus figures the shared musculature of horse and human through a common modeling of light and shade that highlights areas of

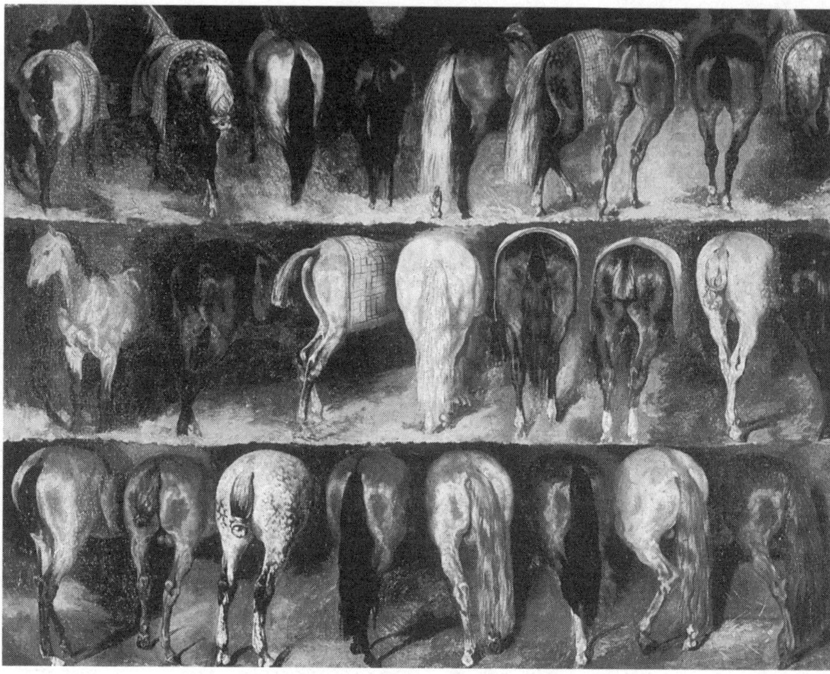

Figure 1.6. Théodore Géricault, *Les croupes, vingt-cinq chevaux dans une écurie*, ca. 1820–22. Image from Nina M. Athanassoglou-Kallmyer, *Théodore Gericault* (London: Phaidon, 2010).

strength: haunches, chest, biceps, as also those unexpected details of seductive beauty such as a glistening tail or lock of hair. It is a fantasy picture of shared physical potency.[44] In these Rome paintings, horses in general and the horse's ass in particular take on a greater share of libidinal investment than was visible in Géricault's earlier work, and this can be only partly explained by the apparent cause for his trip to Italy—a scandalous affair the artist is known to have had with his uncle's wife. In the unfinished project of the *Course de chevaux libres* the horse is at once an eroticized object and an idealized rival. Here the connection between men and horses is located in their shared bodily being. Indeed, physical aliveness is at its height in his Italian project, which was undertaken before his most famous work, *The Raft of the Medusa* (and which borrows from it) and before his studies of severed limbs or of monomaniacs whose attentive if passive stares register a slow drainage of lifeblood. Designated as "riderless," the horses are liberated from any functional value and thrown into a horizontal equivalence with the men that is registered in their bodies beyond any emotional connection.

Figure 1.7. Théodore Géricault, *Horse Market: Five Horses at the Stake*, 1816–19. Image courtesy of RMN-Grand Palais/Art Resource, New York. Photo by Michèle Bellot.

While the project began as a genre painting, the eventual erasure of any specific reference to the Roman race transformed it into a "baffling" composition, according to Lorenz Eitner: "neither genre nor history; of grand style, but without definable subject."[45] Géricault abandoned historical event to focus on the otherwise historical territory and queer fantasy of horse-human relations. Eitner has commented on the development of the series from observed experience, evident in the first sketches, to an idealized "heroic vision concerning the primordial conflict between animal fury and human volition."[46] But the denuding of the humans that accompanies this development, and the switch to a neoclassical rendering, emphasizes less the contest between human and animal than their shared musculature and energy. Unlike his military men whose bodies are effaced beneath inflated armor, the men of the *Race* series are idealized in and through their own bare strength, their Michelangelo-esque muscularity. In his progression of sketches for the project, Géricault eliminated first the spectators and eventually all signs of a public spectacle to position the viewer as participant. At the same time, he shifts the focus from heads to tails, or from faces to haunches, hips, and buttocks: seat of physical and also sexual power. Thus

Figure 1.8. Théodore Géricault, *Entrance to the Adelphi Wharf*, 1821. Image courtesy of HIP/Art Resource, New York.

Le départ (*Horseracing in Rome*), one of the earlier painted sketches, now hanging in Lille (fig. 1.9), depicts what appears to be a contest of psychological stamina visible in the eyes and faces. That test of will is apparently won by the white horse at the center. As we move to the *Cheval arrêté par des esclaves* (*Horse Restrained by Slaves*) (fig. 1.10) and the final stage of the *Course* hanging in Paris, the faces and eyes lose importance and the focus moves, essentially, to the rear.

The various stages of the *Race* thus read as foreplay to a sodomite fantasy where desire and identification are inseparable: wanting to be and wanting to have appear at once as the will to penetrate and to embody the massive hindquarters of the horse. Human and horse, masculine and feminine alternate positions such that sexual as well as species differences lose their value. Is this a primal scene represented otherwise? In Freud's "Wolf Man," a case that is relevant for the displacement of affect between humans and animals, we

Figure 1.9. Théodore Géricault, *Horseracing in Rome*, ca. 1817. Image courtesy of the RMN-Grand Palais/Art Resource, New York. Photo by Michel Urtado.

learn that the primal scene is always viewed as taking place "from behind," *a tergo*, the way animals copulate. The fear (and perhaps also attraction) of that scene is described as a fear of *coitus more ferarum*, or sex in the position of beasts.[47] As Lee Edelman has explained, one of the interesting, if for some disturbing, aspects of this scene is the way the partners involved are sexually undifferentiated, perhaps because the anus shows no sex. He coins the term "(be)hindsight" to describe that formative scene, as well as the way we come to see it: "The most crucial and constitutive dramas of human life are those that can never be viewed head on, those that can never be taken in frontally, but only, as it were, approached from behind."[48] We could say, then, that it is with behindsight that Géricault envisions a sexuality that is at once bestial and idealized in these scenes of athletic men and boys grasping and lifting the tails of horses as they thrust themselves toward them. In such forceful, eroticized scenes, sexual difference is subsumed by species difference, but species difference loses any clear and constant markers or value: men and horses rise diagonally on two legs and share the power to take or the possibility of being taken. Here the artist turns away from the emotional demands

Figure 1.10. Théodore Géricault, *Cheval arrêté par des esclaves*, ca. 1817. Image courtesy of the Musée des Beaux Arts and the Réunion des Museés Métropolitains Rouen Normandie.

elicited by the face while allowing no single identity in the fantasy to be simply taken from behind.

Géricault never realized the final, monumental version of the *Race* project that he is said to have planned—perhaps because the vision was too personal or because his heroic fantasy could not withstand his return to France. The next large work he would begin was *The Raft of the Medusa*, less an antiheroic work than one documenting the death of the heroic. It is interesting, nevertheless, that the bodies hc paints aboard the raft are not the emaciated, sickly ones reported in newspaper accounts but the strong, well-muscled, and beautiful bodies of the *Race* series, now striving desperately to maintain their verticality and so survive. It is as if the identification with equine or animal bodies is still there, although now made evident not in manifestations of physical power, but in a conception of "bare life" or, perhaps, a Benthamite recognition of the capacity for suffering. "Our hopes and desires are nothing but futile dreams here on earth," Géricault wrote to his friend Pierre-Joseph Dedreux-Dorcy: "If there is anything certain on earth, it is our pain. Suffering is real, pleasures are only imagined."[49]

Figure 1.11. Théodore Géricault, *The 1821 Derby at Epsom*, 1821. Paris, the Louvre.

Horses would not disappear from Géricault's work. Indeed, in the paintings and lithographs made in London after 1820 they will once again become the central actors. But these are different animals—workhorses and racehorses, subservient and commodified beings whose power and energy are harnessed and contained for purposes of labor or entertainment. Gone is any physical or emotional connection except that accomplished by the whip. Deindividualized racehorses are stretched horizontally beneath their equally anonymous riders or covered with elegant initialed sheets that evoke the feminine gendering prevalent in both literary and popular discourse. In the most famous work of this period, *The 1821 Derby at Epsom* (fig. 1.11), the horses are different-colored imitations of one another, copies even in their shared glance toward the spectator. Moving in a synchronized but oddly motionless gallop, they have become a fantasy. This is the horse turned whore, now embodying not the artist's fantasy, but that of his paying public. Aliveness becomes matter not through death but through commodification, indicating what Zola would write sixty years later of the racehorse Nana: "She gleamed in the light like a new coin."[50]

Géricault's work in London is strangely premonitory for his generation. In his lithographs as in the Epsom Downs paintings, he assumes the position

Figure 1.12. Théodore Géricault, *A Harnessed Wagon*, from *Various Subjects Drawn from Life*, printed by Charles Joseph Hullmandel and published by Rodwell and Martin, 1821. Image courtesy of the Cleveland Museum of Art.

of the Romantic artist grown up: the gelded artist who acknowledges the necessity of containing or displacing his (sexual) energy or the disillusioned artist whose ideals of love and beauty now turn to thoughts of money. In a letter from England to Dedreux-Dorcy he wrote, "I give up Greek tragedy and Scripture in order to enclose myself in the stables, from which I will only emerge rolling in riches."[51] In this he joins other Romantic writers like Stendhal and later Flaubert, who found compensation for the loss of their illusions in a newly acquired ironic outlook on the world and the self. In Stendhal's *Le rouge et le noir*, Julien Sorel learns that he must turn his passion for horses into discursive capital by making a joke of his otherwise embarrassing fall into the mud. Turning his London lithographs into a book, Géricault displays a similar ironic vision in its frontispiece, where we find the image of a horse-drawn covered wagon viewed from behind (fig. 1.12).

With the title printed over it, the end is transformed into the beginning.[52] More provocatively, the rear of the wagon mimics the rump of the horse if not a human's rear minus the tail. Here, then, Géricault both cites and pokes fun at his own queer obsession and invites the viewer to part the slightly opened canvas and enter through the rear.

CHAPTER TWO

Putting the Horse before Descartes: Sensibility and the War on Pity

The opening pages of Eugène Sue's 1838 novel *Godolphin Arabian* depict an all too "common" and "sad spectacle" of a horse being beaten on the streets of Paris. It is a scene that recalls the one reported in *Le décade* some forty years before.[1] Sue does not spare his reader the gory details as he describes how the weary cart horse struggles to pull his overloaded wagon across the slippery ice, with the driver whipping him mercilessly.

> Breathless, and struggling violently, the poor horse was so exhausted by his continued and severe efforts, that, in spite of the cold, he was covered with sweat and white foam. Now, throwing himself into his collar with desperate exertion, he tugged so vehemently that the stones beneath his feet threw out streams of sparks; now, far from being discouraged by his energetic by vain attempts, he backed a few paces, in order to take breath, and then, once more exerting all his strength, he again essayed but still in vain, to advance with his tremendous load. Twice did he nearly fall, twice did his knees touch the frozen pavement, and twice did the carter, redoubling his blows and imprecations, raise him by a savage tug at the bit, which left the mouth of the unfortunate animal all raw and bleeding.[2]

The scene becomes more painful as the "savage owner" proceeds to "kick the poor creature violently on the nostrils" and then, when that has no effect, strikes a match and raises a burning bundle of straw, saying, "I'll roast the varmint, per'aps that'll make him get up." What is especially surprising, given the potential effect on the reader of this scene of "pitiless savagery," is the reaction of the witnessing crowd who watch with "cruel curiosity or a stupid apathy." Any pity or concern is absent except from a Quaker who happens to be passing by. Belonging to that sect which, according to the narrator, professes "the most generous feelings and the utmost sympathy for animals" (13), the Quaker takes the driver by the hand and asks to buy the horse. The reactions of the crowd and the driver are the same: "they could not comprehend such compassion" and were persuaded that the Quaker was *un fou*, a madman.

Sue was one of the most widely read authors of his time, and the short novel, first published in the popular journal *La presse*, had an instant success with almost immediate translations into English and an abridged version for young readers. The story behind the novel had already become legendary as an equine prince and pauper tale of the stallion who became the first thoroughbred sire. Born in Yemen in 1724, the stallion was given as a gift to the king of France in 1730 by the bey of Tunis, but because of his unruly temperament he ended up as cart horse on the streets of Paris. Scham, as the horse comes to be known, would eventually be rescued and brought to England by the estate of Lord Godolphin. The rest is thoroughbred history, and undoubtedly Sue's novel contributed to the growing cult surrounding the *pur-sang* (pureblood) or thoroughbred horse. His story also brought needed attention to the growing concern over horse flogging in the city of Paris and to animal abuse more generally. A closer look at the novel will show how the status and plight of the horse can be seen to illustrate the conflicting demands of industry and of compassion, a feeling that must now be directed toward animals if they can no longer be regarded as unfeeling machines. As the figure of the Quaker reveals, the new sensibility toward animals faced resistance for being unreasonable, but, as I hope to show, it also initiated a reconsideration of the reasonableness of affect and the emotions more generally.

Pitoyable (pitiful) is a word used to describe the Quaker, as its negation, *impitoyable* (without pity) is repeated in the descriptions of the violence of the scene. *Pitoyable* in French, like "pitiful" in English, has ambiguous meanings and can suggest one who is deserving of pity or compassion, as it can also describe an act or a person as something of an affront to human dignity or, perhaps, reason. The scene thus poses the question whether it is reasonable to pity a horse. According to French historian Maurice Agulhon, the rise of animal protection in France was less a response to animal suffering than a means to condemn the abusive behavior of those who worked with animals. Among them, and as we see in Sue's novel, carriage drivers became the locus and epitome of cruelty, giving rise to expressions such as "to swear like a carter" (*jurer comme un charretier*).[3]

By pitting a Quaker—a sect known for both its compassion and its republican ideals—against the carter, Sue's novel offers an important moment in what Jacques Derrida has called a "war on pity," whose origins he situates toward the end of the eighteenth century. This war, as he describes it, is directly connected to the West's relations with nonhuman animals and to efforts to deny or conceal the violence done to them in the name of industry. If there is no knowledge or proof of harm, there is no need to respond to it, whether for individuals, businesses, or governments. In this, Derrida's work confirms observations made by Keith Thomas at the very end of his pioneering 1983 book *Man and the Natural World*, about the way that by 1800 the "new sensibilities" that had arisen over the course of the eighteenth century came into conflict with "the new material foundations of human society."[4] These new sensibilities include a growing sentimentality toward some animals (especially, but not only, pets), as well a rising appreciation for nature and the creatures within it, who (as Quakers too would say) are all part of God's kingdom. As these new sensibilities grew, however, so too did confusion and anxiety over the growing demands of industrialization and its methods of breeding animals for labor, spectacle, and food. The result was "compromise and concealment," Thomas suggests, referring to efforts to ignore or deny such exploitation, which prevented this conflict from ever being fully resolved.[5]

Thomas's focus is England, but the conflict of sensibilities he describes could also be found in France at the turn of the century and in the clash of eighteenth-century Enlightenment humanism with a growing Romantic celebration of nature and the "natural." Romanticism, as represented first by Rousseau, celebrated those animal sentiments that were being repressed or corrupted by social conventions. Pity in particular, Rousseau writes, is "so natural that even the beasts sometimes show evident signs of it. . . . An animal never goes past a dead animal of his own species without some restlessness."[6] For Rousseau the moral force and utility of pity come from its being "the pure movement of Nature prior to all reflection" (152), indicating that thought and reasoning interfere with the identification with others that is necessary for pity. As we shall see, however, the Romantic promotion of such emotions as compassion or pity would also be blamed for those "natural" passions that stirred the Revolution and were said to lead to the violent and brutish situation of the Terror. Sue's novel, I suggest, gives evidence of unease about the animal origins of sentiment itself and hence a skepticism about the effectiveness of emotions such as sympathy or pity for lending moral clarity or leading to responsible action.

"War is waged over the matter of pity," Derrida writes in *L'animal que donc je suis* (*The Animal That Therefore I Am*), adding that it is "necessary" to "think through this war" because it "concerns what we call thinking."[7] Before returning to Sue's novel, I want to explore the "matter" of pity for animals and its connection, and sometimes opposition, to what we call thinking over the course of this century that established the first anticruelty laws and the Society for the Protection of Animals. One might expect that pity had some role in these efforts, but I will argue that pity, and in particular pity for animals, "mattered" in contradictory ways, influenced on one hand by changes in what historian William Reddy has termed "emotional regimes," referring to historical and cultural shaping of emotional expression, and by changes in the understanding of exactly what pity is and what it can do for humans or for other animals.[8] The Grammont Law condemning cruelty to animals would eventually be passed in July 1850, but if the emotions played a role, it was largely because concern for the animal was lucrative for industry and its image. This was especially true in the case of horses, animals who moved between the status of pet and that of livestock, partner, and enslaved worker. As one English author noted toward the end of the nineteenth century, "The horse is looked on as a machine, for sentiment pays no dividend."[9] Moreover, since the Grammont Law protected only against public displays of cruelty, "compromise and concealment" became, and continues to be, the name of the game.

THE MATTER OF PITY

Critics today tend to dismiss pity as a sign of sentimental "infection" (as Nietzsche called it) or as a display of condescension and disdain in the manner argued by Hannah Arendt.[10] Pity has been replaced by empathy, understood as a productive and altruistic feeling for another, such as that promoted by Barbara Kruger's huge 1994 panel in the Strasbourg train station that greets travelers with the words *L'empathie peut changer le monde* (Empathy can change the world) or in recent books such as Jeremy Rifkin's *The Empathic Civilization* (2010) and primatologist Frans de Waal's *The Age of Empathy* (2009). But the word empathy did not exist before the twentieth century;[11] during the eighteenth century and into the nineteenth it was pity that was regarded as humanity's most honored sentiment: "Nothing lends more honor to humanity than this generous sentiment," reads the 1751 entry on *pitié* in Diderot's *Encyclopédie*.[12] Pity and compassion were described there as "moral sentiments" if not Christian duties, whereas the closely related notion of sympathy was categorized first as a physiological response, an immediate "communication" of feeling.

Outside the *Encyclopédie*, however, the distinctions were not so clear. David Will's translation of Derrida's "subject [*sujet*] of pity" to "*matter* of pity" forges a connection between old and new materialisms by linking pity to the kinds of neural phenomena associated with empathy today: empathy as an automatic mirror-imaging or a material sensation that is prior to cognition. Indeed, in eighteenth-century thought, not unlike today, the "matter" of pity (often referred to as sympathy) is what allowed that sentiment to be shared across species as well as between humans. But perhaps in resistance to such an equation of mind and matter or out of a desire to distinguish human from nonhuman capacities, we also find efforts, then as now, to distinguish the material and automatic sharing of sentiment from a willful imagining oneself into another across boundaries of difference—a deliberate act that requires more than neural firing.

Derrida claims that the war on pity has been waged for some two hundred years, bringing us to the turn of the eighteenth century and to the rise of industrial and experimental practices using animals for food and medicine. More specifically, I would argue, the war has also to do with questions regarding the subject of pity (*sujet de la pitié*)[13] in terms of who experiences it and toward whom. With regard to nonhuman animals, how might that subject determine the experience, and how might the essence of pity as material or animal affect change the way one thinks it could or should be directed toward other species? Descartes affirmed the wrongness, if not irrationality, of showing pity for animals, since, as he put it, they are incapable of "real" feelings. They only react like machines, don't feel pain, and cannot suffer. But Descartes's dualist approach to human-animal difference would be contested by the eighteenth century's cult of sensibility (*sensibilité*), which worked to elide neat distinctions between body and mind. As the essential link between the physical and moral realms, moreover, and between the body and man's ethical faculties, the ideas that developed around the cult of sensibility worked to overturn Descartes's opposition between feeling and reason, giving political and moral importance to those "natural" emotions like "pity" that, as Rousseau and other Enlightenment figures suggested, humans shared with animals.

In *The Animal Claim: Sensibility and the Creaturely Voice*, Tobias Menely writes of sensibility as a direct response to Descartes's *bête-machine* and intriguingly characterizes it as a kind of "semiosis," a communicative capacity that is shared across species. Especially focused on the British tradition, Menely reminds us that for Shaftesbury "sympathy" was synonymous with "communication." The ability to recognize the "impassioned voice" signifies "the elemental medium of community," "the pre-cultural origin of sociability."[14] Anne Vila has put forth a similar argument with respect to the French tradition, writing that sensibility as "a means of establishing causal connections between the physical and moral realms . . . was seen as the innate and active principle of sociability that gave rise to human society."[15] This principle of original and natural sociability worked its way into the ideals of the Revolution when, according to William Reddy, there was no better way for the Revolutionary supporter Madame Rolande to prove that the Convention ought to hear her than to "hug a stray dog."[16] Such a gesture would exhibit the "natural source" of her feeling, hence its necessary authenticity and goodness. Indeed, praise for the natural sociability of animals and their affections would find its ultimate political spokesperson in Louis-Antoine de Saint-Just.[17] But as Saint-Just and the Jacobins took it upon themselves to legislate correct displays of pity and to separate true, emotional communication from its false and "purchased" expression, so Madame Roland would be imprisoned with her dog and eventually executed with her husband for treason.[18] As Reddy and others have argued, the violent, emotional extremes of the Terror would lead to a retreat from sentimentalism and the demise of an emotionally informed politics. Cartesian rationality and an honor code would return as the generating principles of government.[19]

Menely's understanding of sensibility also emphasizes that "creaturely expression" and "the passionate voice" are "irreducible to semantic convention."[20] While this will have bearing for the process by which "creaturely claims" will be recognized and politically constituted, it will also affect the ways basic emotions can be understood and communicated and so influence what it could mean to hug a dog. Reddy speaks of "multiple languages within the self or within 'experience'" that are a "precondition to the existence of meaningful speech."[21] "Emotive" is the term he uses to reference the language with which emotions are expressed and also managed, whether by individuals or by the larger society in which they must be understood. Emotions, he emphasizes, are "activated" and regulated by the very norms that try to make them understandable. Always prior to and in excess of the emotives with which we try to describe them, emotions are also changed by those very utterances, creating something of an ongoing dialectic between emotions as "thought material" but not yet thought and the expression of that material. The political importance of emotives is especially apparent in relation to the standards or norms by which "emotional suffering" is judged or measured, and by which we recognize such suffering in the first place.[22] Reddy, it should be noted, reserves the term "emotive" for human expression, indeed for expression that derives from intentional decisions if not from a deliberate act of translation.[23] I shall return to the issue of translation at the end of this chapter, but here I simply want to emphasize its importance with regard to human-animal relations. To the extent that "we are their voices," as PETA advocates with regard to other nonhuman voices, "emotive" can describe acts of translation of nonhuman suffering and nonhuman needs into human language, acts that must also negotiate stiff forms of linguistic and political control. Such control was especially active when it came to defining boundaries between what was and wasn't accepted as "natural."

For much of the nineteenth century our relations with animals in general and with horses in particular provided a testing ground for determining what role, if any, pity should play in public life. Writings from the turn of the century describe both how and for whom pity would or would not be activated and how it was judged legitimate by virtue of the particular suffering it recognized and claimed to know or represent. What we find is evidence for the ways pity as an immediate sharing of suffering was set in opposition to thought and rational intention and so discounted as having a positive role in politics, art, or literature. This is exemplified in the works of Flaubert, where the "natural" feelings of Catherine Leroux for her cows in *Madame Bovary*, or of Félicité for her parrots in "A Simple Heart"—two women whose work ethic far exceeds their intellect—take the brunt of his modernist irony. In these women we see the distance that midcentury French realism has traveled from sentimentalism, as they also expose the way animal sympathy (especially from women) could be and was exploited.[24] But if pity or sympathy is sentimental and unreasonable, how does one stimulate what Edmund Burke, in his *Reflections on the French Revolution*, called the "moral imagination" that separates man from animals? What sort of thinking and of thinking about suffering can lead to moral clarity and action? Can those who lack such thinking themselves be worthy of pity? Who, indeed, are the rightful subjects of pity?

SENSIBILITY, READING, AND ANIMAL PROTECTION

In 1802 the issue of pity toward animals was explicitly raised in an essay contest proposed by members of the Academy or Institute for Moral and Political Science (called *deuxième classe* or Idéologues), a group founded in 1795 and disbanded by Napoleon in 1803. Led by Antoine-Louis-Claude Destutt de Tracy and Pierre-Jean-Georges Cabanis, the Idéologues were mostly "sensationalists," accepting John Locke's and Étienne Bonnot de Condillac's view on the primacy of the sensations for ideas. But the group also included Jacques-Henri Bernardin de Saint-Pierre, whose 1788 novel *Paul et Virginie* remained a sentimentalist icon throughout the nineteenth century. It was Saint-Pierre who explicitly turned animal sensibility into a question of political sentiment and posed the following question for a "Prix de Morale": "To what extent should the barbarian treatments imposed on animals be of interest to public morality?" Twenty-seven essays were submitted in response, and these were insightfully excerpted and analyzed by the French sociologist Valentin Pelosse.[25] As Pelosse explains, most of the responses were written not by animal professionals or those who worked with animals, but by those who saw themselves as writers and thinkers. This created what he calls a "stylistic homogeneity" among the essays, which he attributes to the "Delille effect," or popularity of the prerevolutionary poet Jacques Delille. Delille's poem *Pity* (*La pitié*), was published in 1803, the very year of the contest. It is a long poem (over a thousand lines followed by notes), divided into four "chants" or psalms, the first of which begins in praise of pity as an essentially human gift and the foundation of human dominion over the animal world:

> Glorious attribute of man, king of the world,
> Of all his traits, pity is the fertile source,
> Force is not what makes him king of the animals
> No, it is that pity that moans over sorrows.[26]

Delille's praise for the glory of pity echoes Louis de Jaucourt's entry on pity in Diderot's *Encyclopédie*, even as the poem resituates eighteenth-century materialist views within a religious or metaphysical framework of dominion. Referring readers to the "touching" (*attendrissant*) prints of animal cruelty by Hogarth, the First Chant clearly has horses in mind as it focuses on those animals that "serve" man, in war and at home, and implores that "they should be our aids, even our friends, but not our victims." "It is above all to you that we owe our pity / Generous Animal, model of friendship" (27).

The publication of Delille's poem was a "political event" according to the well-known nineteenth-century critic Charles Augustin Sainte-Beuve, and its juxtaposition of the sufferings of kings and the suffering of animals raised the attention of Napoleon's advisers.[27] The poem even included a eulogy for Madame Roland's dog, who had been imprisoned with her:

> Oh you! Who, consoling your royal mistress,
> Until her last sigh, proved to her your tenderness
> Who charmed her unhappiness, distracted her from prison:
> Oh, the farewells of a brother, unique and sad gift . . .

For you who, almost alone in this century of ingrates,
In the hours of unhappiness did not abandon her,
Go to the Élysée, where your shadow reposes,
Enjoy the sweet honors of your apotheosis! (27–28)

Delille refers to a "right to pity" (*droit à la pitié*) in the poem's preface, but most of the poem gives less attention to rights than to the responsibilities of the sensitive man, *l'homme sensible*, who figures, as Pelosse indicates, as the hero of the Delille's poem and of many of the prize essays. *Sensibilité*, as in Rousseau, is represented as the "quality shared with the suffering animal," and it is the very quality that the contestants for the prize wish themselves to exemplify through their expressive witnessing of that suffering.[28] *Sensibilité*, or sensitivity to the sufferings of others, is upheld as a mark of distinction in the modern age, since it no longer appears natural in men or, as Rousseau warned, has been lost.

Many essays look for ways that *sensibilité* can be newly cultivated, while others look to identify ways to discriminate between quantities, if not qualities, of sensibility toward animals. Thus, for example, the sensible man is offered as the ideal to be emulated and is contrasted with the sensible woman, who tends to show an overabundance of pity toward animals, often at the expense of attention to other humans (such as her own family). Sensibility could be a useful sentiment toward animals in the home, but it was up to the *homme sensible* to determine its just function in the public realm and, more specifically, to determine when an animal's "signs" of distress merit our attention.[29] Pelosse also points to an ambiguity in the meaning of *sensibilité* that runs throughout the essays and that has relevance for its gendered as well as classed manifestations. Much like the pity Rousseau describes in *Émile*, *sensibilité* could be at once a purely physical faculty of feeling or sensitivity (associated especially with women) and something more reflective: "the effect of an impression on an internal sentiment, which has its source in an act of intelligence and belongs only to the moral sentiments."[30]

This distinction between physical reaction and moral reflection will also influence opinions on how and whether sensibility can be taught or legislated. Where some respondents requested laws in the hopes of rehabilitating our treatment of animals, others wrote against any form of repressive legislation for fear it would only force violent impulses underground or into private spaces or, worse, redirect them to other humans. Thus, wrote one respondent:

> It could happen, that the cruel, in order to take revenge on laws that they can't avoid and whose menace they can't endure, impose suffering on innocent animals when they're alone. Unable to assert their propensities as they wish, they may become even more bent on creating victims. . . . Since cruelty is an active and violent passion that needs feeding, wouldn't it be better for it to be nourished on animals than on men? (28–29)

To legislate pity, then, could backfire. Instead, it should be taught or modeled. Such a pedagogical, if not sentimental, project would thus also be a republican project, contributing to *la morale universelle* and a love of justice. It was what the working class or *peuple* needed in particular. "Europe is covered with theaters consecrated to the instruction of the rich; I find none for the *peuple*," wrote one contestant (29). Their "spectacles" are of butchery and "barbarian" acts toward animals.

Identification was central to these spectacles where readers and viewers were supposed to feel their own eyes being punched or their own arms and legs being pulled out from the body, as one writer put it. But identification was also risky because, as one warned, "cruelty is contagious to the point where the fictive spectacle of cruel actions is enough to plant the seed" (32). *L'homme sensible*, in other words, might be as receptive to cruelty as to pity. Indeed, in *Émile* Rousseau cautioned against assuming identification and sympathy with the victim of injustice rather than the perpetrator. He advises against having children read La Fontaine's fable "The Ant and Grasshopper" because they will not have "sufficient reason" to understand the moral—the value both of art and of generosity. Rather than sympathize with the hungry artist/grasshopper, they will want to imitate the industrious, if selfish, ant who teaches the child "not merely to refuse [the grasshopper] but to revile him."[31] As soon as there is "spectacle," writes Pelosse, the process of identification loses its pedagogical value because of the uncertainty of psychological investment in the object, whether food or power. Sensibility can be a basis for community, but it might also breed division.

THE PITIFUL AND THE PITILESS IN SUE'S *GODOLPHIN ARABIAN*

The essay contest on the role of pity for animals had no immediate political consequences. Napoleon dissolved the Academy even before a prizewinner could be announced, and it would be almost fifty years before France would pass its first law against cruelty to animals. This law punished the public abuse of domestic animals with either a fine or a prison sentence depending on the severity of the abuse or its outcome.[32] Acts of cruelty committed in the home or out of view were not considered to be of public concern and so were not included as criminal offenses.

The Grammont Law raised the status of domestic animals from things to creatures of some sentience, but the harm done to the animals themselves was not the primary focus. Rather, it was directed to proper public behavior and how to teach and encourage correct displays of sympathy. Much as today, discussions led to the role literature and theater might play in "expanding the circle of moral concern," to borrow a phrase from Peter Singer.[33] The psychologist Steven Pinker and the literary critic Elaine Scarry have recently argued that literature plays a vital role in developing our faculties for empathy and for putting ourselves into the position of some one very different from ourselves.[34] Nineteenth-century views were more cautious, perhaps recalling Rousseau's warnings about readers who take the side of the selfish ant rather than the hungry grasshopper. Thus the prolific novelist Honoré de Balzac waxed eloquent over the seductive value of vice in literature, whose multifaceted representations were far more interesting than the monotonous, if not boring, face of virtue. "Do you know what our immorality consists in?" he asked, referring to novelists like himself. "In rendering faults seductive. In excusing them."[35] Such warnings about the seductive value of vice, if not of violence, bring us to question what significance must be given to the increasing representation of horse beatings by midcentury. Might the "pleasure" of compassion, as described a century before in the *Encyclopédie*, offer a ploy for expanding readership or, worse, for enticing us to take the viewpoint of the abusive worker who beats the horse rather than that of the suffering animal? Such a problem of shifting perspectives was what Raskolnikov experienced in a dream of horse flogging in the streets of Petersburg, in Dostoyevsky's *Crime and Punishment*. Imagination may activate pity, but evidence suggests it may also entice us toward its opposite. The violent opening of Sue's novel might serve as an enticement for readership rather than engaging the reader's compassion toward horses.

Written almost forty years before Anna Sewell's *Black Beauty* (1877), Sue's tale illustrates how horses have been caught up in a political realm from which they are excluded as agents.[36] A creature between *zoe* and *bios* or between species life and the life worthy of a biography, the Godolphin Arabian is defined at once by his geographical provenance (the Arab world) and by his owner, Lord Godolphin.[37] The name signals the British appropriation of Arab blood, and questions of race and breeding are integral to Sue's story, which like *Black Beauty* has also been read as a slave narrative. In the background is the rivalry between the French and British empires that extended even to horse breeding and a larger traffic in animals. Enmeshed in this rivalry of nations is also a contest over the true meaning and correct display of pity.

Two characters in the novel can be said to represent animal compassion: the Quaker and a mute Arab boy, Agba, who has traveled with Scham from Yemen and refuses to part from him. Building on the view of pity as an "innate component of the feminine personality,"[38] the novel illustrates through these two strangers the otherness of pity for animals on French soil, if not the foreignness of animal affection. If the novel does make a plea for such affection, it is by illustrating that such concern will be good for breeding and consequently for the nation. To this end, the narrative charts a shift in the meaning and value of blood such that the blood that flows in the opening scene as a result of a beating becomes increasingly important not for what it reveals about the capacity for human violence, but for what it hides in terms of symbolic capital. This is the value of blood for breeding.

The shifting meaning of blood will also be relevant for the intersections and rivalries between ideas of class and species at the time. Sue was a dandy, a founding member of the Jockey Club, and a socialist who increasingly turned his attention to the plight of the working class. In his popular tale, the contest of the horse as symbolic capital or blood with the horse as labor power is intertwined with and opposed to matters of affection or more specifically pity—pity for horses as modeled on but also in contest with empathy for other humans. As Harriet Ritvo and Kathleen Kete have discussed, depictions of animal abuse could inspire distrust of the very zoophilia they appear to support by promoting condemnation of those "dangerous laboring classes" who beat their horses, over and above any understanding of the subjectivity and needs of the animals.[39] Socialists of the time, including Karl Marx, feared that a growing animal protection movement would reduce sympathy for the working class—those for whom horses were their livelihood—if not shore up the moral superiority of the middle class and their love of pets.[40] Thus Marx included members of societies for the prevention of cruelty to animals among those who are "desirous of redressing social grievances [only] in order to secure the continued existence of bourgeois society."[41]

Animal suffering, nevertheless, grew as a focus of representation about the same time as the discourse around misery—what it is and what causes it—became the focus of essay contests and literature such as Balzac's *Splendeurs et misères des courtisanes* or Hugo's *Les misérables*, both of 1845. The same year that Sue's novel appeared, Victor Hugo published his poem "Melancholia," which included a less graphic but still emotionally disturbing depiction of a beaten horse among a series of scenes of the sufferings of working-class children and families. Human and animal suffering were thus placed on a comparable scale. Sue's novel enters the discourse but complicates it in that the horse is both likened to a worker and abused by one. In his version of the story, the horse's misery is ascribed at once to his own behavior (revealing him to be a creature of agency) and to the cruelty of his keepers, who have turned him into an unfeeling object. As if unable to decide between these two, the author also ascribes his misery to fate: "two prophetic and contradictory signs" on Scham's body that, Agba explains, could either doom the horse to misery or signal a long and illustrious life.

As the causes of Scham's misery are thus unclear, so are the potential cures. Pity will play an ambiguous role. While the Quaker represents certain republican ideals of equality, we have also seen that the crowd regards him as a "madman" because of his concern for the horse. Pity is further called into question when its most loyal incarnation is found in the character of Agba—referred to in racialized terms as *le mauricaud*, or blackamoor in English translation. Indeed, it is in his muteness that Agba embodies questions about the possibility and function of sympathetic understanding at this time, or what Richard Nash has called "affective modes of knowledge." While others are said to treat Agba as "a Jew, a renegade, a heretic, a para" (43), the Quaker is fascinated by his intimacy with the horse and what he believes to be his "singular intelligence" (31). Orientalism shades into animality, moreover, as Agba's "attachment" to Scham is repeated in a cat named Grimalkin who is inseparable from the horse. Describing the affection between cat and horse, the carter explains, "the blackamoor may make himself a fool about the horse, that I'll allow, because he is himself a human being, and they both come from the same place in foreign parts; but a cat! Why it ain't believable" (17). Indeed, what he finds especially unbelievable, and *bête*, is that Agba would groom and take care of Scham for nothing. "But what's the use of rubbing and cleaning? Do I rub myself down? Do I take any care of myself? Pooh, to be sure not, what's the use of rubbing and cleaning—nothing but a set of useless rubbish, only fit to make horses as tender and delicate as women . . . why should an animal want rubbing and cleaning?" (21). The carter's jealousy reveals his own indignation that an animal could be treated better than he is or that the desires of an animal could be comparable to those of the worker.

But Agba's intimacy and identification with the horse will be crucial to the novel's turning point and lead to the horse's prodigious and profitable (at least for his owner) future as a sire. Such intimacy had become something of an orientalist trope by this point, one that emphasized the shared "ani-

Figure 2.1. Jean-Baptiste Mauzaisse, *The Arab Lamenting the Death of His Steed*, ca. 1812. Image courtesy of the Birmingham Museum of Art. Photo by Sean Pathasema.

mal" sensibilities of Arabian horse and Arab (usually referring to a range of peoples from North Africa and the Middle East). Charles Hubert Millevoye's poem "L'Arabe au tombeau de son coursier" (1812) describes the intense sadness of an Arab over his horse's death in battle. The scene was subsequently and erotically illustrated in a painting by Jean-Baptiste Mauzaisse titled *Arabe pleurant son coursier* (*The Arab Lamenting the Death of His Steed*)(fig. 2.1).[42] Some twelve years later Eugène Delacroix would reverse subject and object and show an Arabian horse's intense concern for his rider in his watercolor *Turk Resting, Watched by His Horse* (fig. 2.2). Today we might use the term "emotional intelligence" to describe the recognition between Arab and Arabian horse. But as Donna Landry suggests, the British, and perhaps the French too, failed "to recognize Oriental knowledges as knowledge."[43] The people who bred, trained, and rode Eastern horses were regarded as creatures of nature, not of culture. In Sue's book nature, in the shape of Agba and Scham (Arab and horse), will triumph over culture, only to be reappropriated as a new form of capital.

Scham is eventually sold to Lord Godolphin as a "teaser" to excite Roxana

Figure 2.2. Eugène Delacroix, *Turk Resting, Watched by His Horse,* 1824. Image courtesy of the Rhode Island School of Design Museum.

and prepare the mare for insemination by her intended mate, Hobgoblin. The latter, we are told, "was to have the unappreciable honor of regenerating the blood of the English race-horse" (79). Here the novel turns from slave narrative to animal romance, if not to an account of animal magnetism. Politics makes way for triangulated desire as Agba "identifies" with his horse to the point where he "desired [Roxana] for Scham with an ardour which hardly fell short of passion" (91). In that fit of passion that instinctively recognizes the "nobleness and worth" of such an alliance, Agba opens the gate to allow Scham to defeat Hobgoblin and mate with the beautiful Roxana, who awaits him with a desire matching his own. The rest is thoroughbred history, as "no colt ever showed finer qualities," and the lovers, first punished for their behavior, are ultimately returned to favor and given luxurious care. Scham, the Godolphin Arabian, takes the place of Hobgoblin, now relegated to the status of teaser, and continues to triumph with two more colts and generations of renowned race winners.

Animal magnetism, Arab love, and intuition are thus aligned with animal passion to lend support to the biopolitical arena of thoroughbred breeding. Sympathy and unmediated affect triumph as investments, albeit of a new form. The animal body, regarded as material labor and as such alternately identified with and subservient to the working and "dangerous" classes, has now been transformed into capital and identified with and available to the upper classes as a product of breeding—a "pureblood" (*pur-sang*)—to be displayed in the realm of sport or spectacle. The moral of the story, as Sue expresses it at the end of the novel, is more in line with later decadent works: "In spite of the apparent uselessness of this biographical narrative, we think it may be advantageous to note the necessary conclusion of these facts, for they demonstrate the undeniable power of pure blood as the means of regenerating bastard races, and thus affect a grave question of agriculture, commerce and national interest" (113). The answer to horse beatings is thus to breed better horses, or to breed compassion by way of eugenic policies that will serve national interests.

THE ENDS OF PITY AND BEGINNINGS OF TRANSLATION

The instituting of anticruelty laws in France reflected less a new sensibility toward nature or toward animals than a concern for humanity and what constituted humane behavior. Behind the laws was the recognition that the potential violence of humans and the contagion of that violence could be bad for business. "The massacre of horses by the cart drivers is a true loss for the national economy," the authors of the Grammont Law argued.[44] In this regard, showing pity was as much a form of cultural and political capital as a display of virtue or character. Such was also the understanding of Charles Baudelaire, who in the 1860s addressed the question of pity with an irony absent in Sue and reminiscent of Rousseau's views—if initially in an inverted form. Rousseau, we saw above, praised pity as an antidote to reason's calculated selfishness. Baudelaire would recode pity not as affective identification, but as another form of calculation, that is, as profitable affect. In his prose poem "Counterfeit," the narrator reads a gesture of offering alms to a beggar on the street as speculation, calculated "to do a good deed while at the same time making a good deal." It is an attempt "to win paradise economically."[45] The beggar's solicitation of pity, moreover, is compared to the look of a beaten dog: "For the man of feeling who is able to read them, I know nothing more distressing than the mute eloquence of a pauper's pleading eyes, so full of humility and reproach. There is in them something of the profound and complex emotion to be seen in the tear-filled eyes of a dog being beaten" (58).

Much in this poem will revolve around attending to, or ignoring, the eyes and face of the other—animal or beggar—and reading the vulnerability they express, if not around how to respond to that vulnerability and take responsibility for it. Reading those eyes, and not just sensing their pain, has become the special capacity of Baudelaire's *homme sensible*, who has the ability to determine the best gesture of compassion.

Baudelaire thus poses the very question Derrida asks in *L'animal que donc je suis*: How do I respond to the look of the other? "An animal looks at me. What am I to think of this sentence?"[46] To what extent should the animal other concern me? This is a question Baudelaire raises in other prose poems as well, although his narrators sometimes take joy in adding to another's suffering rather than trying to relieve it.[47] What is troubling to the narrator of this poem is his discovery that the coin his friend gave the beggar was counterfeit and thus that its outcome, perhaps like speculation itself, could either "multiply into good money" (*multiplier en pièces variées*) or land the beggar in jail. The narrator thus blames his friend for the "ineptitude of his calculation." Deliberate cruelty may have some aesthetic merit, the narrator claims, but it is "an unforgiveable vice to do harm from stupidity," from *bêtise*. Calculation, weighing the good against the bad, produces a self-serving expression of pity, understood not only as economic or cultural investment, but as a spiritual investment as well. A form of stupidity, if not of a certain type of animality (as suggested by the literal translation of *bête* as animal or beast), this calculation as *bêtise*, is opposed to a different kind of thinking, produced by a close attention to and reading of the other's eyes. Such is the compulsive but also imaginative reasoning we see in the narrator who can't stop thinking, whose "fancy," as he calls it, "lends wings to his friend's imagination, . . . drawing all possible deductions from all possible hypotheses" as to what this coin might do to the beggar.

Here, as in Rousseau, imagination is what brings one to consider the situation of the other/beggar/dog and to consider that other's point of view. Indeed, we might say, invoking Emmanuel Levinas, that Baudelaire's narrator is made hostage to the face and look of the other by his "miserable brain" and the "exhausting faculty" of thought that activates his imagination regarding the eyes before him.[48] Levinas, we must remember, is equivocal about whether the face of an animal can and should have the same ethical effect as the face of a human. "The priority is not found in the animal, but in the human face. We understand the animal, the face of the animal, in accordance with Dasein."[49] Baudelaire's narrator understands the dog's expression by way of that of a human, as indicated by the anthropocentric reference to the eyes as "tear-filled": dogs do not make tears. But if the dog's emotion is read in accordance with a human's, the beggar's face is acknowledged and read through the priority of the dog he is compared to. We might then ask whether the mention of tears is another sign of *bêtise* or a productive metaphor.

The question brings us back to emotives, to the difficulty of understanding not only what one feels but also what the other feels, and how thinking and feeling are intertwined in the brain so that it is not always clear which activates which. Reddy describes an incident in 1816 in which the philosopher Maine de Biran was asked to give to the poor and, on learning that his offering was smaller than most others, experienced a whirlwind of reactions. He "had penetrated a typically nineteenth-century type of internal space, a space where moral uncertainty and ambiguity has supplanted the fervent clarity of late sentimentalism, and where shame has a new power."[50] That power is to make him reflect not only on how much he gave but also on the uncertainty over how others will judge that gesture. Reddy adds that Maine de Biran concluded later in life that "the human soul was not as so many eighteenth-century thinkers had thought, inherently good, but—ineffable" (212).

Moral uncertainty and ineffability are also what Baudelaire's poet experiences. Maine de Biran's reflection was largely focused on the uncertainty about how others perceived him. Baudelaire's poet, by contrast, is concerned with the uncertain status of the beggar whose own "ineffable" consciousness is reflected in the "mute eloquence" of the dog's eyes and their combined look of need and reproach.

In Baudelaire, true pity or compassion is not opposed to thinking (as Rousseau first claimed) but rather is integral to the duty of thinking itself as a kind of suffering of the other, a suffering that comes from the imagination.[51] While the friend's calculated gesture deflects or protects him from such thinking (and is thus *bêtise*), the narrator suffers from the look of the other, indeed from the recognition that the animal other *me regarde* in the double sense of looks at me and concerns me. Whereas some twenty years later Nietzsche will dismiss pity as an infection, Baudelaire represents thinking as an infection of pity.[52] It is why his thinking poet looks on beggars, but also dogs and horses, with a "brotherly eye."[53] Perhaps this is why, for Derrida, "Thinking concerning the animal, if there is such a thing, derives from poetry . . . what philosophy has had to deprive itself of.[54] Pity confronts us with the ineffable, and consequently the undecidable.

Philosophy, Derrida writes, may be that "calculated forgetting" that the animal can look at me—that the animal concerns me.[55] This may be because philosophy refuses to accept sensibility as a matter of thinking or refuses to risk anthropomorphic translations of the other's look.[56] Toward the end of *The Beast and the Sovereign*, and in a statement about the function of imagination reminiscent of Rousseau, Derrida insists that "everything we have spoken about comes down to problems of translation. . . . It's in our way of translating what are called animal reactions that we believe ourselves able—but this is a risk of translation—to discern or trace a limit between animality and humanity, reactive animality and responsive or responsible humanity."[57] To be sure, the translations necessitated by human-animal relations, translations from one sense to another, from touch or smell to words and back again, might be the most difficult we confront. They force us to see the uniqueness of human language, but also how it is limited by all that we don't know of nonhuman languages, whether of dogs, horses, rats, or bees. Translation, perhaps like pity, Derrida suggests, is both necessary and impossible.[58] It is necessary because of the ways we are indebted to the many creatures who activate our imagination and our senses, thus giving us wings like Baudelaire's poet. "To be human," Menely writes referencing Rousseau, "is to find one's volition . . . in one's responsiveness to a prior voice," that voice of "creaturely being."[59] But it is not only humans who thus become responsive, and responsible, because animals also respond to us, translating our eyes, our voice, our gestures, our smell, and other signs we are unconscious of.[60] Translation is nevertheless impossible because of what, in the other and in ourselves, remains opaque to understanding, if not in excess of what we willingly or unwillingly perceive. Emotion, Reddy reminds us, is always in excess of its emotive. It is only through attention to the necessity and impossibility of translation that empathy can become an ethical force.

Any ethical obligation, Judith Butler has argued, demands translation, "otherwise we are ethically bound only to those who already speak as we do, in the language we already know."[61] This is especially true for those who live in what she calls "unwilled proximity and unchosen cohabitation," referring to the everyday experience of Jews and Palestinians. Risking a "dreaded comparison," I suggest the aptness of these terms to describe the situation of domestic animals in particular, if not all animals of the Anthropocene who live in "unchosen cohabitation" with humans. It underscores what some see as the injustice behind all domestication—that our freedoms are so unevenly distributed and that some have freedoms others lack. Citing Levinas, who also figures largely in Butler's book, Vicki Hearne writes that "freedom can never be justified, but it can be rendered just."[62] Translation, in the form of reading and thinking the mute eloquence of those animals we cohabit with, is our impossible obligation, a necessary step toward rendering our freedom, and our pity, just.

CHAPTER THREE

Making *Horse*work Visible: Domestication and Labor from Buffon to Bonheur

In 1895, when Rosa Bonheur's soon to be partner and biographer, Anna Klumpke, visited her studio for the second time, the seventy-three-year-old artist was working on a painting that she admitted to struggling with for years.[1] That painting, *The Duel*, was inspired by Eugène Sue's still popular story of the Godolphin Arabian (discussed in chapter 2). It shows the stallion at the moment of his fight with Hobgoblin over the beautiful Roxana, who is seen in the distance awaiting her suitor/sire (see fig. 3.1).

Referring to Roxanna as "the lovely Helen of Troy," Bonheur also describes the Godolphin Arabian as "this heroic horse" whose portrait she wants to get "right."[2] For Bonheur, then, the horse is not only a historical actor, as we saw in Géricault, but also a heroic, named individual worthy of a portrait. In what way he is heroic, however, we are not told. Perhaps heroism is inherent in his survival of abuse. Some forty years earlier Bonheur had illustrated the very kinds of cruelty depicted in Sue's novel. The sketch *Cartload of Stones* (1850), for example, shows a fallen cart horse writhing in agony as one man raises a whip over him while another man attempts to release him from his harness (see fig. 3.2).

In *The Duel*, however, equine heroism is linked to classical romance: boy fights boy to mate with girl and create a new family in his name, or in this case a new family or line of thoroughbreds. This story might seem odd for a painter whose own fame in recent decades has been tied as much to her lesbian feminism as to her art. Bonheur's legacy is that of an eccentric cross-dresser (she obtained legal permission to wear trousers) who loved women and posed for the camera with the ferocious animals she also painted—displacements, it has been argued, for a love that could not be represented.[3]

As Klumpke recalls this meeting, she writes that Bonheur said the white horse in the painting was the Godolphin Arabian and that she was lucky to

Figure 3.1. Rosa Bonheur, *The Duel*, 1895. Image from François Castre, *Rosa Bonheur*, trans. Frederic Taber Cooper (New York: Frederick A. Stokes, 1913).

Figure 3.2. Rosa Bonheur, *The Cartload of Stones*, 1870. Image from Dore Ashton, *Rosa Bonheur: A Life and a Legend* (New York: Viking, 1981).

have found an engraving of him by George Stubbs to ensure her accuracy. In Stubbs's engraving, however, the Godolphin Arabian appears as a dark bay, much like the dominant horse in Bonheur's rendition. Indeed, one can see the resemblance between the two bays even in the hint of white socks on the hind legs. Was this Anna Klumpke's mistake, perhaps motivated by the heroic model of Plato's white horse, or even Napoleon's? Or is it simply that Bonheur has put the white horse in the role of underdog, making his triumph all the more remarkable and worthy of Roxana? I don't have the answers, but I raise these questions because they are relevant to larger concerns regarding Bonheur's conception of heroism and of what heroic models and acts are open to men, women, and other species at this time in France. The Godolphin Arabian's triumph, we can assume, is related to his passion (in this case for Roxana) and to the strength of a desire that allows no one, man or animal, to stand in its way. On Bonheur's canvas, furthermore, this passion is implicated in a scene of animal violence that had become something of a tradition in the art world, visible in works from Stubbs to Géricault or Delacroix and the animalier sculptor Antoine-Louis Barye. This violence might be understood as queer "biological exuberance"[4] except that the outcome of the scene and of the Arabian's passion, as we saw in Sue's story, will be normative reproduction, indeed reproduction in the service of man and of capital by virtue of the birth of the thoroughbred. What makes this significant for Bonheur, however, is that the agency and the labor behind the making of the breed are animal.

Art historians have noted changes in Romantic depictions of equestrianism that are especially visible in Bonheur's attribution of agency to the horse over and above the rider.[5] Agency, moreover, is visible not only in scenes of a riderless, rearing horse (also painted earlier by Stubbs), but also in the depictions of working relations between horses and other domestic animals.[6] One of Bonheur's earliest works, *Ploughing in the Nivernais* of 1849 (fig. 3.4), paints the hardworking and some might even say enslaved oxen, who are also referred to as "heroes" on the Musée d'Orsay's website. "It is primarily an animal painting, and the heroes are the oxen themselves, leaving little room for the men."[7] Are they heroes simply because they are the main actors, or do they represent a different kind of heroism, one that is also a function of their labor and thus different from that of the Godolphin Arabian? These are questions raised by Bonheur and her contemporaries, for whom the role of domestic animals and their labor within human history was an ongoing topic of discussion. My claim in this chapter is that it was the artistic mission of this female animalier to reveal the ways animals were integral to and instructive for understanding a larger world order—both natural and spiritual. The art critic Albert Boime writes that "her commitment to the animal world was founded on mystical ideals," but those mystical ideals were themselves implicated in contemporary theories of natural history and notions of progress that linked the natural world to the world of industry and labor.[8]

"Do animals work?" Historian of science Vincianne Despret and sociologist Jocelyne Porcher posed this question to various farmers and breeders and received mixed responses.[9] Animals are often thought to do what they do naturally, if not mechanically, rather than by intelligence or knowledge. It is only in moments of resistance or refusal that their will is revealed or acknowledged. Rosa Bonheur, by contrast, seeks to make this work visible not only in animal resistance but also in the very capacity for cooperation and partnership that such moments of resistance can make apparent. She does so in part because of her Saint-Simonian–inspired belief that work was essential to notions of progress and a more just world order. "Work" included the work performed by nonhuman animals. At the same time, Bonheur questioned the conditions under which animals could both work and thrive physically and emotionally, and thus she emphasized their status as conscious subjects and not machines. In this way she takes the recognition of animal sensibility that we saw with Géricault one step further, questioning what role we humans play in an animal's livelihood, not only the role they play in ours. Many of her paintings include scenes of recognition where a momentary glance from an animal catches the viewer's eye and reminds us that, as Derrida says, they have a point of view regarding us and our ways. In this, moreover, she was unique among the renowned animaliers of her time.

BONHEUR: *ANIMALIÈRE* AND *SAINT-SIMONIENNE*

While animals have been subjects of artistic production since the cave paintings at Lascaux, the animalier—a painter or sculptor of animals—became especially popular in the nineteenth century because of new occasions for observing "exotic" animals up close in public zoos.[10] Animal art, in other words, grew as a consequence of the "liberation" of the king's menagerie at Versailles after the Revolution and the animals' eventual move to the municipal Jardin des plantes—what would become the National Museum of Natural History. Antoine-Louis Barye is perhaps the best-known representative of those artists skilled at offering a "realistic" portrayal of animals. Whether sculpted or painted, this realism most often portrayed the imagined violence of the animal kingdom, such as Barye's large *Tiger Devouring a Gavial Crocodile* or his *Lion Crushing a Serpent*. While Bonheur would eventually install her own menagerie, including lions and tigers, behind her studio in the town of By, the initial focus of her art was on domestic animals: sheep, oxen, and of course horses. These were animals she regarded as her companions, friends, and even coworkers. To be sure, Bonheur's relationships with animals may have been at times performative (like those of Adah Menken, discussed in chapter 5), allowing her, as Mary Lou Roberts has argued, to capitalize on her image as an eccentric.[11] But such displays of a love that exceeded normative boundaries were also linked to a worldview in which animals were present in their own right, not only as symbols or stand-ins for unconventional human relationships.[12] If her art offers "a radical intervention in the visual and cultural construction of nineteenth-century femininity and masculinity," as James Saslow suggests, it also offers a prescient intervention into contemporary debates about animal nature and domestication—debates that directed attention to animal agency and its role in both the natural and cultural worlds.[13] That is to say, it was not just animal "freedom" or wild nature as unencumbered by social constraints that was relevant for Bonheur, but animal freedom as necessarily structured and restrained by relations with other animals and humans.[14] Rather than animal liberation, Bonheur envisioned a kind of interspecies collaboration in which the freedoms of disparate partners may not be equal, but nevertheless inspire the curiosity, reciprocity, and affection that many theorists today consider to be our obligation.[15]

Bonheur's biographies make frequent reference to her deep affection for animals. "I was only happy in the company of these animals. I really got into studying their ways, especially the expression in their eyes," Klumpke reports her as saying.[16] In his *Reminiscences of Rosa Bonheur*, Theodore Stanton found it necessary to devote an entire chapter to her "love of animals," a love that is not without its contradictions. She accepted the "necessity" of killing animals in her menagerie if they became dangerous to her or to others. Shooting contributed to Bonheur's transgressive image as a woman, as did hunting, although opinion is mixed on whether she actually participated in (or enjoyed) the kill.[17] She describes how she hated seeing animals suffer and would shoot them, if need be, to put them out of their misery. But there were also times when she couldn't go through with it, as with her very old blind and paralyzed dog or with an old deer who had an abscess over her eye and whose rheumatism left her so lame she could barely walk. "I have not the courage to kill her on account of the pictures I have painted of her or with her," Bonheur said. "They are friends, don't you see, they have worked with me."[18] Regarded as friends and collaborators, they were also soul mates. "I find it monstrous that animals should be said to have no soul. My lioness loved. She, therefore, had more soul than certain people who do not love."[19]

The reference to animal souls was not mere metaphor. Bonheur's belief was fostered by her readings of Félicité Robert de Lamennais, a Catholic priest turned philosopher who was known for bringing Catholicism in touch with a Rousseauist faith in the natural world. Lamennais believed all animals possessed souls, emanating from an "infinite beauty" that it was the artist's duty to reveal.[20] According to Bonheur, "Lamennais defined everything I searched for."[21] She was introduced to his writings by her father, Raymond Bonheur, a struggling painter of landscapes and portraits from Bordeaux. He moved to Paris and found inspiration in the Saint-Simonian movement that was gaining influence in Paris under its new "Father," Barthélemy Prosper Enfantin. When Rosa was only ten, her father joined sixty-nine other disciples of the Saint-Simonian group who had taken vows of celibacy in the all-male commune at Ménilmontant, to the north of Paris. Whether because of or in spite of the fact that Rosa's mother, like so many Saint-Simonian women, was left alone to take care of and support Rosa and her siblings in their small apartment in Paris, Rosa reported that "this Saint-Simonian episode in our life had influences that I now perceive were much more far-reaching than any of us imagined at the time. . . . The moral brace which I received from Saint Simonian connections has remained with me to this day."[22]

The belief that art should have a social role was present in Henri de Saint-Simon's writings of the first decades of the century, and these were more systematically and emphatically developed by his followers in a series of lectures given in 1828 to 1830.[23] Whereas Saint-Simon had given priority to science and industry or, relatedly, to reason and action, it was the importance of the capacity for feeling or "sympathy" (perhaps recalling the Idéologues) and for determining the moral goals of society that was stressed by the movement's chief aesthetician, Émile Barrault, and by members such as Léon Halévy, brother of the composer Fromental Halévy.[24] For a brief time it appeared the artists would take on the role of "priests" in the new Saint-Simonian religion.

Insofar as the importance of the artist was more theorized than actualized, however, it bears analogies to the role ascribed to women in the movement.[25] Under the leadership of Enfantin, the Saint-Simonians promoted belief in an androgynous god and began the search for a female messiah to accompany Father Enfantin in his mission to "rehabilitate the flesh" and thereby improve the human race. Although the female messiah would (and could) never be found, these ideas would have direct effect on Rosa, resulting not only in her adoption of the nontraditional dress that included culottes for women and tight-fitting, collarless frock coats for men, but also in her mission as an artist. As she recalls, "My father, that enthusiastic apostle of humanity, told me again and again that it was woman's mission to improve the human race. . . . to his doctrines I owe my great and glorious ambition for the sex to which I proudly belong."[26] It was thus the woman's and the artist's role to educate and guide humanity by revealing natural truths in a language that all could grasp, unlike the scientists who "couch[ed] their revelations in formulas that few people can understand."[27]

NATURAL SCIENCE, INDUSTRY, AND THE QUESTION OF THE ANIMAL

Bonheur believed her particular mission was to interpret "the magnificent book of nature" in a way that science could not do. Questions of interpretation, moreover, drove debates over the place of comparative anatomy within the fields of natural history and especially natural philosophy, and these in turn put the study and representation of animals at the center of larger questions concerning the laws of nature and the place of humans and animals within the natural world. In this regard the matter of the spirit or soul was crucial, especially insofar as the soul itself had been naturalized and materialized by major thinkers of the eighteenth century. Whether it was possible to find evidence of the soul or of some divine spirit in the natural world, and whether it was the scientist's job to do so, were questions at the heart of the famous Cuvier-Geoffroy debate of 1830, whose influence was felt in science, philosophy, literature, and the arts. "It would be wrong to believe that the big debate that developed between Georges Cuvier and Étienne Geoffroy Saint-Hilaire rested on scientific innovation. The 'unity of composition' had already occupied, in other terms, the greatest minds of the preceding two centuries," writes Balzac in his preface to the *Comédie humaine* (1842). Declaring that the idea behind his grand work came from Geoffroy's comparison between humanity and animality, Balzac cites the influence of a number of thinkers, including Leibnitz, Buffon, and Goethe, who were influential for Geoffroy and the idea of the "unity of composition," which he explains in these terms:

> There is only one animal. The Creator used one and the same model for all organized beings. The animal is a principle that derives its exterior form or, to speak more exactly, the differences of its form, from the environment where it is called on to develop. Zoological species result from these differences. The proclamation and the support for this system, which is in

> harmony with divine power, will be the eternal honor of Geoffroy Saint-Hilaire, the victor over Cuvier on this point of high science, and whose triumph was saluted by the last article written by the great Goethe.[28]

The two most prominent zoologists of their time, Étienne Geoffroy Saint-Hilaire and Georges Cuvier, were colleagues, friends, and eventually rivals. Geoffroy was appointed to the first chair of zoology at the new Jardin des plantes in 1793 (what was to become in essence the first modern zoo), was a member of Napoleon's scientific expedition to Egypt in 1798, and was elected a member of the French Academy of Sciences in 1807. Cuvier was the first naturalist to conclusively demonstrate the fact of extinction and would also be appointed to the Jardin des plantes in 1802, following previous appointments as a member of the Academy of Sciences in 1795 and professor of natural history at the Collège de France in 1799. Fundamental differences between these two zoologists would reveal themselves over the next two decades, culminating in the debate over scientific method, the purpose of scientific inquiry, and most crucially, as evident in Balzac's brief account, over the identities and differences between animal and human worlds. In his 1847 biography of his father, Isidore Geoffroy Saint-Hilaire characterized the debate as a confrontation between "the school of facts and the school of ideas."[29] Cuvier represented the school of facts, within which the role of the scientist was to observe nature and document his observation through the collection of evidence. It was not man's place to question the mysteries behind what was observed. For Geoffroy, on the other hand, the role of the scientist was to build on this evidence in order to "seek the harmony, affinity and the true reason of things."[30] Thus, whereas for Cuvier anatomical evidence confirmed the functional differences between species, Geoffroy saw formal analogies between species that led to the idea of a divinely inspired "unity of composition." Inspired greatly by Buffon, this was a pre-Darwinian account of evolution as the transmutation of matter and of species through time and in space that resulted from the effects of environment and attraction—forces he understood to be the "universal soul of nature." Here too we can see Geoffroy's affinity with Balzac, who understood observing "reality" to be only one part of his role as author. The second part was to penetrate that reality in order to apprehend and translate the truth behind the visible world. This was the goal of the trilogy of novels making up Balzac's *Livre mystique*, which he completed in 1835. There, in a manner that recalls the Saint-Simonian god, truth is figured as androgyne (Seraphita/us), a "unity" composed of differences if not oppositions (female/male; body/spirit, animal/human), all emanating from a single divine force.[31]

Figure 3.3. Édouard Louis Dubufe, *Portrait of Rosa Bonheur*, 1857. Image courtesy of RMN-Grand Palais/Art Resource, New York.

Along with his son Isidore, an aspiring naturalist, Geoffroy became friends with the Bonheur family. Rosa's father had been asked to make illustrations for Geoffroy, and Rosa often joined him at the Jardin des plantes to study the animals. When she began to teach drawing in a girl's school she admitted having "the confidence of Geoffroy Saint-Hilaire" to assist her in the natural history class.[32] Her own art is characterized both by Geoffroy's commitment to anatomical truth (which he shared with Cuvier), and to moving beyond observation to reveal the divine spark that illuminates the animal body. Such is the light that illuminates the head of the bull in the 1857 portrait of Bonheur by Édouard Louis Dubufe (who also painted the portraits of the emperor and empress), in which Bonheur intervened to paint herself (fig. 3.3). Showing the artist with one hand draped over the bull,

Figure 3.4. Rosa Bonheur, *Ploughing in the Nivernais*, 1849. Image courtesy of the RMN-Grand Palais/Art Resource, New York. Photo by Michel Urtado.

holding a paintbrush, and the other holding her sketchbook, the portrait confirms the bull as a partner in her art.[33]

A more encompassing light embraces the entire composition of men, oxen, and landscape in the painting *Ploughing in the Nivernais*, Bonheur's first Salon success of 1849, a work that inspired comparisons to the writings of George Sand (fig. 3.4). The critic Émile Cantrel writes, "George Sand has a special genius for landscapes; and in her paintings, Rosa Bonheur gives song to the trees and eloquent speech to the animals, grass, and clouds. Both can understand the mute symphonies of creation and render them in the passionate harmonious language of art."[34] Both are praised for respiritualizing nature and the animals, if at the expense of the human figures that critics found to be awkward or effaced. Thus in *Ploughing* it is the bright and expressive eye of one of the oxen that holds the focus, emphasizing Bonheur's faith in the animal soul and where to find it. "Isn't the eye the mirror of the soul for each and every living creature? Nature didn't give them any other way to express their thoughts, so that's where their feelings and desires get reflected."[35] *Ploughing in the Nivernais* moves beyond a simple aesthetic appreciation of nature to endorse a scene of communal labor, a tilling of the earth in which the animals exceed the men even as they are guided (or forcibly moved) by them. In this, moreover, it both endorses contemporary views concerning the role of domestic animals within (human) history and goes beyond them by attending to animals' agency, well-being, and point of view within these debates.

Domestication was addressed in numerous writings by Geoffroy's son Isidore, beginning with his entry on the topic in the *Encyclopédie nouvelle* of 1836. Building on his father's understanding of the variability of species, Isidore considered the work of taming, shaping, and "acclimatizing" entire species as a necessary and vital force of historical, social, and even religious progress.[36] His description of this "conquest" of nature differs significantly from Buffon's view that the "domestic animal is a slave that we play with, use, abuse, and change, and one that we disorient and denature."[37] As Buffon's and other eighteenth-century taxonomies affirmed, however, man's dominance over the animal world was uncontested and legitimized by the empire of spirit over matter. Domestication was a right of nature and a gift of God. Insofar as Isidore insisted that domestic animals are "gifted with will and intelligence," he changed this conquest from one of mind over matter to a civilizing mission for educating our "inferior brothers."[38] Nevertheless, it was man who was to benefit from this mission, both symbolically and practically. As "veritable works of man, domestication proves the supremacy of our species," Isidore wrote.[39] Its purpose was to turn a wild and unusable nature into resources and even food for those in greatest need.[40] Domestication would thus become one version of that "rehabilitation of the flesh" advanced by Father Enfantin and his Saint-Simonian disciples.

As a necessary part of domestication, acclimatizing animals would thus be proclaimed one of the major functions of zoos and menageries such as the Jardin des plantes.[41] Isidore succeeded his father as director of the Museum of Natural History in 1841, and in 1854 he became president of the newly founded Société zoologique d'acclimatation, created to help introduce foreign species and breeds into Europe and endorsed by Napoleon III for its public utility. As he explained in *Acclimatation et domestication des animaux utiles*, one part of a larger project was to import "useful animals" to places where they would be needed, whether sending yaks from Asia to Europe, along with llamas and alpacas from the Andes, or camels from North Africa to Brazil. Acclimation and colonization, in other words, went hand in hand, as foreseen in Napoleon's 1798 expedition to Egypt, joined by Isidore's father. By 1859 the menagerie of the National Museum witnessed the birth of two generations of yaks—animals in which Bonheur took a particular interest. According to Isidore, Bonheur came often to the museum's menagerie and created a series of representations of the yak for the society. This was followed by a drawing that he describes as "remarkable from the point of view of zoological exactitude and of artistic execution. This drawing is incontestably the best representation we have of the yak."[42] Often described as a buffalo with a horse's tail, one might suppose that it was actually a yak she painted into Dubufe's portrait of her. It would then be the acclimated yak whom she anoints with the light of progress.

THE *SAINT-SIMONIENNE* ON HORSEBACK AND REHABILITATION OF THE ANIMAL

The Horse Fair was the painting that launched Rosa Bonheur's career. Its display of trotting and rearing horses trades on the painterly influences of Géricault, and in its larger composition we can read both the impact of naturalist theories of animal domestication and the social politics of Second Empire Paris. Commentators have noted a discrepancy between Bonheur's Saint-Simonian background, with its republican ideals and emphasis on the communal advance of society, and the success she claimed for herself beginning with this painting.[43] Saint-Simon, of course, put industry first, and whereas his followers during the July Monarchy emphasized the idealist and communal aspects of his writings, under Napoleon III many emerged as bankers and technicians working to connect life on earth through railways, canals, and electricity. Incongruities and tensions between social good (understood in some instances to be inclusive of if not dependent on animal good) and individual advancement were thus displaced to the background of Second Empire politics, and it is only with some irony that Sainte-Beuve called Napoleon III Saint-Simon on horseback. Talent and industry would be crucial to imperial progress, and horse breeding would figure importantly as both social and cultural capital.

In the wake of Bonheur's initial successes in the art market, the director of fine arts at the National Museum approached her about commissioning a work. She proposed a horse fair, one of two works she had in the making. But the director chose the painting *Haymaking* instead, explaining that Bonheur had painted far too few horses "for a scene as turbulent as a horse fair. We've not seen enough of your horses," he said.[44] Undeterred, Bonheur proceeded with her horse painting, and its huge success proved the director wrong. Realizing his mistake, he tried to purchase the painting for the museum, but it had already been sold to a private buyer. In 1887 it would be sold again to Cornelius Vanderbilt, who presented it to the Metropolitan Museum of Art in New York, where it still hangs.[45]

Of all the animals Bonheur studied and painted, horses held a special significance. They were integral to her feminist persona, as they were for a growing number of women riders, especially those who contested convention to ride astride or to write about it, as did Bonheur and one of her favorite authors, George Sand. Since riding astride necessitated breeches, it went hand in hand with cross-dressing. But the sheer physical agility needed to partner with a horse afforded women a new image of feminine strength that was threatening to some and exciting to others. Such was the case with Sand's androgynous character Gabriel in her dialogic novel, or with the performer Adah Menken (as we will see in chapter 5).[46] Bonheur rode *en chevalier* rather than *en amazone*, and she did so with passion, whether traveling with her "companion" Nathalie Micas or on brief rides through the Bois de Boulogne with the Saint-Simonian Gustave D'Eichthal, one of the few men, she said, who would ride with her.

Bonheur's love for horses and demand for knowledge about them joined in her sense of mission as an artist and brought her, ironically, to spend hours in the slaughter yards. This made wearing men's clothes a necessity. "Don't forget, I used to spend days and days in slaughterhouses. Oh! You've got to be devoted to art to live in pools of blood, surrounded by butchers. I was also passionate about horses; and what better place to study them than at horse fairs, mingling with all those traders? Women's clothes were quite simply in the way."[47] Horses offered mobility, a purpose, and a sense of freedom, even as Bonheur recognized how far the horse's own freedom was tightly circumscribed by human abuse. "Like man, the horse is the most beautiful or the most wretched of creatures. Yet man becomes ugly and shameful through vice or poverty; he is almost responsible for his decadence. The horse, on the other hand, is just a slave that the Creator entrusted to man and that man abuses in his ingratitude and cowardly, selfish wretchedness, even to the point of making himself lower than the most brutish beast."[48]

The reference to the horse as slave is reminiscent of Buffon's equation of domestication with slavery, warning of the human tendency to abuse those powers we have received as a gift from God. But if Buffon admitted that for the animals the centuries-old "stigmata of their captivity" might be beyond repair or "rehabilitation," a word he himself uses, Bonheur's work is far more ambiguous concerning the long-term effects of domestication.[49] Few of the animals in her major works are shown in harness or under tight control, and while the horses and oxen work and live in the company of humans, they appear to retain their will and spirit, suggesting that under the right conditions domestication can allow an animal to flourish, if not reveal its divinely inspired place in nature.

For Bonheur, in other words, domestication is the animal equivalent of what the Saint-Simonians would refer to as "rehabilitation" for humans, referring to the disciplined expression of bodily appetites. The connection between the education of the passions and the disciplining of horses is not a new theme and can be traced back to Plato's *Phaedrus*. In Bonheur's canvas, the connection might also help explain an architectural element that appears only in the final composition of *The Horse Fair*—the Salpêtrière Hospital. Absent in many of the sketches for the *Fair*, the hospital hovers over a darkened corner to the left of the canvas, out of which the horses move toward the center and right and into the light. Critics have noted how the hospital situates the scene in Paris but have otherwise paid it little attention. Known for housing and treating *aliénés*, or the insane, the hospital nevertheless has a curious connection to the understanding and fate of animals during the late eighteenth and nineteenth centuries. Bonheur may be referencing Géricault's own portraits of monomaniacs from the 1820s, of which Jan Goldstein writes that "the tension in their faces betrays a powerful inner agitation held back, momentarily, from active expression."[50] This sympathetic view contrasts with and challenges what had been the accepted, almost demonic, view of monomaniacs before the Revolution. Matthew Senior has written about the parallel between the Salpêtrière and Louis XIV's menagerie at Versailles, both designed by the architect Louis Le Vau. As structures of enclosure and captivity, the menagerie was designed for putting wild animals and nature on display for the king and his guests, while the hospital confined those charged with indigence, prostitution, or mental illness. Foucault describes it as a place where "mad women given to episodes of fury are chained up like dogs" and where "those who are chained to the walls of the cells are not really men who have lost their reason, but rather beasts fallen prey to a natural rage."[51] As Senior describes it, insanity was thus linked to brute passion. Madness "was identified with pure animal violence and liberty. It was this pure animal liberty that was most feared and constrained by classical reason."[52]

The almost simultaneous dismantling of the Salpêtrière and the king's menagerie in the aftermath of the Revolution furthered the parallel between the insane in chains and animals in cages. Whereas insanity and animal brutality had been regarded as predetermined, unchangeable fates, under the influence of new theories of the embodied mind and "animal economy" (*oeconomie animale*) shared by humans and animals alike, both the insane and nonhuman animals were understood to be susceptible to at least a modicum of education or rehabilitation through changes in environment and manners. Geoffroy Saint-Hilaire himself had professed malleability to be at the core of species (and a reason to be skeptical of taxonomy). Such ideas were also the basis of ideas introduced by Philippe Pinel, the celebrated doctor and eventual chief physician at the Salpêtrière, who, following the Idéologues, stressed the intimate connections between body and mind (*phy-*

sique et moral).[53] Author of what would come to be known as mental and "moral medicine," Pinel argued that insanity was not an incurable state but an illness that could be cured through sympathetic and nonviolent treatment. Pinel himself had worked closely with Geoffroy and Cuvier at the Jardin du roi, studying the function of the physical or "animal economy" shared by humans and animals and teaching animal anatomy, or *zootomie*, before he turned his attention to human "neuroses." From his work at the Jardin he learned the importance of serious and attentive observation for discovering the etiology of illness. In addition to observation, however, Pinel advanced the role of sympathetic listening. As Goldstein writes, it was largely thanks to Pinel that the French government began to recognize the importance of introducing more humanitarian methods in the treatment of the insane. This included treating them with "pity," much as Delille and the Idéologues would demand for animals shortly thereafter.[54] It would also include understanding the "therapeutic power of work."[55]

For later supporters of the Second and Third Republics, Pinel became a heroic figure who had "liberated the insane from their chains," and the Salpêtrière Hospital commissioned two paintings depicting either him or his assistant in this act. Politics was certainly behind this legend even if Pinel himself was not, as Dora Weiner points out, political.[56] His efforts stood out in the politically charged atmosphere of postrevolutionary Paris, raising concerns over correct forms of "sensibility" and the "moral" treatment of others. As Pierre Serna writes, "manners" (*moeurs*) constituted "the cardinal notion, . . . the plural cement of the directorial Republic. The rethought regime owes it to itself to be moral."[57] Influenced by eighteenth-century thinking about the animal economy, and perhaps also by the knowledge that the English had already taken steps toward animal protection, Republican thinkers, Serna explains, wanted to take away the privileging of intelligence and intellect in order "to forge a natural morality that would make the body and its animal functions the foundation of our being in the world." These would be "screened by a reasonable morality, translated in a simple and effective language."[58] With this as the foundation, the next step was to ask, as the Idéologues did, whether all "inferiors," including "inferior brothers," as nonhuman animals were referred to, must have the right to a moral treatment.

The "liberation" of the animals from the king's menagerie and their eventual move to the national garden would, of course, offer little in the way of freedom. Freedom from chains, whether for the mad or for the animal, was not meant to signal the liberation of the repressed beast but rather, in accordance with Rousseauist notions of freedom, meant having the capacity to obey a law you give to yourself. In nineteenth-century terms, terms that already had relevance for Isidore's theories of domestication, it meant participating in the social contract through work as a form of rehabilitation.

The relevance that Pinel and moral medicine may have for horses and animals more generally becomes even clearer with the realization that one of Pinel's close associates and students at the Salpêtrière, who became his replacement in charge of the "commission for the amelioration of *aliénés*" during the Restoration, was Étienne Pariset.[59] Elected to the Academy of Sciences in the section of zoology in 1842, Pariset would become a founding member and first president of the French Society for the Protection of Animals, created in 1845 to address the deplorable treatment of horses in the streets (Rosa Bonheur and Isidore Geoffroy Saint-Hilaire were also active members).[60] In his history of the SPA, Georges Fleury writes that while some members of the SPA reserved their attention for horses, Pariset's "compassion," which had been visible in his care for the *aliénés*, was "extended to all animals."[61] Pariset thus links Pinel's moral medicine to Isidore's understanding of domestication as the moral treatment by which animals would be "rehabilitated" and their bodies and talents nurtured for the good of the nation and of the world beyond.

THE HORSE FAIR: DANCING IN THE STREETS

In contrast to Bonheur's sketches of beaten and abused horses, *The Horse Fair* (plate 4) puts horses on display at the moment before they are sold, when they are most free to parade their physical beauty and power, but also their capacity for something we might call moral agency, here revealed in their spirited resistance as well as their capacity for shared, synchronized movement. What we witness is a "joint dance of being," to borrow from Erica Fudge's description of the partnership of humans and animals on a farm or in training. Building on Donna Haraway and Charis Cussins, Fudge describes this partnership as a "choreographing of different ontologies into a collaborative movement."[62]

Ontological choreography is a joining of the physical and moral through a partnership that calls on the mutual capacities for affecting and being affected by others, or what Haraway calls "the oxymoron of disciplined spontaneity." It is the ability to "take the initiative and to respond obediently to the other."[63] The dance depends, in other words, on those shared interrogative capacities of humans and animals that, for Maurice Merleau-Ponty, reveal our "strange kinship."[64] John Ruskin described the human element in Bonheur's composition as "disagreeably hidden," thus emphasizing her attention to the greater, if unacknowledged, role of the horses within it.

A comparison with Géricault's renditions of the subject is revealing, and not only because Bonheur's massive painting overpowers the viewer with the horses' agility.[65] Bonheur studied and admired Géricault, and she had purchased his *Study of a White Horse* for her own collection.[66] Both preferred Percherons, native French horses with large, muscular haunches better suited for work than for racing or sport. Both valued anatomical correctness to the point that in Géricault's lithograph *Horses Going to a Fair* (1821) the central horse could be said to be posing to show off his proportions. But the sense of thrust and impulsion that Géricault had painted so boldly in his *Race* series is muted in these scenes. In his *Horse Market* (1816–17), shown in figure 1.7, horses are chained to a pole, with only minimal possibilities for resistance. They move slowly and individually uphill, their expressions, like the darkened skies, registering an ominous if unknown fate. Bonheur's canvas, by contrast, shows horses rearing and running from left to right across the canvas, mostly in groups of two or more, their handlers struggling to keep up or to control them. This is the horses' moment of frolic and display, when they can show off their strength and passion—much like the Godolphin Arabian—but also their capacity to compose themselves and perform. Thus a brilliant white pair trot together in rhythm, with little evidence of the rider's incentive. Only one horse is mounted.

Whereas Géricault's scenes most often take place in unrecognizable landscapes, Bonheur identifies the location of the horse fair by the dome of the Salpêtrière Hospital that looms in the distance. This architectural symbol of "moral medicine," linked as we have seen to the founding of the French SPA and a moral treatment of animals, changes what is to be seen as "disagreeable" in the painting. A rider's whipping of a rearing horse, for instance, would be known to encourage even more violent behavior. The visible contrast between that rider, with his raised arm and frenzied horse, and the calm of the central horse and rider is striking and might offer a further rationale for reading the latter as a self-portrait of Bonheur in masculine attire.[67] "To conquer them one must love them," said Bonheur about the way she tamed her own animals. Even lions "are formidable only when they are feared or when we hurt them."[68] Convention and accuracy, of course, would not allow for a mounted woman at the horse fair, which has led to reading the portrait as signaling a "proto-lesbian" identity and the horse as symbol of a love that cannot be fully "image-ined." We might also assume, however, that what cannot be imagined or accepted by either artistic or historical convention are women and animals as actors in history. As Whitney Chadwick writes, "that nature (passion/temperament) might be brought under control by a 'feminine' hand, was inconceivable within an aesthetic discourse in which masculinity served as the agent for the transformation of nature into culture."[69] Bonheur is the *Saint-Simonienne* on horseback who partners with her mount to "rehabilitate the flesh" (human and animal) and turn both toward the collaborative task at hand.

This unfamiliar partnership of woman and horse is also one of identification, an affinity that appears with increasing frequency in Bonheur's writings.[70] Different from Géricault's imitative positioning of taut legs and muscular haunches, identification here is revealed through a parallel tilt of the heads of rider and the central white horse, suggesting a shared, knowing glance. But whereas the rider's eyes are cast in shadow, the horse holds the viewer's gaze, attracting our attention through his (or her) animated expression of fear or surprise, if not concern for the horse being whipped.[71] If there is displacement, it is of this expression of passion from human to horse, where it is conveyed with unrestrained force and attraction. This is not to deny that human and horse also share the capacity for self-restraint and what, for Bonheur (as for Plato), is at the core of their moral agency. Klumpke once remarked on the energy of Bonheur's horses, saying they were "a sign of their author's fiery nature," and Bonheur responded by speaking of the need to "dominate" her own nature when she painted her horses. "No doubt some artists let their inner self take over against their will; but I know how to resist that and yield to the subject."[72]

This transfer of her own restraint and compulsion to her horses is what Chadwick goes on to describe in comparing the preliminary drawings with the finished work. The horses' gait, which was undramatic in the drawings, becomes "a romanticized expression of coiled energy and motion," such that the heightened flexion and elevation "articulate the power of these laboring beasts under a play of light that sculpts and etches muscles and tendons."[73] These are movements that are usually induced by a rider, and that these horses achieve them on their own is indicative not only of Bonheur's controlled brush but also of the horses' self-determination. This combination of freedom and training is what Bonheur sought in one of her last efforts as well, a painting titled *Treading Wheat in the Camargue* (fig. 3.5), planned for the Universal Exhibition of 1900. It depicts a method of threshing used in the Camargue in the south of France: "treading back and forth, these nine horses crush the husks with their hooves and squeeze out the kernels that are gathered up later on."[74]

Much of the labor, as she describes it, involves herds of "well-trained horses left loose. . . . It's enough to call the horses by name and give them hand and voice commands. I wanted to paint this scene, since it gives a better idea about how smart these wonderful beasts are."[75] Of course, the

Figure 3.5. Rosa Bonheur, *Treading Wheat in the Camargue*, unfinished in the painter's lifetime. Image from François Castre, *Rosa Bonheur*, trans. Frederic Taber Cooper (New York: Frederick A. Stokes, 1913).

celebratory "liberation" of the horses that is visible in *The Horse Fair* will be circumscribed by their eventual purchase by the unknown, faceless traders faintly visible at the top right of the canvas, in whose hands rests the fate of these "smart and wonderful beasts."

As an animalier, Bonheur was dedicated to revealing not only the beauty of animal form, but also the intelligence and spirit within that form. As an artist she believed her mission was to be absolutely faithful to what science knows about the nature of animals and their anatomy. But that mission also involved looking into their eyes to see and attempt to reveal who they are and what they can do. This was especially true of the horses she rode with passion and painted in hopes of revealing their beauty, their intelligence, and their cooperation in a mission of history. While riding astride and painting in pants challenged gender norms of the day and helped prove that a woman could be a great artist, Bonheur was also challenging conventions regarding the relations between women and horses and the love that could exist between them. Such love had yet to become conventional or to find favor within the Academy.

Influenced by Saint-Simonian ideas about talent, art, and women (ideas that the group itself often belied) and by Geoffroy Saint-Hilaire's notions about the divinely inspired rapport between human and animal form, Bonheur developed a vaguely theological and republican notion of a universal history in which both women and animals were necessary actors, driven by passion but able to direct that passion toward cooperation and work. According to the entry "Le cheval" for the *Encyclopédie nouvelle* of 1840, written by Victor Meunier, the horse was recognized as one of the animals most "useful" to man and, with the dog and donkey, one whose domestication was most "complete."[76] Domestication, as we have seen, was viewed as both a natural capacity of these "intelligent" animals and a social mission. "Who has not dreamed of all the advantages man has taken from this association," Meunier continues, even as he warns that their faithfulness and services give them a "right" to be properly cared for. "Bad treatment, hitting, and negligence only inspire fear and hatred; it dazes and ruins them."[77] In similar terms Jules Michelet wrote in *Le peuple* (1846) that "all of nature protests against the barbarity of man, who ignores, debases, and tortures his inferior brother; she accuses him before the One who created both of them," and he advises continuing the "grand work of animal education" that will be outlined in Isidore Saint-Hilaire's article on domestication.[78]

Bonheur's work thus took place in the thick of ongoing debates concerning the nature and function of domestication, a subject whose importance was signaled in Buffon's *Histoire naturelle* of the eighteenth century and continued through to Isidore Geoffroy Saint-Hilaire's many publications in the middle of the century. These biopolitical debates involved questions that continue to be raised today: Should there be domestic animals at all? Under what terms, if any, can the "relationship" created by domestication be "rendered just"? Sue Donaldson and Will Kymlicka ask these questions in *Zoopolis*.[79] What kinds of treatment does their nature require and deserve? What are they owed for their labor? To the first question, nineteenth-century natural scientists and social thinkers answered a resounding yes. An abolitionist voice, if it existed, was not to be heard. Rather, domestication was seen as good for both the animal and the human. Much as Donaldson and Kymlicka also argue, domestication was said to build on the natural, pro-social capacities of certain animals if not for "co-citizenship," then at least for a co-partnership.[80] Bonheur, we might remember, referred to her animals as partners in her art. Indeed, her works give evidence both of their social behavior—whether in the peaceful grazing of sheep or the synchronized gaits of the horses—and of their useful labor, from the oxen's plowing to the horses' threshing. Celebrating agriculture at a moment before its complete domination by industrial capitalism, she insists on the important role of animals as actors within industry. Indeed, she makes animal work visible, and she does so not only in the moments of their resistance or refusal, but also in their "intelligent cooperation," giving further evidence of her belief that "if we don't always understand animals, they always understand us."[81] Bonheur thus seconds Vincianne Despret's observation that they often know what we want from them better than we do. It was not human ingenuity that created the thoroughbred, but the Godolphin Arabian's combination of passion and talent, one he pursued in defiance of the "better knowledge" of the humans.[82]

That humans were the ultimate beneficiaries of the talents of animals went without saying. As we see in the next chapter, it was only three years after *The Horse Fair* that Isidore Geoffroy Saint-Hilaire would begin his campaign to legalize horsemeat for human consumption, affirming that the animals' ultimate utility might come as dead meat. It is difficult to see Bonheur lending support to such a campaign, given her own "mournful contemplation" of slaughtered animals and of the "living flesh" she witnessed during her rides on horseback.

> I mournfully contemplated all this living flesh, all the blood of these poor beasts, bellowing and bleating in a cloud of dust. Soon they'd all fall under the butcher's knife.
>
> Poor innocent creatures, born only to die that miserable death! I wondered why there were so many victims. Had these mute beings already had a life? Had they been people like us and earned this horrible punishment because of their crimes and errors? What a wretched fate? And how awful to have to kill them.[83]

Indeed, even though she spent much time in slaughter yards, it is clearly the life of the horse that she celebrates, a life whose power, passion, and potential are visible not only in the body but especially, as we have seen, in the face and in the eyes that say so much, and so much more than their humans' eyes. In her art horses, oxen, bulls, and rams regard the viewer with an unmistakable point of view and with a look that is an appeal to those who should no longer ignore their service and their spirit.

CHAPTER FOUR

Let Them Eat Horse

What makes something good to eat? Taste is certainly important but is notoriously fickle. Tastes change with age and experience, and the acquisition of certain tastes can be seen as a mark of maturity or of a changed identity, whether of an individual, a community, or even a nation. In a nation like France, whose reputation and cultural dominance depended for centuries on its role as an arbiter of taste, what one ate and how one ate became crucial markers of social standing. Roland Barthes wrote in the 1950s that in France steak is "a basic element, nationalized even more than socialized." Served bloody rare, it is thought to impart "bull-like strength." Eating one's *bifteck* he saw as a marker of Frenchness, except that, at the time, French markets and restaurants were experiencing an "invasion of American steaks."[1]

If steak threatened to be regarded as an American meal, it might be more appropriate to identify the Gallic nation with another meat, one that Americans (among others) didn't eat and that many don't want to taste: horse. True, a taboo against eating horse dates back to the Mosaic laws, which classified it as an impure meat. This was reaffirmed in the fourth century AD by Christians who decreed horsemeat a food of heathens. According to Daniel Roche, while Gauls, Celts, and Germans ate horsemeat, Romans banished it from the table, largely because of the horse's closeness to human society and of the privileges associated with chevaliers: "the horse categorizes the social world."[2] It was only in the middle of the nineteenth century that France officially acquired the taste for horse, but then as now it was considered a *basse viande* or inferior meat compared with beef, eaten mostly by the working and lower-middle classes.[3] Nevertheless during the century promoting and legalizing horsemeat became a national endeavor, and by 1910 France had become the "horseflesh center of the Western World."[4]

How certain nonhuman animals come to be seen as edible or good to eat is a fraught question that reveals not only the instability of associations between taste and social identity, but also the shifting boundaries of what (or who) is good to eat. Indeed, we might ask whether, for something to be deemed good to eat, it is important to ensure that that something not be regarded as a someone. If eating someone immediately connotes cannibalism, this may be a reason we humans have tried for so long to reserve certain markers of subjectivity (including pronouns) for ourselves and deny them to nonhuman animals.[5]

In an interview titled "Eating Well, or The Calculation of the Subject," Jacques Derrida explores the meaning of "eating well" and its relation to the construction of human subjectivity. "Eating well," with all the cultural ritual it implies, might be one means of ensuring that we humans are subjects who eat rather than objects that are eaten. To eat well, Derrida argues further, is not only an aesthetic or health imperative for the individual gastronome but also an ethical imperative to take responsibility for those others one eats with, including those who risk being eaten—literally or metaphorically. "One must eat well" does not mean above all taking in and grasping for oneself, but means learning and giving to eat, "learning to give the other to eat." One never eats entirely on one's own: this constitutes the rule underlying the statement "One must eat well." It is a rule offering infinite hospitality.[6]

This necessary relation between eating well and hospitality is an imperative to take the other into account, to make sure one does not eat at the expense of another by taking responsibility for the other's ability to eat well too. Such was the major argument behind the legalizing of horsemeat, that it was to enable the working classes to also eat well, or at least well enough. By this line of reasoning, the horse was either not other enough or too other.

Derrida suggests that this ethical imperative to "give the other to eat" can even go so far as to call on the reciprocal willingness to be eaten, at least in the sense that one might have or be what is needed to nourish the other.[7] "The question is no longer one of knowing if it is 'good' to eat the other or if the other is 'good' to eat, nor of knowing which other. One eats him regardless and lets oneself be eaten by him" (282). Perhaps this is why Derrida admits he doesn't know who is "who" anymore (283). Such a notion of responsibility tends toward a potential identification, if not confusion, between who and what and, by extension, between the animal I am and the animal I eat or feed. This is a confusion that debates about eating horse during the first half of the nineteenth century both incited and warded off. The reciprocity promoted by Derrida's notions of hospitality was hardly a willed possibility for the horse, nor was it possible for the hungry classes for whom horsemeat was promoted and who thereby gained in sustenance what they lost in distinction from their food.

The introduction of horsemeat into French cuisine was one of the rare instances of an enforced change in attitude, if not taste, from general aversion to official (if not general) acceptance.[8] The first real efforts to legalize hippophagy took place in 1856 when the SPA petitioned the Paris police, who referred the matter to the minister of agriculture and the Council on Public Hygiene and Health. Although the verdict was favorable, it would be ten years before the prefect of police issued a decree legalizing horsemeat for human consumption. The decree included several articles requiring that slaughter of horses take place separately from that of other animals and under the surveillance of a police inspector or a veterinarian. As animal slaughter would be increasingly hidden from view during the century, however, the name Montfaucon was ingrained in the French imaginary and difficult to separate from the horsemeat on the plate. This hill on the outskirts of Paris earned a particularly sinister image because of its dual function as site of the gibbet and site for horse slaughter. In what follows I want to ask not only why France became a nation that ate horsemeat but also what the controversies surrounding the idea of hippophagy reveal about nineteenth-century French culture and the status of the horse within it.

At first glance the rationale behind the practice, which was supported even by the Society for the Protection of Animals, was logical, ethical, and persuasive. Horseflesh was plentiful in the nation, and introducing it into markets would help support the health of workers who, according to recent research of public hygienists, were said to be suffering from dangerously low levels of protein, a substance only recently discovered as the primary nutritional component of meat.[9] Meat protein was necessary, but since beef was too expensive for many, it was reasoned, "let them eat horse." Because of the unique status of the horse, however, persuading the public was not so simple. Unlike snails, which (who?) slipped unproblematically into the dishes of haute cuisine, hippophagy never quite made the grade, and its mere introduction onto the French table was a matter of intense debate. That debate had to do not only with the status and taste of French cuisine (many described horsemeat as sweet and tender), but also with the status of the horse, with whom the nation had complex, affective relations and whose "conquest" at the dinner table threatened that "nobility" associated with the animal. Indeed, it is both curious and telling that it was in the middle of the century, when the horse was at the height of popularity for riding or racing and when an ever increasing number of well-to-do citizens groomed, saddled, and pampered their horses, endowing them with names, person-

Figure 4.1. Storefront of Boucherie Chevaline, Paris, on French postcard.

alities, and intimate care, that they were also turned into dinner. In what follows I will suggest that the legalizing of horsemeat for human consumption in 1866, and the newly promoted practice of hippophagy, went hand in hand with an increasingly ambivalent attitude toward the subjectivity of the horse, especially since the horse could, in turn, point to the questionable subjectivity of certain "breeds" of humans.

KIN AND KIND

That eating horse still strikes us as somewhat distasteful is evident in a postcard I received some years ago (fig. 4.1). The postcard depicts a line of women shoppers at the *boucherie chevaline*, or horse butcher, and a man in full equestrian attire—breeches, boots, riding helmet—but with a shopping bag in place of a whip. While the well-dressed and tidy appearance of the women, with their stockings and high-heeled shoes, suggests that in the twentieth century buying horsemeat had become a middle-class practice, the equestrian begs us to ask, What's wrong with this picture? What is it that makes us chuckle, or perhaps cringe? What might this apparently conflicted relation to the animal world say about our subjectivity, or for that matter about the horse's?

According to anthropologist Marshall Sahlins horses, like dogs, are deemed inedible in America because they "participate in American society in the capacity of subjects. They have proper personal names, and indeed we are in the habit of conversing with them, unlike pigs and cattle."[10] If "Mr. Ed" was any indication, horses not only converse but also participate as personalities in America, and so are deemed inedible. In France dogs are common dinner companions but are not considered food. How then do we understand the edibility of a horse? Does it have less than subject status because, unlike other pets, it is not allowed in the house?[11] Or should we assume that the horse changed status in the nineteenth century so that when it was deemed edible it was no longer considered a subject? These questions point toward the increasingly ambiguous status not only of the horse but also of pets in general, who hover on the borders of our kin and kind.[12] In a book whose title, *L'homnivore* (The omnivorous human), recalls a deconstructed boundary between eater and eaten, Claude Fischler describes our relation to animals as a modern paradox; they have become "at the same time more object and more subject than ever."[13] On the one hand, animals in modern industrial society have a newfound role and place in the family such that each is accorded individuality, an identity, and a personality. At the same time science, and in particular the agricultural and food sciences, has reified animals by turning them into "deanimalized matter" such that we need not identify the steak on our plate with the steer it came from. Grocery stores further absent the animal through their tidy packaging.[14]

Contemporary culinary desire, as the anthropologist Noélie Vialles writes, is for animal flesh even as we refuse to recognize the animal in the flesh.[15] In her book *Le sang et la chair* (Blood and flesh), Vialles distinguishes between "zoophagy," or eating recognizable animals, and "sarcophagy," or eating flesh that cannot be identified with an animal, and she charts a general shift to sarcophagy in the early nineteenth century, coinciding with new regulations affecting the practice and location of slaughter.[16] She also suggests that the horse "is certainly, at least to the extent that one consents to eat it, one of the animals one hopes most not to recognize"[17] on the plate, and thus that the practice of "sarcophagy"—or disguising the animal in the meat—would make hippophagy more possible. The point seems to be contradicted by the horse heads that hang at the entrance to horse butchers in France, seen also in the postcard. How and why, then, did the horse become edible in the first place? What were the arguments and what the resistances?

MONTFAUCON: PUTTING THE CART BEFORE THE HORSE

It is perhaps prescient that the witty nineteenth-century journalist Albert Cler ends his book on the "follies" of the horsey world with a chapter on Montfaucon, the slaughter yards to the northeast of Paris that closed in 1842. Montfaucon was, as he described it, a "theater" of another sort, where working and noble horses met their gruesome end and where every body part, including the blood, was turned into glue, oil, or a particular paint known as "Prussian blue." Cler's satirical tone does not detract from the horror of this final chapter, and one can only wonder how the public came to accept that a "dashing and brilliant steed, winner at the hippodrome and applauded with military solemnity, or that favorite mare, caressed by the hand of a lovely amazon, could from one day to the next be rushed from glory and honor into the mire of the butcher."[18] Horsemeat was bought or stolen from Montfaucon not just for other carnivorous animals, but also for humans, although the establishment's prime function was not as a butchery. Indeed, the separation of the job of the butcher from that of the *écorcheur*, or knacker—a new euphemism that replaced *tueur*, or killer, at the turn of the century—was one effect of laws put in place under Napoleon I. While it had previously been common practice to slaughter animals in the city streets, under the First Empire ordinances were passed to relocate such killings to specific areas designated and controlled by the state. The reason was not animal protection but to protect humans from the sight of violent, inhumane behavior. It was necessary to hide killing so as not to give others the idea.[19] To view a pig being slaughtered, it was feared, might lead a boy to turn a knife on his sister (as one newspaper had reported happening), or more seriously, lead a worker to take vengeance on his master. (The memory of the guillotine is not far off.)

The link between slaughter and criminal activity also dates back to the thirteenth century, when Montfaucon was the site of the royal gibbet. Criminals were hanged on the racks, their bodies displayed as symbols of royal justice and power. During the eighteenth century the gibbet fell into disuse and disrepair, and the site developed a more important use as a cesspit for the city, where garbage was dumped and fecal matter collected through various city streams and paths. Excrement, it was believed, could be put to productive use as fertilizer, but it also contributed to the putrid smell associated with Montfaucon. By the nineteenth century such odors were feared to carry diseases that could infect any who come in contact with them. In addition to the fecal matter, putrefying animal flesh added to the stench. Since the seventeenth century, Montfaucon was also the site where horses were slaughtered, skinned, and dismembered so that every ounce of flesh, bone, hair, and fat could be sold on the market, whether for hides, tallow, or dog food or, eventually, as meat for the animals at the Jardin des plantes. Estimates suggest that by the 1830s, about 13,000 horses met their end at Montfaucon each year.[20] What crime had these equines committed, one might ask, to be splayed and hung on the gallows for all to see? Or were they more simply a reminder of the "carnivorous virility" of the state, even though the state did not yet officially eat horsemeat?[21]

The underside of the horse's nobility was thus manifest in the odorific association of excrement and rotting flesh, whose infectious emanations raised the concern of officials. Fears surrounding the emanations resulted in a number of police ordinances, dating back to 1739, that moved to shut down or move the site, but without success. In 1811 a committee was once again sent to investigate the potential hazards, and among the signers of the report was Étienne Pariset. Pariset, recall, had been Pinel's assistant in psychological medicine at the Salpêtrière, and his research led him to the study of infectious diseases. He would also become one of the founders of the Paris SPA.[22] The report of 1811 was followed by a series of investigations during the first quarter of the century, culminating in the report on the slaughter yards of Paris by the public hygienist Alexandre Parent-Duchâtelet, published first in 1832 and then again within his extensive report on public hygiene of 1836. In a first chapter, Parent-Duchâtelet covers in detail the many complaints brought against this site that had become famous for its "pernicious" air and for its "cartloads of dead horses and pestilential matter, or other wagons filled with infected and half-gangrenous horses that have fallen on the ground from the beatings of their drivers."[23] His point, however, is not to raise sympathy for the horses—far from it—but to substantiate the claims regarding Montfaucon's risk to the health of its workers or to those living in nearby neighborhoods, and to suggest measures to reduce it. Significantly, he writes that closing Montfaucon, as many had demanded, was unnecessary. Rather, it could be an example of how art and science must be applied to turn the site into a clean, efficient, and profitable operation. Parent-Duchâtelet cites a report that shows just how this can be done:

> The animals' blood is carefully collected, and as soon as the skin and all the products that are useful to the arts have been removed, the carcass is cut into pieces and transported in an iron case with the blood and other products; big enough to hold four horses, the case is transferred to a steam boiler. . . . [E]levated to a high temperature, the vapor acts on the flesh and separates it from the bones, which it whitens and from which it extracts a good part of fat. In the space of an hour and a half to two hours, the

> operation is finished, and what remains is, on one side, the bones that have been perfectly defleshed and, on the other, flesh . . . reduced to the state of mincemeat.[24]
>
> The process is remarkable not only for the speed with which it is accomplished, but also for the fact that the flesh produced has no odor and "can be conserved for an unlimited time and easily transported to immense distances."[25]

Here, then, is a perfect example of a "deanimalization" of flesh, even to the point of eliminating its most tenacious and lingering quality—its smell.[26] If absenting the animal is a goal for the site of *équarrissage*, butchery, it is also a goal for Parent-Duchâtelet's study, insofar as it removes obstacles to both the scientific and the economic value of its findings. There is no recognition here of that noble animal, as there would be in a later report on Montfaucon by an engineer from Lyon who, citing Buffon, writes, "It is an atrocious savagery, this manner in which, in his final moments, one treats this useful animal . . . the most noble conquest that man has ever made."[27]

"Words don't smell," or so says the proverb, writes Théophile Gautier in his own account of a *voyage* to Montfaucon. Yet he warns his female readers to have a bottle of smelling salts and a jar of disinfectant ready when they finish reading his description and begs their pardon for his crime against smell—what he calls, *lèse-odorat*. Gautier writes against or in defiance of that new "field of the visible" launched by naturalist writers of the eighteenth century, in whose works, Foucault has argued, words must be purged of all that does not partake of sheer observation, including taste and flavor and so also odor.[28] Rather, with attention to the poetic possibilities of the odors and flavors of death and decay that will find its counterpart in Baudelaire's poem "A Carcass," Gautier launches into a prefiguration of naturalism's effort to look deeply into the ugly and cruel aspects of life and to translate the simultaneously "ultrapicturesque" and "nauseating" details of this "last circle of hell" where death has become a spectacle for the entertainment of tourists.[29] First published in 1838 in the widely read newspaper *La presse*, Gautier's indelicate travelogue lends support to Montfaucon's significance in the popular imagination, if not to an apprehension of the accounts offered by the officials of hygiene as themselves overly sterile. Here the rhetoric used to describe the surrounding hillsides warns readers of the horror that lies ahead: "The horizon is cut off by bald hills, crouching at the horizon in all sorts of awkward and deformed positions; their shoulders are hunched, their nipples wrinkled and covered with . . . a greenish clay that resembles flesh beginning to rot—one would say cadavers of hills stripped of their skin of plants and thrown here and there by the hand of a gigantic knacker."[30]

Many of the details of Parent-Duchâtelet's account—details about dogs sneaking away with bits of stolen horsemeat or the problem of rat infestations—find their way into Gautier's account, but with an almost surrealist amplification of the ugly. The effect is an aestheticizing of animal subjects and objects, whos and whats, that confuses distinctions between species as between life and death. Some of this occurs under the sign of "eating well," although for and by whom is not always clear. In the "cascades of liquid, amber mud, perfumed with long veins of blood," there can be perceived, we are told, a *paté de maison*, accompanied by the various "scrofulous and sinister physiognomies." Indeed, the *paté* seems to include the remains of the now defunct gallows as well as of the current *tuerie* or kill factory; Gautier does not euphemize. It is "incongruous" that human flesh is not meat (*viande*), Vialles suggests, but for Gautier and the other animals at Montfaucon it certainly is, even if, as we are told in the second "chapter" of this visit, it is regarded as an "inferior meat" by both the dogs and the rats. Because of that, moreover, we are supposed to be thankful that the knackery exists and provides these nonhuman gastronomes with their preferred meat: horse. The rats in particular are assiduous in their cuisine, and the "chefs" of the band head right for the horses' eyes, "slitting the cornea and emptying the socket to obtain that little ball of fat that lines the bottom of the cavity." This is like candy for them or a delicacy comparable, we are told, to a "truffled partridge or a terrine of Nérac" (27). Rat gastronomy follows in the grand French tradition.

This focus on horses' eyes as meat and matter is a shift from earlier reports about blindfolding horses at the moment of killing, which suggests they could indeed see what was coming and was one of the few concessions toward their subjectivity. Beyond that they are offered no "last supper, for "What's the use of feeding those today who will die tomorrow?" the knacker argues. Gautier describes the horses as "condemned" (*condamnés*) (18), thus reiterating their identification with the criminals who were executed and hung on the gibbet. But condemned for what? What crime did they commit? Here, moreover, the guilt seems to shift slightly to the tourist, who is asked if he would like to see one or two horses killed "for amusement" (18). Once the act is performed, the word "kill" again comes under scrutiny. "One didn't kill him, one conjured away his life, and that so quickly, so efficiently, that he didn't even notice" (19).

"Who really kills," Vialles asks, raising a doubt that Gautier's text also underscores. "No one," she answers. "No one kills. The first man doesn't kill, he knocks out. The last doesn't kill either, he bleeds the animal that arrives, as one regularly says, as if dead."[31] Gautier directs attention to the bleeding and "gleaming" flesh that hangs from one carcass, and readers might wonder how far the focus on color is calculated as fulfillment of the promised "picturesque" or, alternatively, as a means to avoid seeing through to the color's source. His narrator claims to see the most "splendid color" imaginable: "tones of pearl, rose, lacquer, violet, sky blue, apple green, and with silver tints like the richest and most exotic shell." When he finally witnesses the actual act of bleeding, death is signaled only by the change of color that "flowed scarlet first, then violet, then black" (19).[32] The artist's eye thus reveals what the scientist's observations avoid, that this is a place of "horror" not because of the odor and infection and waste, but because it is where lives are taken, all color annihilated.

If Montfaucon is thus a place of both beauty and horror for the narrator, his sensibility and manner, including his appreciation for the sensibility of his readers, is to be contrasted with that of the "gallant" knacker" he encounters. A man of "exquisite manners," he offers some "grilled horse" that he had made for his own lunch (20), but the narrator declines the offer, saying politely that he has tasted horse in restaurants. To this the knacker replies that he must have been given bad beef, not horse. Confirming his own knowledge in matters of taste, he affirms that horsemeat is superior in texture, tenderness, and taste to the finest beef, an opinion that throws the narrator into great confusion and into admitting that his own views on the tenderness of meat have been "singularly disturbed." More disturbing, however, is learning of the discriminating palates of those around him, notably the dogs and the rats who, despite their preference for horse, are said to eat humans when the horsemeat runs out. Gautier's writing thus deliberately confuses the who and what of gastronomy, as of the table manners once thought to be reserved for bourgeois dining. This is a world where any and all may be meat for another, so that it becomes imperative to determine the terms on which we should or should not accept Derrida's imperative to "give the other to eat."

HIPPOPHAGY AND EATING WELL

Gautier's gallant, horse-eating knacker would contest Vialles's claim that the horse is the animal one least wants to recognize on the plate. Prioritizing matters of taste and economy, he is inured to the violence he participates in and that Gautier's narrator bears witness to. The rats too produce a "spectacle of combat," giving the lie to the often-cited claim that "animals don't rip each other apart," proffered by the seventeenth-century poet Nicolas Boileau (31). Reflecting on the shared brutishness of humans and animals alike, and consequently on our shared fate of being "devoured" (32), the narrator also hints that the arts—and perhaps literature in particular—can do more than simply invent ways to clean and economize the conditions of the slaughter yards. They can alert us to the horror of the carnage and, by extension, bring us to question the value of animal life and the justice of condemning animals merely for living. That Gautier's text was published the same year and in the same journal (*La presse*) as Eugène Sue's *Godolphin Arabian* (discussed in chapter 2) demonstrates the growing concern for animal abuse among writers and what such abuse reveals about the animality of humans.

To abuse and to eat, however, were different matters. To be sure, the question of animal suffering was frequently raised within growing discussions surrounding hippophagy. Some questioned the hypocrisy of the SPA, writing, "One must not believe the Animal Protection Society is composed only of vegetarians; eh! My G-d no; there like elsewhere one laments the lot of the beasts, and one consoles oneself over their misfortune while eating them."[33] But animal suffering was a secondary consideration. The first step toward legalizing horsemeat for human consumption concerned the prejudices regarding the meat itself—the very same intuited by Gautier's knacker—that it was feared might even incite workers to revolt against the administration for proposing it. This was the prejudice that Parent-Duchâtelet set out to combat, having discovered in the course of his studies that many poor people living in the vicinity of the yards were regularly eating horsemeat with no ill effects.[34] He also noted that more horsemeat had been eaten during the winter of 1835 than ever before and that the only cause for concern was the ease with which it slipped illegally into the market.

Already in 1825 the health commission had noted the benefits of horsemeat, which was sold in other European countries, and suggested that measures be taken to regularize and legalize its sale in France. But no action was taken. More than twenty years later, Isidore Geoffroy Saint-Hilaire, son of the famous zoologist and himself a natural historian, made the legal consumption of horses into a personal crusade. For Geoffroy the issue was above all socioeconomic: "Is it not absurd to lose, each month, in all of France, millions of kilos of good meat while all over France, there are millions of men who lack meat?"[35] Meat, according to contemporary theories, was the essential food for repairing and restoring what the body lost in work, and it was precisely what workers could not afford. Horsemeat could solve this problem and help sustain the working class. Concern for the working class was thus the first, humanitarian argument for legalizing horsemeat. The second argument took horses' interests into consideration and suggested that killing them might be in their best interest. Nothing could be worse than the deaths suffered by most horses, who either collapsed on the street from overwork or were sold to the renderer only to be starved in the truck that hauled other horses to a similar fate. Such inhumane deaths, it was argued, would be illegal at the abattoir, where, moreover, the higher price per pound for better-quality meat would ensure that more horses be spared the brutal abuses that were all too common and be kept in good condition until sold. It is because we don't eat them, Geoffroy argued, that horses are overworked and mistreated.

The arguments for eating horsemeat thus relied, paradoxically, on acknowledging the suffering of animals, if not their humanity, and the inhumanity of humans whose abuses of them would be deterred only by the possibility of economic gain. While these were the opinions that eventually won over the government, however, they did little to address a second, pervasive objection to eating horsemeat, which had to do with the less arguable matter of taste or, one might say, of "eating well." Indeed, despite the early efforts of Parent-Duchâtelet, the suspicions toward the meat that were expressed by Gautier's narrator persisted for years.

In 1865 the former chief of police came before the newly formed hippophagic committee and announced, "We have come here, sirs, to attempt to destroy a prejudice of the stomach that is as tenacious, and as unjust, as all the prejudices of caste and nation."[36] To address this prejudice was of great concern, especially because gastronomy was already integral to France's national identity. For France to officially approve of eating horsemeat, it had to be considered up to French gastronomic standards, and Geoffroy suggested that the example must come from the top. That year a series of "hippophagic banquets" were held for those who "by virtue of their important social status, could exert a salutary influence on public opinion."[37] The dignitaries dined on such delicacies as vermicelli with consommé of horse, paté of horse liver with truffles, and saddle of horse with *sauce au xérès*, all accompanied by appropriate garnishes and wines. For the most part the dignitaries pronounced the meal "exquisite," and it was in the following year, 1866, that the first legal horse butchery opened. But as the mandatory horse head above its doors indicated, only a minimum of prejudice was conquered. French culinary pride afforded horsemeat separate but not equal status, thus responding to consumers' fears that they might be slipped a filet of horse in place of beefsteak.

Despite the successful outcome of the campaign, reactions to the banquets themselves were mixed. Some newspapers reported that "the prejudice against horsemeat will fall,"[38] others were not convinced. For example, the reporter from the satirical paper *La lune* described how even the most courageous tester "had a little worried wrinkle in the corner of his mouth—we looked at each other with a smile that tried to be frank but couldn't quite make it."[39] This was not because of the taste alone, which he admitted could be "exquisite," but because of the idea of it. As Claude Lévi-Strauss claimed, for something to be good to eat it must be good to think, and the thought of eating horse unleashed a whole set of cultural transgressions. "What makes me shout a cry of alarm is that the promoters of hippophagy will prevent all the underclasses from sleeping. And it will soon be announced . . . that the meat of dog is far superior to that of lamb. And they will prove it."[40] Once they have moved to the dog, the reporter continued, it was a short step to the donkey, the rat, the caterpillar, and who knows what next.

Simultaneous with the slippery slope argument, the specific meaning and status of the horse were also at stake. If indeed the horse is the animal one would least want to recognize in the meat, the mid-nineteenth century is the moment when it would be most difficult not to do so. At no time in history was the horse so ubiquitous in France's urban areas, and no one was spared the smells, the sounds, and the sight of the daily traffic jams of coaches, carts, omnibuses, and saddle horses, all moving in every direction. If the image of the horse head above the butcher shop did not linger into the dining room, the smells of manure probably did. For the upper classes, horses were pets to parade through the streets and especially around the Bois de Boulogne, where in 1860 one enterprising photographer named Jean Delton began a successful business making horse portraits. While anthropologists suggest that the best way to prevent an animal from finding its way to the dining table is to "give it a proper name," horses were given names that not only enhanced their subjectivity but often established the connection to their human breeders. The year before the legalizing of hippophagy, the name of one horse in particular was known throughout the land: Gladiator. Having won both the English Derby and the Paris Grand Prix, Gladiator became a national symbol and proof that French horses were at least as worthy as the renowned English thoroughbreds, whose value had never been culinary.

While such events obviously did not stop the eating of horses, they made it difficult to separate the meat on the plate from the animal who won yesterday's Derby, as the popular illustrator Cham suggested in his references to the racetrack. Cham's humor, like that of the *boucherie chevaline* postcard, depends on a certain uneasiness, if not disgust, provoked by a transgression of boundaries (see figs. 4.2 and 4.3).

But which boundaries? Anthropologists have stressed the similarity

Figure 4.2. Cham (Count Amédée-Charles-Henry de Noé), *La chronique du jour: Album de soixante caricatures par Cham* (Paris: Arnauld de Vresse, 1865), 231. "Françoise, how have you prepared the meat for me?—Why Madame, à la Daumont."

between sexual and food prohibitions, suggesting that the foods we eat, like our sexual partners, must be at "intermediate distances," neither too close nor too far.[41] "Very similar and hence rejected items include other humans, primates, and pets (which are emotionally close to humans, though not very similar in form)."[42] Eating those who are too "close" is cannibalism, or at least means we ourselves fall to a kind of animal state by not knowing or not paying heed to such distinctions. Horses seem to slip in and out of the category of pet, and hence of family, which may be one reason horsemeat remained primarily a food of necessity, not one of choice, to use Pierre Bourdieu's categories.[43] According to a popular song written in response to the hippophagic banquet, horsemeat is regarded as a "taste of necessity turned into a virtue," since eating it is better than waiting for the ever elusive chicken in every pot, especially since that waiting was rhetorically figured as the activity of another beaked creature.[44]

Manger du cheval, jeune ou vieux, ferme ou tendre,
Vaut mieux que toujours attendre
Le Bec dans l'eau,
Cette fameuse poule au pot.

Figure 4.3. Cham (Count Amédée-Charles-Henry de Noé), *La chronique du jour: Album de soixante caricatures par Cham* (Paris: Arnauld de Vresse, 1865), 233. "It's not possible, Françoise. All that horsemeat I bought yesterday is already eaten?—It was a racehorse. Nothing goes faster!"

[To eat horse, young or old, tough or tender,
Is better than always waiting,
Beak in the water,
For that famous chicken in the pot.]

Like Gautier's rats, we are feathered friends who eat horse so as not to eat, or perhaps be eaten by, our own kind. But here the we is a particular "we," since horsemeat was sanctioned by the upper classes but designated for the workers who most needed meat and could not afford beef. The working classes should eat horse, perhaps so they will not eat each other, or more likely so they will not revolt against the hands that feed them.

Conversely, to secure a strict hierarchy of foods might itself incite dangerous reactions, as was indicated in Paret-Duchâtelet's report: "Nothing will happen if, in a dirty restaurant, workers eat horse flesh without knowing it, without suspecting it; but if the sale of that food is authorized, they will see horse flesh everywhere and will say that the important people, the rich people, make them eat horse so they can have beef at a better price. The consequences of such an innovation are too dangerous to allow it to pass."[45]

Eating well is thus a precarious practice to prescribe across markers of difference. In a gesture reminiscent of Derrida's "giving the other to eat," legalizing hippophagy may appear to have been a gesture of hospitality, offering the working classes the privileges of "carnivorous virility," but only insofar as these very privileges, and the subjecthood they afforded, according to Derrida, were of a distinctly lesser order.

The importance of eating animals for the construction of human subjectivity and for discriminating between subjects is the focus of a section of Walter Benjamin's "One-Way Street," titled "Gloves." Benjamin suggests that eating animals is one way of overcoming our "disgust" at being like them. "In an aversion to animals the predominant feeling is fear of being recognized by them through contact. The horror that stirs deep in man is an obscure awareness that in him something lives so akin to the animal that it might be recognized. All disgust is originally disgust at touching."[46]

Whereas feminist thinkers like Luce Irigaray have described "touch" in positive terms as a sensual relating to otherness that allows for reciprocity, Benjamin alerts us to the (perhaps more masculine) fear of a disgusting proximity to the animal other. One way to overcome this fear and disgust is to eat the animal. It is "a drastic gesture that overleaps its mark: the nauseous is violently engulfed, eaten, while the zone of finest epidermal contact remains taboo. Only in this way is the paradox of the moral demand to be met, exacting simultaneously the overcoming and the subtlest elaboration of man's sense of disgust. He may not deny his bestial relationship with animals, the invocation of which revolts him: he must make himself its master."[47]

What is not described in Benjamin's comment is the desire that brings us to touch what disgusts us in the first place. The attraction to the "low" is the flip side of disgust. The simultaneous attraction/repulsion to animals and to women underlies the structure of what Derrida refers to as "carnophallogocentrism," or the idea that eating animal flesh is a show of mastery necessary to the construction of virile, human subjectivity.[48] Might it be that in nineteenth-century France the horse was that creature who most revealed man's intimate and bestial relationship with animals, such that activities like pleasure riding required subsequently a drastic means of separation, sending our postcard equestrian immediately to the *chevaline* to eat his disgusting mate and so prove himself its master?

"Disgust," writes William Miller, "helps define boundaries between us and them, me and you." But as he writes in *The Anatomy of Disgust*, the story about disgust can cut two ways. "For all the concern to claim ourselves superior to animals and our horror that we are assimilable to them, there is a countervailing admiration and envy of them, a desire to live *up* to them. Their bodies can do anything ours can do better and they do it clothed."[49]

To be sure, at a time when bodily performance was becoming increasingly important for bourgeois subjectivity, the horse was often regarded as a human ideal. Literary fiction from Gautier's *Mademoiselle de Maupin* (1835) to Maupassant's 1882 story "Fou" (Crazy) is replete with horses whose beauty and attraction are unparalleled and thus causes for jealousy. For some a sexual rival, for others, like the frustrated workers in Sue's *Godolphin Arabian* (1838) or Maupassant's *Coco* (1884), the horse was a symbol of a pampered, idle, and feminized leisure class: "But of course groom him," bemoans an envious and embittered coachman in Sue's novel: "So many delicacies are good for making a horse as soft as a woman. On the other hand, do I groom myself? Do I take care of myself like that? Then why would a horse be so cared for?"[50] Sue's bourgeois narrator, on the other hand, finds that the racehorse exemplified a "male and useful beauty" achieved not through labor but through blood, "the pure and unadulterated transmission of the precious blood of the noble son of the Kings of Jarret."[51]

From Géricault to Degas, Stendhal or Gautier to Zola and Maupassant, nineteenth-century representations of horses more often looked away from the horse as an object of abuse to show the horse as an envied rival: better as lover, better as worker (and sometimes better treated), better even as aristocrat—his pure bloodlines transmitted without adulteration. Bred to perfection, in the French cultural imagination horses revealed by comparison an imperfection in the French male body. As Miller emphasizes, "We make a pathetic animal."[52]

The "elaboration of disgust" with regard to horsemeat, then, must take into account both sides: disgust with animals that are too much like us and disgust with our own bodies, whose performance pales beside that of other animals. To overcome that disgust we may turn the horse into an edible object so as to bolster our own subjectivity by opposition. Or we may try to eat horse in an effort to become more horse ("you are what you eat"). In either case, what Benjamin alluded to as mastery over the animal, similar to what Derrida calls "carnivorous virility," is a tenuous achievement. As Gautier's descriptions of the slaughter yards acknowledged, we eat so as not to be eaten and to affirm a phallic subjectivity that may be easily shaken by being shared with the (feminine) animal other. A classed as well as a gendered activity, "eating well" can be a gesture of hospitality or even friendship, but it can also be a mechanism of asserting difference and privilege. By authorizing the consumption of horsemeat principally for the working class, the bourgeois dignitaries acknowledged the ongoing needs of the working class while denying fraternity with those needs. "Giving the horse/other to eat" worked not only to demote the horse from its status as subject but also to diminish the value of its breeding. The pure blood (the literal translation of *pur-sang*) that established a rhetorical link between certain horses and the aristocracy was indistinguishable on the plate. Hippophagy could thus be a means for the bourgeoisie to assert its carnivorous subjectivity without eating the family pet.

As for the virility of that subjectivity, its tenuousness was equally at stake. In a century when the classed and gendered associations of horsemanship were in flux and when the increasingly visible woman rider or amazon was as likely to be a courtesan as a woman of means, the availability of horsemeat fed fears concerning disguised and transgressive sexualities. Gautier's narrator remarks that many of the workers at Montfaucon were women dressed as men (17–18). Nor is it coincidental that Parent-Duchâtelet conducted his investigation of the horse slaughter yards simultaneously with his well-known study of prostitution, and the two are linked in a number of ways. Like prostitution, eating horsemeat occurred daily and should, claimed Parent-Duchâtelet, similarly be considered a "necessity" (155). Indeed, proof of the widespread practice of hippophagy was to be found in a brothel: "We end these details proving that the consumption of horsemeat in Paris is daily and considerable, by saying that the sanitary commission of the observatory quarter noted last February, as a cause of insalubrity, a house overflowing with prostitutes, in which was found considerable masses of horse flesh destined for the food of the inhabitants of the neighborhood" (154).

His observation did not stop there but continued to describe a courtyard filled with chickens and ducks that were also fed "exclusively with horsemeat, but principally with horse liver." No waiting "beak in the water" for these fowl. Given such observations and the apparent health benefits of horsemeat (if not prostitution), Parent-Duchâtelet proposed legalization for both accompanied by similar strategies of containment and regulation to ensure sanitary conditions and to limit the spread of disease.[53]

The associations between eating horse and an encroaching and indomitable female sexuality have lingered into the present, and both are marked by a notion of Frenchness, understood to be a deviant and undemocratic culture because it permits hippophagy. In a post to a website called "From Horses to Horsemeat's Dreambook," a French woman named Camille wrote:

> How do you find horsemeat in the United States? I innocently asked some markets that I wanted it and they looked at me as though I commited a felony. . . . Thanks for the website! I cannot tell you how many times I've been called a frog, horse killer and French eurotrash because I want to supply my immigrating family with horsemeat. I've gotten nasty email from people telling me "you're a horse eatin' French slut who should die!!!" . . . Thank you for any help at all. I know how you feel about the American taboo.[54]

Perhaps we all need taboos, and to argue about them may be as futile as arguing about taste. The tastes and taboos that determine what it means to eat well are the foundations not only for how we constitute ourselves in contradistinction to our edible others, but also for how we distinguish ourselves as subjects of gender, class, and nation.

CHAPTER FIVE

Purebreds and Amazons: Race, Gender, and Species from the Second Empire to the Third Republic

HORSES AND WOMEN ON SHOW

In 1867 Paris held the second of its universal or world exhibitions (the first was in 1855), which were designed, ostensibly, to make known the major scientific and technological advances of the day. Attracting some eleven million visitors, the exhibition and its sequels also allowed the French to show off their own technological and aesthetic conquests and so ensure the status of Paris as the cultural capital of the world.[1] Indeed, as we might glean from Édouard Manet's own painting of the event, *View of the 1867 Exposition Universelle* (fig. 5.1), Paris put itself on display with its newly formed parks and roads (the product of "Hausmannization"), its monuments and domes gleaming under a hydrogen balloon sun, and above all its array of inhabitants enjoying the city and the apparent bounties it had to offer.[2] As T. J. Clark remarks, the people are "enjoying the exhibition and making sure their enjoyment is noticed: gaping, strolling, sprawling on makeshift grass, pointing things out to one another with umbrellas, looking well on a horse, showing off pets and wearing (they hope) outlandish shades of yellow."[3] The painting fits into Clark's larger argument about the 1860s as an "epoch of transition" during which the city is being made over into a "spectacle," an image to be looked at, but one in which the "the great categories of collective life—for instance, class, city, neighborhood, sex, nation, place on the 'occupational ladder'—have not yet been made over into commodity form, though the effort to do so is impressive."[4] The image of Paris that these spectators are searching for is not yet in clear focus, hence the tenuousness or sketchiness of the brushstrokes.

At the very center of Manet's painting is the figure of a woman on horseback—an amazon, as she would have been known. While Clark men-

Figure 5.1. Édouard Manet, *View of the 1867 Exposition Universelle*, 1867. Image courtesy of the National Museum of Art, Architecture and Design, Oslo.

tions this pairing of woman and horse only in passing, the two are in fact central to the transitional image of this period and, I would argue, to the ambivalence this painting expresses regarding the apparent progress and future of France.[5] The figure is one whose movement itself is ambiguous; with both human and horse heads turned away from the road to face the fenced-in grass, it is impossible to tell which way the two are actually proceeding and whether we are witnessing a momentary loss of control or a display of haute école dressage. With regard to their placement vis-à-vis the other people in the painting, the amazon and horse occupy a transitional space between those at leisure who are watching the exhibition, and those otherwise occupied in daily activities or work: walking the dog or tending the garden. One could say that the first group is tending to the spectacle while the second is tending to nature—although nature that is also trimmed for viewing. Whether the amazon is a woman of leisure on her pleasure ride or a professional rider exercising one of the horses for the nearby hippodrome or circus is uncertain.[6] The way her torso and head carriage repeat the gardener's might seem to link her with a category of labor, while the dandified dress of the young boy walking the dog reminds us that animals are indeed forms of commodified display. The uncertainty over the amazon's class affiliation, moreover, is linked to an uncertainty over her sexuality. Patricia Mainardi quite rightly asserts that she "could be harlot or lady of fashion."[7] By 1867 the professional amazon or *écuyère* was often the

Figure 5.2. Antoine-Auguste Préault, *Gaulish Horseman*, installed at Pont d'Iéna, Paris, 1853.

most sought-after of courtesans. At the same time, however, Paris was rife with stories of such *écuyères* marrying their adoring counts, and it was not unheard of for girls of the upper classes to train for the haute école.[8] In this way the *écuyère* is emblematic of the transitional epoch of Second Empire Paris, with its increasingly fluid social and sexual orders. For many she is a disturbing emblem precisely because of the visibility of her "enjoyment," to return to Clark's word. Unlike what could be assumed of the harlot, the amazon's enjoyment depended not on a man, but on a horse. This displacement of man in the sexual-social order may also be hinted at by Manet's painting. The actual center of the city view is occupied by one of the bridge's two equestrian statues, Antoine-Auguste Préault's *Gaulish Horseman* (fig. 5.2). With a countenance of virile power and self-assured authority, man and horse are, as Clark says, "perched there at the picture's center as a noble (and illegible) reminder of the republic."[9] And yet this statue is barely visible, replaced by the amazon and her horse.

By 1867 the woman rider was a familiar sight in Paris, although her status was not always apparent. Initially it was male riders who would perform the difficult exercises at the hippodromes, but in 1835 Caroline Loyo became the first of successive generations of *écuyères* who would dominate the circus. This opening of riding to women was part of the larger expansion of horse culture that took place in Paris over the course of the century. Under the Empire, horseback riding was above all a practice reserved for the military and secondarily a pastime of the nobility. But under the influence of French Anglomania and the establishment in 1834 of the Jockey Club, a meeting place for the *jeunesse doré* or golden youth of Paris, equestrianism became a bourgeois sport. Its popularity grew especially under Napoleon III, an avid horseman like his wife, who purchased the Bois de Boulogne in 1852 as a kind of horse playground for the city of Paris. Depending on whom one wanted to see or for whom one wanted to show off his or her horse and fashion, one had a specific time slot for appearing in the Bois. Alfred Delvau's 1867 *Les plaisirs de Paris* documents the lifestyle of "le tout Paris" when, he affirms, the ride through the Bois became "the privileged promenade of a good half of Paris, the richer half, of course."[10] But it becomes clear that it was not only the rich but also the would-be wealthy who would sport their attire and horsemanship.

> I wouldn't want to affirm that the princesses who fluff up their skirts in these carriages are women of the best world, or that the cavaliers prancing around them are the cream of the crop of French gentlemanry. No! I know well that all the pretty women are equal before us, and that there is nothing that resembles a dandy as much as another dandy, such that distinguishing is difficult. However, at my risk and peril, I would ask you . . . not to take these elegant men and women for what they are not, but rather for what they are, fake dandies and stablewomen.[11]

Horses for riding or for driving were to became the center of a dandified public lifestyle that brought various worlds together, combining elements of both "high society" and the world of *le spectacle* while making the distinctions between these worlds, and the classes of people frequenting them, increasingly difficult to ascertain.[12] If the arcade became the haven for the *flâneur* or stroller, this was partly, as Walter Benjamin suggests, to get away from the carriages "that did not recognize pedestrians as rivals."[13] The promenade of horse and carriage through the boulevards and the Bois thus established new rules and signs of (social) mobility (fig. 5.3). The photographer Jean Delton set up shop in the Bois in 1860 to make his living exclusively on equestrian portraits. In his preface he writes,

> The day will come, have no doubts, when the collectioners, the historians, the moralists will purchase at auctions for the price of gold this "Tour of the Bois," sketched from nature, in the aristocratic movement

Figure 5.3. Cham (Count Amédée-Charles-Henry de Noé), "He's riding a horse worth fifteen thousand francs. Do you want me to bring him to you?—The horse? Absolutely!"

> of the promenade on horseback where the old nobleman as well as the gentleman will see themselves, the grande dame of the faubourg as well as the upper-middle-class lady of the Parc Monceau, the man of the sword and the man of the balcony, in a word, everyone from that class of society who looks, rightly or wrongly, with pride at the mass of *promeneurs* rolling or straddling beneath them, for whom the wheel of fortune has not yet turned.[14]

The prominence of the amazon within this spectacle was due in large part to the special, potentially passionate relationship said to exist between women and horses.[15] The writings of Céleste Mogador, a prostitute turned *écuyère* who published her memoirs in 1858 to prove that she could "please otherwise than by charming the senses," admits that her "true passion" for horses was also her means of healing the wounds of an abused childhood.[16] Comparing herself to Mogador, the author of the anonymously published collection of stories titled *Les amazones de Paris* (1866) claims to be a former *écuyère* at the hippodrome and a woman who "loves horses with passion."[17]

Having realized, however, that she could make a far better living with a "position," she leaves the hippodrome to try her luck. "But I rode horses so ravishingly, that I resolved to exploit this new talent in my own way."[18] A very savvy woman, this *écuyère* turned courtesan feigns stupidity to attract the great names of Paris as her escorts and patrons. They in turn must learn to ride to keep their position with her. But the "salutary labor" of the training brings them to see the "abyss" into which they were falling, so that they eventually return to their families. In short, she says proudly, her "work" is to turn lovers into "men" and herself into a rich woman. In other stories, love between woman and horse is portrayed as constant and true even as it defies bourgeois conventions. In one instance alone is the amazon a victim of her mount: the Lady Seyton was a daring child and adolescent and the only person able to ride a certain Tom, but in the end he kills her. This turning on his mistress, however, is represented as an act of saving grace by the horse, rescuing her from a melancholy future as wife and mother.

Such stories of horse love and horse agency might be regarded as nineteenth-century precursors to the kinds of dog love written about by Donna Haraway, Marjorie Garber, and Alice Kuzniar. As Kuzniar writes, "trans-species love transcends the constrictions that gender and sexuality place upon the human body," and "pet devotion has the potential to question the regulating strictures and categories by which we define sexuality, eroticism and love, though not in the banal sense that it offers different forms of genital stimulation."[19] Even before Freud, it was the fear of alternative eroticism and genital stimulation that made riding, or rather straddling a horse, a transgressive act for women. When the title character of George Sand's *Indiana* dons her amazon riding habit and joins the hunt, she experiences a mixture of "terror" and "pleasure" and demonstrates a "masculine courage" unknown to her lover, Raymon. "Raymon was frightened to see her thus, giving herself fearlessly to the fury of this horse whom she barely knew."[20] Flaubert describes the "particular brutality" that comes from handling "thoroughbred horses and the society of fallen women," and the comparison leads us to understand why Emma Bovary's adulterous affair is initiated by a gallop through the woods: "she abandoned herself to the cadence of the movement, which rocked her in the saddle."[21] As more and more women took up riding, they inevitably came up against its associations with the kinds of physical, social, and sexual mobility that were the prerogative of men or the wrong kind of women. Perhaps this is why Albert Cler suggests that a woman of leisure would never let such passion get out of hand. According to him, one could distinguish the *femme du monde* from the *lorette*, or courtesan, by the way the former "doesn't appear to care about her horse, except to stroke him occasionally with her hand. The *femme du monde* likes riding, but the pleasure she takes from it is calm; she easily contains it and does not let it burst out in noisy or exaggerated expressions."[22] It was against such exhortations that Gautier's celebrated character Mademoiselle de Maupin had already rebelled: "My horse is a hundred times more beautiful and I should find it less repugnant to kiss him than to kiss certain fops who think themselves most charming."[23]

As the aristocratic associations of the amazon weakened, the term *amazone* itself, referring either to the woman rider, her sidesaddle position, or the masculine riding habit, indicated both a specificity and a confusion of gender. At the beginning of the century the *amazone* was a woman who joined clubs and was politically active. Amazons were regarded as virile like their ancestral namesakes who shaved off one breast to take part in combat. When referring to a woman rider, the term amazon lost its political significance and denoted the specific way women were to sit on a horse, with their legs tightly together on one side. To ride, *en amazone* was to have restraints both on one's mobility and on one's contact with the horse's motion, reducing especially that "excitation of the genital organs and the propensity for pleasures of love" that contemporary *gymnastique médicale* confirmed was stimulated by riding.[24] The top of the riding habit was modeled on the male riding coat (redingote) and did its job of tightly buttoning in and shaping the chest. The skirt was made of an especially heavy material and often tied around the woman's legs so as not to fly up with the wind and risk exposing part of the leg.[25] The amazon's means of getting into the saddle was such that she always needed a groom to ride with her in case she should fall or simply wish to dismount and get back on—or so she was instructed by the standard *Reasoned Dictionary of Equitation* (1859) written by the riding master François Baucher. To compensate for the loss of efficient use of her legs, the amazon always had to carry a whip, a ready phallic symbol that completed the image of transgression. For the amazon, as we shall see in the case of one of the most famous professional women riders of the Second Empire, the confusion of gender, class, and often of race made her all the more seductive, if also more threatening to the bourgeois society that produced her.

In 1867 one particular amazon became the hit of the Parisian stage and the focus of attention both on the streets and in the press. Much ink was spilled over whether such hippodrama was suitable to follow in the tradition of Racine or whether it was mere commercial spectacle. The question of high and low art was compounded by a question of race. In addition to the star's gender and costume, her ambiguous ethnic origin, while not immediately obvious and only tangentially relevant to the "exotic" setting of the play, was featured in the playbill that served as advance publicity for the performance. Her name was Adah Isaacs Menken: she was an American, a Jew, and a woman playing the role of a man.

La Menken, as she would be known, became the hit of Paris by virtue of a short scene in which she was strapped, *à la Mazeppa*, to the back of a black horse who galloped across the stage. Her performance was a culmination of many trends in the "horse culture" of Second Empire France, even as its reception in the press reveals how the newly popular woman rider preyed on the fantasies and fears of the Parisian public. These fears would feed into efforts under the Third Republic to rehabilitate horse breeds and equestrian culture in the name of rehabilitating the nation. Menken's performance and its repercussions thus demonstrate the way the horse functioned as a kind of "transitional object" for talking not only about aesthetics but also about gender, race, and sexuality (or breeding) in French society.

MAZEPPA IN FRANCE: FROM ROMANTIC GENIUS TO EQUESTRIAN CIRCUS

Mazeppa is the tale of a young Ukrainian gentleman who had an adulterous affair with the wife of a count and as punishment was tied naked to the back of a horse set loose across the steppes. The tale inspired a generation of authors and painters from England and France. Byron's 1819 poem of that name launched the notion of what Nigel Leask has called an "equestrian sublime": a new Romantic celebration of the horse not as the submissive "workaday engine of society," or as the servant of war popularized in the eighteenth century, but as an image of fury that was wild and animalistic, if also poetic.[26] The equestrian sublime draws on Plato's dark horse from the *Phaedrus*, symbol of uncontrolled appetites and bodily lust, to celebrate Romanticism's resistance to aesthetic and political authority. French paintings of the Mazeppa legend by Géricault and Delacroix focused on a passive but eroticized male figure with legs splayed across the back of a frenzied horse. In a more cautious manner, Victor Hugo wrote his own version of the Mazeppa story, published in *Les orientales* of 1829, in which he insisted that the horse was only a symbol for the artist's "genius" and thus forestalled any hint of bestiality in the myth.

> Thus, when a mortal whom God protects,
> Is bound alive to your fateful back,
> Genius ardent steed,
> In vain he struggles, alas! You leap, you carry him off

Away from the real world, whose barriers you smash
With your hooves of steel![27]

The sublimity of this equestrian image, however, became something less symbolic and more physical in the newly established equestrian circus. And when the equestrian was revealed to be an equestrienne, the sublime materialized into an alluring but potentially dangerous spectacle of interspecies corporeality—an image male riders were only beginning to be burdened with.

Whether harnessed to a carriage or ridden in the streets or the Bois de Boulogne, horses were omnipresent in Second Empire Paris and became the focus of a dandified public lifestyle that brought together the worlds of the *grand monde* and of entertainment. Horses and their riders were objects of admiration, of envy, and of satire, as we have seen in Albert Cler's *La comédie à cheval, ou Manies et travers du monde équestre* (The comedy on horseback: Fads and follies in the equestrian world), which bemoans the horse's fall from Buffon's image of nobility to bourgeois sport and spectacle.[28] It is Plato's dark horse who lies behind Cler's equine world, with its emphasis on the animal's unpredictable temperament, but also on the growing numbers of bourgeois riders who are unable to govern themselves or their horses. Where riding schools once prepared well-bred men and horses for the military, they now equipped men and women with the latest fashions in riding styles and riding gear to attract the envious eyes of onlookers in the city streets and parks, if not also on the stage.

The penultimate chapter of Cler's book focuses on one of those forms of entertainment and what was indeed a literal theater of the horse known as the Cirque Olympique. Opened in 1807 by the Franconi Brothers in the midst of the "hippomania" that spread from London to Paris, it drew on France's unique equestrian traditions, especially the amazing and beautiful feats of haute école dressage. Laurent Franconi was considered the most accomplished horseman of the times, although he departed from the former classical and neoclassical image.[29]

It was in the Olympic circus of 1825 that the Mazeppa legend made its first translation to the stage in a new *mimo-drame*, half play, half equestrian spectacle, starring Franconi in the title role. Franconi's performance brought the legend to a popular audience but also muddled the historical background. As Mainardi explains, the Cossack was turned into a Tartar and the story of ethnic and sexual tension was supplanted by a more classic tale of prince and pauper. Instead of focusing on the Romantic symbolism of the horse, moreover, the *mimo-drame* attracted crowds with the excitement generated by

Franconi's now famous equestrian tricks so that the conflation of man and horse suggested by the title, *Mazeppa, or the Tartar Horse*, showcased the man and his skill while the horse functioned as his tool of self-recognition.

Some forty years later a different version of the Mazeppa story again found its way to the Paris stage, this time with Adah Menken in the equestrian role. The play was titled *Les pirates de la savanne*, and its most thrilling scene starred Menken strapped to the back of a horse who "gallops" across the stage. Decried by one critic as a "female phenomenon" (*femme phénomène*) Menken became the hit of Paris as she indulged her Parisian audience and revealed the strength and power a woman could discover in partnership with her horse. Taking advance publicity into her own hands, she worked to transform the image of shared vulnerability and victimization of man and horse suggested by previous literary and visual representations of Mazeppa into a performance of bodily agency and mastery uncommon for women on the stage.

ADAH ISAACS MENKEN: SEX, RACE, SPECIES, AND THE AMAZON

Within more recent theater history, the name Mazeppa probably brings to mind the accomplished, if bawdy, stripper from the 1959 musical *Gypsy* and the song "You Gotta Have a Gimmick," written by Stephen Sondheim. "Once I was a schlepper, now I'm Miss Mazeppa" the song goes, describing how one needs a publicity stunt to get ahead in show business. Sung by a brash and belting alto, Mazeppa's "ballsy" stage presence in *Gypsy* was heightened by her particular gimmick: she would "bump it with a trumpet," and *Gypsy* was advertised as the burlesque response to Shakespeare.[30]

Almost a century before *Gypsy*, Adah Isaacs Menken's performance also combined elements of high and low in the new form of the hippodrama. And this Mazeppa also had a gimmick: she would "bump" with her horse, or at least that was how a central scene of the play was represented in the press of the time (fig. 5.4). In the scene, "La Menken" boldly rode her horse across the stage wearing only a revealing body suit. For the audience this fleshly appearance highlighted a certain nakedness she was said to share with her mount. Performing together, Adah and her horse transgressed categories not only of gender and race but also of species.

An American born in New Orleans of mixed, if ambiguous, racial ancestry and a converted Jew, Menken's "creole" identity inspired commentaries and fantasies about the relation between race and species. Newspaper reports translated Mazeppa's "sublime passion" into the affections of kiss-

Figure 5.4. Cartoon of Adah Menken dancing with a horse published in *La lune*, February 10, 1867.

ing kin. Indeed, Menken's success turned to scandal as the "phenomenon" of this *écuyère* inspired stories regarding the perverse passions of women and horses, raising the specter of bestial miscegenation. The partnership of woman and horse on the stage was thus as striking as the way the press perverted that partnership into a forbidden passion of interspecies intimacy.

Menken began her role as "Miss Mazeppa" in 1861 in Albany, New York, and her exciting ride on the Tartar steed was seen on stages across the United States and in London before she made her debut in Paris. When she arrived in the fall of 1866, she was visibly pregnant, but without a husband, and appeared eager to take on whichever lovers or horses were worthy of her. Celebrated as poetess, horsewoman, and lover, she was, as one writer in *Le mousquetaire* called her, the "example of a new species." Menken herself suggested that men, but not women, should be married: "Somehow they all sink into nonentities after this epoch in their existence. That is the fault of the female education. They are taught from their cradles to look upon marriage as the one event in their lives. That accomplished, nothing else remains."[31] This amazon was out to prove that there was more to her life than marriage, and that something more often involved a horse.

On December 30, 1866, Menken opened in *Les pirates de la savanne*, in the "breeches role" of Léo, loosely based on the Mazeppa legend and written expressly for her. Léo is described as Mexican and mute, a decision that solved the problem presented by Adah's American accent even as it also furthered identification between man (or in her case woman) and animal. The story takes place in Mexico where, with the help of the local pirates, the nephew of an old French colonist attempts to steal his uncle's property from the rightful hands of his cousin Eva. A battle ensues in which the nephew is killed and, with Léo's help, Eva's inheritance is returned to her. Subsequently captured by the pirates himself, Léo is tied naked to the back of a wild horse let loose across the plains. As she played Léo, Menken's femininity was made all the more apparent by her sheer costume, and the play sold out for a dazzling 150 performances.

Almost overnight Menken's image hit the market and decorated everything from shaving mugs to scarf pins.[32] Advance publicity had much to do with the attraction as circulars were floated showing an all but nude woman, her shapely curves set off by the blackness of the galloping horse to which she lay strapped, back to back. Menken herself took part in creating and defending her image, and in response to accusations of indecency by her English critics, she compared the aesthetic value of her bodily poses and nudity to that of the ballet or of sculpture. "My costume, or rather want of costume, as might be inferred, is not in the least indelicate and in no way more open to invidious comment than the dress worn by Cerito [or] Rosati. . . . I have long been a student of sculpture, and my attitudes, selected from the works of Canova, present a classicality which has been invariably recognized by the foremost of American critics."[33] To be sure, Menken's pink body stocking was an extended version of the ballerina's tights, those "prerequisites for the transformation of carnal flesh into the sublimated, sculptural form of aesthetic, albeit eroticized, delectation," according to Abigail Solomon-Godeau.[34] French reviewers were in awe of her "sculptural" qualities: "There are stars and stars" wrote one critic, "this one has nothing to say; she appears and she seduces, she mimes and she carries you away. . . . She is surprising, this *amazone* with her supple body whose forms are worthy of the admiration of a sculptor" (*Le centaure*, January 10, 1867).

Even as she compared her act to the art of ballerinas, Menken insisted on advertising her physical, if not animal, presence and power, as if to contrast the ballerina's spiritualization with the *écuyère*'s material transformation with her horse. Before her arrival, the theater published a fourteen-page biographical notice, approved by Menken, telling of her successes at translating Greek or at fending off buffalo in Texas, her adventures being captured by Indians, and her marriages to a series of husbands. Upon her arrival in Paris she reportedly donned her amazon habit, leased the most spirited horse to be had, and took to the streets on horseback to prove to the public that she could handle her horses as well as her men. Adding to stories of her agility with horses, men, and pistols were the newspaper reports of the large sums of money she made for herself and her directors. Smoker, rider, poet, and moneymaker, she incarnated the new woman who was to be judged not only by who or what she was, but also by what she did, and in this horses were central. Daphne Brooks argues that it was her ride across the stage that "transformed what could have been a scene of violent abjection and prurient delight for spectators into the pinnacle of her performance."[35] It was nevertheless a performance that many regarded as threatening, and while the whip and habit gave the suggestion of masculine mastery, it was as "mistress" of the horse, with all the term's sexual connotations, that Adah was represented in the press.

Shortly after she arrived in Paris, the journal *L'illustration* reported that her horse had turned angry and unmanageable from being left in London. When he finally joined his mistress in Paris, however, he "whinnied insanely with joy and began like a dog to lick Miss Menken's hands and face" (*L'illustration*, January 5, 1867). This scene was quickly and prominently featured on the first page of the newspaper *La lune*, as we saw in figure 5.4, with Menken dancing arm in arm with her horse. He is in white tie and she in a revealing tunic as he eagerly licks her face. The caption reads "Miss Dada Menken," playing on the nickname given to Adah by her French public, whose meaning of hobbyhorse or pet topic identifies woman with equine and both with a form of "insane" obsession. The licking horse (an uncommon sight) might remind us of the now well-known passage at the opening of *When Species Meet* where Donna Haraway describes the "darter-tongue kisses" of her Australian shepherd and wonders about the "becomings" produced by their mutual affection, the way her cells may have been colonized by her dog and what record or "traces in the world" their touch might leave.[36] In 1860s France any idea of symbiogenesis was far in the future, but fantasies of a different sort of coevolution and multispecies organism were figured in a cartoon image that appeared on the first page of the satirical newspaper *Le hanneton* (fig. 5.5). Whereas the "centaur ideal" was integral to constructions of masculinity in the eighteenth century, here that ideal is feminized and racialized as Menken is depicted as a centauress with a black

Figure 5.5. Cartoon of Adah Menken as a centauress published in *Le hanneton*, May 23, 1867.

horse body, a small white torso dressed in African garb, and an enlarged head whose ethnic origins are marked by dark curls and large hoop earrings.[37]

Part of the appeal of Menken's performance was, not surprisingly, the pleasure of anticipating her destruction. Théophile Gautier reviewed the play for *Le moniteur* and described the charm of such potential danger to a beautiful horse and a beautiful woman together: "If his foot slipped, if a plank broke, the audience would have the pleasure of seeing a superb beast and a charming woman of intelligence, level-headedness and bravery, break together in bits. What greater attraction could one imagine?" (*Le moniteur universel*, January 7, 1867). Fantasies about the destruction of this body were inspired not only by its physical and, I should add, financial potential, but also by the uncertainty over exactly what kind of body Menken's was. The equine-woman partnership accentuated her own ambiguous "breed" and the very ethnic attributes that had been washed out of Franconi's *Mazeppa* except in vague, orientalizing ways. Regarded as hermaphroditic in its exploits and capabilities, Menken's body was also regarded as racially impure, leading to disagreements over her beauty and talent. The theater's pamphlet coupled its account of Menken's exploits with details of her exotic heritage, both creole and Israelite. While some critics extolled her classic beauty[38] and a charm that "belonged to no nationality" (*Le monde pour rire*, July 7, 1868), others called on this exotic background to describe Miss Mazeppa as an "artist both foreign and strange [*étrangère et étrange*], a woman whose beauty is also a curiosity." Born in New Orleans, she was understood to be the result of "one of those crossings that constitute the American race" (*Le constitutionnel*, January 7, 1867), and so it was Adah's breeding, not her black horse's, that the press focused on. Her charm and her danger were constituted both by what her body did and by what it was.

Thus, at the same time that "Oriental" horses were being imported to improve European breeds, Adah's Semitic and "Oriental" features turned her into something other than, and for some less than, a woman. Her horsemanship and her race alike contributed to this. The reviewer for the illustrated newspaper *La lune* was hyperbolic but explicit on this issue. An article signed by Biloquet Fils and titled "Women Phenomena" focused on both Adah Menken and Cora Pearl, a British actress/equestrian and famous *cocotte* (tart) currently playing at the Bouffes Parisiennes. According to the author, these women were interchangeable: "Pearl or Menken, Menken or Pearl, it's all the same," because neither was a "real woman." The author continues to deliver a eulogy on the real woman, the mother Eve with "elegant limbs," Venus dressed in her blond hair. "She has to be white, our mother Eve, white with that whiteness beneath which life and blood circulate." But the women of today are neither white nor really women: "This is where the taste for phenomena like Cora Pearl and Miss Adah leads us. Today it is English women on horseback, tomorrow it will be Germans playing the clarinet, then Italians climbing a greased pole, which brings us to Lapps and Hottentots; we will come to . . . acrobats, tightrope walkers, horsewomen, . . . sword swallowers, women with two heads, seals, androgynes, monsters, this is what we need" (*La lune*, February 10, 1867). From Menken on horseback it is a short step to the androgyne and the Hottentot, unsexed or oversexed, racially other if not of another species.

The final scandal over Menken was initiated by the reproduction and widespread display of a number of photographs of her in the lap of her presumed lover, Alexandre Dumas père.[39] In response, the well-known poet Paul Verlaine published a jingle repeated throughout Paris. In its lyrics the rhetoric of horsemanship is used to contrast Adah's sexual vitality with the aging Dumas's questionable potency, while Dumas's own black ancestry is invoked with the name of "Uncle Tom."[40]

L'oncle Tom avec Miss Ada
C'est un spectacle dont on rêve
Quel photographe fou soude
L'oncle Tom avec Miss Ada?
Ada peut rester à Dada,
Mais Tom, chevauche-t-il sans trêve?
L'oncle Tom avec Miss Ada,
C'est un spectacle dont on rêve.[41]

[Uncle Tom with Miss Ada,
It's a spectacle one dreams about.
What crazy photographer soldered
Uncle Tom with Miss Ada?
Ada can stay on her hobbyhorse,
But can Tom mount forever?
Uncle Tom with Miss Ada.
It's a spectacle one dreams about.]

Menken and Dumas's dreamed-of equestrian "spectacle" thus appears to invoke the more nightmarish specter of bestial miscegenation. Not surprisingly Dumas's own journal, *Le mousquetaire*, defended Menken's racial purity in an article concerning her temporary replacement by Sarah l'Africaine from the hippodrome after an accident on stage: "How is it believable that one could dream of replacing Miss Menken, who plays or at least mimes an important role, an intelligent artist and a woman who is beauty itself, by a negress who is absolute ugliness everywhere except in Guinea or Senegambia and who has probably had no other teachers than the monkeys from whom she took courses in the Coconut trees?" The response of the hippodrome's director is remarkable in revealing the way racial otherness has itself become a commodity, at least in its feminine form: "What! You want my African! Never! Never in the world will you abduct my black pearl, the most beautiful of my jewel box" (*Le mousquetaire*, January 25, 1867).

BLOOD, STUDS, AND NATURALIST HORSEPOWER

Verlaine's reference to an aging Uncle Tom to mock Dumas's sexual escapades with Menken reveals that where sexual potency and breeding were at issue, the question of race was not far off. The exchange over Sarah l'Africaine also shows how race itself was fetishized, at least on stage. Nowhere was this so evident as in the horse business itself. Since the beginning of the century and especially since the foundation in 1833 of the "Society for the Encouragement of the Betterment of the Race of Horses in France" and the Jockey Club in 1834 (itself a racially exclusive club), France was engaged in competition with England to produce the best "race" of horses, and to this end it imported more and more "pure"-breds, mostly thoroughbreds from England but also Arabians from North Africa. The otherwise imprecise nineteenth-century definition of "race" was given "scientific" explanation in its application to the equine population.[42] The "studbook," created in 1833 and first published in 1838, documented both the paternal and the maternal lineage of all purebreds, including work or draft horses. Some fifty years after its conception, one equine specialist, H. V. de Loncey, wrote that "the studbook shows better than any rationale the importance that must be attached to the ancestry and confirmed race of the reproducers we use . . . and we remain convinced of the mathematical truth of the old axiom: Good blood cannot lie."[43] From his observations of horses the author concluded that, contrary to the opinion of some skeptics, races do exist. They are not the same as species, which are the result of climate and environment. Race, he explained in Lamarckian fashion, is the result of function, "the expression of the needs of an epoch. Races thus do not remain constant but evolve to adapt to those particular needs."[44] De Loncey's rhetoric links horse breeding to a pressing issue facing French thinkers of the end of the century: the future of the human race in general and of the French race in particular. Thanks to the encouragement of various agricultural associations, de Loncey states, we can proudly say that the evolution of the horse in France is "everywhere progressing. . . . The majority of the species that is better bred, better educated, better nourished, the object of greater attention and care, tends to shed its vulgar exterior to acquire another one that is better suited to other destinations."[45] What the equine example demonstrates, in other words, is that the development of a species (or race) can be controlled by managing the hereditary characteristics to be passed on. This is progress, and welcome news at a time when most signs seemed to point to the decline of the French race. "The art of creating a thoroughbred human," as one book title would announce (discussed in chapter 6), was within human capability.[46]

Figure 5.6. Cham (Count Amédée-Charles-Henry de Noé), *Inconvénients de l'exposition peintures et chevaux*, from *Le Salon de 1866* (Paris: Arnauld de Vresse, 1866). "Imbecile, not that horse! You were asked to put varnish on a horse painting that is on the next floor."

In his enthusiasm over the progress in horse breeding, de Loncey nevertheless points to an irony behind the situation, that such improvements did not lead to more efficient or productive animals, but rather met the demands of a consumer market concerned above all with image.[47] This was true even for the French draft horses known as Percherons, which were considered a national treasure and the one French breed that could rival the English. Having become such a "vogue" both in Europe and in the United States, France's own Percheron population was being depleted. Entered in the 1867 Universal Exhibition, French horses did not represent France's productive capacities but rather, as the popular cartoonist Cham frequently suggested, had become denatured articles of display (fig. 5.6).

Already in the literature of Balzac, the cult of purity, especially in terms of blood or breeding, and the danger of its dissimulation find expression in terms of an equestrian rhetoric that distinguishes horses according to the classed, gendered, and racial hierarchies that worked to organize bourgeois sexuality. In *Le Père Goriot* (1834), for instance, Balzac's narrator refers to

Goriot's daughter Anasthasie as a "purebred horse," and as Rastignac joins the other "cavaliers" on her dance list, the narrator explains that such "locutions" as "thoroughbred, woman of breeding [*cheval de pur sang, femme de race*] have begun to replace angels from heaven, Ossianic figures, and all the ancient, amorous mythology pushed out by dandyism."[48]

A question of rhetoric in Balzac becomes a question of pathology in the work of later naturalists. For writers like Maupassant or Zola, the presence of a saddle horse could signal the beau monde associated with these practices and a counterpoint to the symptoms of degeneration both authors describe and claim to observe. On the other hand, practices of breeding and crossbreeding could be both sign and symptom of a more general national degeneration that unsettled relations of class, gender, and race through an erotic and sometimes violent triangle of man, woman, and animal.

Whether regarded as oversexed or as desexed, amazons were figured as the enemy of the family and of the domestic (and reproductive) duties of women until late in the century.[49] In a story of 1882 by Maupassant titled "Crazy?" (*Fou?*), for example, the narrator identifies his former lover with her horse, seeing in both the essence of bestiality and damned sensuality: "The perfume of her sweaty body, as after the warmth of bed, mixed under [his] nostrils with the acrid and wild odor of the beast."[50] At the same time, the lover credits the horse with an ability to excite this woman, a power he no longer possesses and that makes him intensely jealous: "One evening, I told you, one evening as she returned from a long horseback ride, she fell, her cheeks red, chest pounding, legs collapsed, eyes bruised, onto a low chair facing me. I had seen her like that before! She was in love. I couldn't be mistaken."[51]

To avenge the humiliation he endures, he schemes "to fight a duel," though one of a different sort. After rigging a trap that throws both horse and woman rider to the ground, he draws his pistol and shoots the horse "like a man." When his mistress tries to intervene by flogging him with her whip, he turns the pistol on her and shoots her in the stomach. "Am I crazy?" the lover/narrator asks in what begins as confession. But as he implores readers to sympathize with his plight, the onus and the guilt shift to the woman and her horse and the bestial possibilities that warrant his actions. Ultimately what is revealed in this unromantic representation of triangular desire is not only the gendering of madness as a kind of hysteria—the narrator blaming his act on the "unfathomable . . . perversions of female sensuality"[52]—but also the instability of such identities as man and human that are maintained only through the abjection of woman and animal. The narrator's killing the horse brings him into even closer identification with the equine as a result of the "whipping" he receives from his mistress and hence to identification with that feminine, "sensual and false animal that has no soul."[53]

In Zola's *Nana* (1880), which, like Manet's painting, is set during the 1867 Universal Exhibition, horse culture is emblematic of modernity by virtue of its identification of female desire and the degeneration of the French race. As in Maupassant's short story "À cheval," mobility takes on a contradictory significance, especially in light of the new accessibility of rental carriages and horses to men and women of various means. When a group of high-society women choose to walk instead of ride on a Sunday afternoon, they and their conversations are abruptly immobilized before a "superb parade of Nana and her crowd." With their "skirts billowing over the wheels" of their horse-drawn carriages, they take over the road with only "disdainful eyes for those honest women who were on foot."[54] Throughout the novel horses function literally and figuratively to expose the particularly bestial nature of the courtesan. Nana's friend Lucy Stewart is described as having the "head of a horse" (115), and Nana herself is eyed by the pimp Labordette "with the surprised air of a horse dealer admiring a perfect mare" (49). Courtesan and horse are identified as commodified bodies, and the golden Grand Prix mare named after Nana is said to gleam "in the light like a new coin" (374).[55] At other moments their bodies move in like manner, as when, at the height of the race, Nana "put her thighs and loins in a balanced position as if she herself had run. She gave belly thrusts that seemed to her to help the filly" (378–79). In a much-cited passage in which Nana performs her toilette before her dazed lover Muffat, femininity itself is represented as pure animality, trapping its male prey through the sheer force of instinct and unwittingly infecting him with its rabidity.

> Nana was hairy everywhere: a reddish down turned her body into velvet, while under her haunches and in her mare's thighs, in the fleshy bulges furrowed with deep folds that gave to her sex the troubling veil of their shadow, there was bestiality. It was the golden beast, unconscious like a force and whose odor alone rotted the world. Muffat continued to look, obsessed, possessed to the point where having closed his eyelids so as not to see, the animal reappeared in the depths of the darkness, large, terrible, exaggerating its build. Now he would be there, in front of its eyes, forever. (226)

Covered in a "veil of shadow," Nana's sex is not only invisible but also, as such, bestialized and demonized in its "unconscious" hold on the male gaze and in its penetrating odor from which Muffat is unable to escape. Closing his eyes before her, Muffat sees a mare instead.[56] Unable to resist or conquer the feminine, Muffat's effort to uncover woman's difference, perhaps like Zola's own, is engulfed by both desire and repulsion. Like Maupassant, Zola's persistent metaphors linking women and animals belie the naturalist's claim to scientific observation and reveal his own seduction by the unconscious pull of animal magnetism.

The culminating scenes of *Nana* at the Longchamps racetrack are acts of animalistic frenzy and crowd contagion: "the fever rose, an anxiousness whipped the crowd" (364). The race is seen, furthermore, as a test of national pride pitting methods of schooling and breeding against each other in order to determine which can best control and make use of the beast. Nana's win is claimed as a national victory, sending the crowd into convulsive cries of "Long live Nana! Long live France! Down with England." And as "they loudly took up again: 'Nana! Nana! Nana!' . . . one no longer knew if it was the animal or the woman that filled the hearts" (379, 381). The irony of the victory is suggested in the names as the English horse, Spirit, is defeated by Nana. Nana's victory marks also the defeat of *esprit*, the mark of France's greatness, lost to the reign of bestial women and the emasculated men who fall prey to them. The worn and spent body of Nana's jockey, Price, reveals the cost: "This old shriveled child, that long, hard, and dead face, threw off flames. And in a burst of furious daring, of triumphant will, he gave his heart to the filly. He supported it, he carried it, drenched in foam, his eyes bloody" (379).

Price represents a generation of men who have given their last ounce of potency to sustain the Nanas of their desires, only to destroy themselves in the process. The death of Nana's own young son, seen early in the novel "straddling a broom handle," suggests that the next generation of jockeys will never make it past their *dada* or hobbyhorse. Humanity in general will be consumed by their mother's or their female lover's animalistic desire.

Many of Zola's critics have commented on the importance of bestial imagery in his works. I suggest that the horse has a special importance in this imagery because of the equine's capacity to represent, within realist conventions, ideologies of power, sexuality, and the relations between them. The sexualized nature of riding comes to the foreground during the races when even Nana, the woman this time, responds with laughter to the circulating pun, "Who will mount Nana?" Zola's novel figures the prostitute as *amazone*, as we learn of a passion that has spread from the horse-headed Lucy to all of Nana's crowd, separating them from the men. "Ever since Lucy began taking the morning tour through the Bois on horseback that launched her, everybody rode horses, a rage took over them" (133). This "rage" is most evident in the courtesan La Tricon, who, we are told, goes to the horse races not to work (although Longchamps is obviously fertile ground for picking up tricks) but "out of pleasure, a fanatic [*enragé*] gambler having the passion for horses" (354). Standing on the driver's seat of her carriage, she is not only spectacle but also spectator and successful speculator, for while "she seemed to reign over her people of women," she uses her superior vantage point and vision to choose the winning horse and make her bet. For Zola this "rage" virilizes the courtesan, making her the subject of both gaze and desire. In Nana herself Zola brings together the two meanings of *amazone*: "her amazon chest, whose pink tips were held raised and rigid like lances," bodies forth the female warrior engaged in a fight against patriarchy, while the woman rider takes her whip to le Comte Muffat, driving him onward in jest as her female scent has dominated him in life, yelling, "Hee yah, Hee yah, You are the horse, giddy up you dirty nag, move on!" (446).

Nana the amazon moves Nana the actress outdoors and even beyond the city walls, where she can claim a greater public visibility, mobility, and sense of bodily power. Indeed, it is in her daily drives through the Bois that Nana "reclaims total freedom," no longer answering to the rich but becoming the envied model for the duchesses and wealthy bourgeoise. It is thus that the amazon, like the prostitute and the actress, embodies Zola's and Maupassant's ambivalent responses to woman in modernity. She is both image and instigator of the disruptions and degeneracy that Zola saw as the Second Empire's legacy to the fin de siècle—a figure who defies categorical distinctions between human and animal, between "honest" aristocrat and fallen prostitute, and between man and woman. What is at once compelling and disturbing in the amazon is not simply the way horses and riding have become suffused with capital or with image, as Clark might say, but rather that the amazon's desire appears to surpass her image (despite common opinion that, as Flaubert said of Emma Bovary, the habit was the deciding factor); that it was not only the spectacle she enjoyed but also something more physical if perhaps invisible between her and her horse.[57]

This is especially true of the character of La Thompkins in Edmond de Goncourt's *Les Frères Zemganno*, who is apparently modeled on Adah Menken.[58] Written after the death of his brother Jules, the novel is about the circus and about a brother team of acrobats whose relationship is a patterned on that of the Goncourt brothers.[59] They are portrayed as artists whose career is brought to an early close when an American equestrienne known as "La Thompkins" interferes in the grand feat that the brothers have labored to prepare and in doing so permanently injures the younger brother. Like "La" Menken, "La" Thompkins has performed in London and Paris, speaks a *français-nègre* (Creole French), is an insatiable spendthrift (no doubt an oblique reference also to her Jewishness), a smoker, and a "bizarre woman . . . taken by the ambition to do the impossible, the superhuman, things forbidden by nature and God, all that with the brutal volition of the American race that has come into money."[60]

In La Thompkins, Goncourt incorporates his hatred for the modern American woman—regarded as both cause and symptom of the vulgarity of the modern world—and a strangely related aversion to horses.[61] Comments in his journal about horses, or more specifically horsemeat, render Edmond's disgust with France during and after 1870. An entry for October 1, 1870, for instance, sums up the effect of the Prussian occupation of Paris by the "underhanded" method of slipping horsemeat onto the Parisian table, which he lavishly describes as "an aqueous meat with no fat, striped with white nerves, and whose blackish red my painterly eyes discern as so different from the pink red of beef."[62] Edmond's refusal to eat the meat, signaling his resistance to the political situation, is opposed to the mediocrity of the Parisians' reaction, evinced also in their culinary habits: "Let posterity guard itself against telling future generations about the heroism of the Parisian in 1870," he writes on November 12. "His entire heroism consisted of eating . . . roast horse instead of beef—and barely noticing it, the Parisian has little discernment of what he eats."[63]

Moving from journal to novel, the repulsive colorless meat is revitalized into Thompkins's two horses, one white, one black. Having more in common with the black horse (at least insofar as he is modeled on Plato's dark horse), her singular "passion" for them, combined with her lack of taste in clothes or jewelry, evokes an anti-aesthetic of sensual pleasure and a dangerous female sexuality that is opposed to the homoerotic yet spiritual bond between the brothers, founded on a love of hard work and beauty. Echoing the opinions of one of the women in *Les amazones de Paris*, she finds that men are *stupide* unless on horseback.[64] Above all, Thompkins prefers to be alone, not to ride, but to give herself wholly to her horses in a kind of equine orgy.

> Breathing in distracted puffs of tobacco in this stable that one believed to belong to everybody but that was hers, at the sight of her horses that she never rode in public and that were paraded during Paris's sleep, "La Thompkins" savored the royally egotistical rapture [*jouissance*], the solitary pleasure of the secret possession of beautiful and unique things

> unknown to the world. . . . From time to time the woman called to herself Erèbe or Snow and, without moving, lifting her head, held a piece of sugar out to the horse between her teeth, then kissed it on the muzzle.[65]

Whereas Nana eventually destroys her lovers though the metaphoric contagion of her diseased body, Thompkins's weapon is her health. "One would say that this woman was the explosion of muscular activity. . . . There was in that body an impetuous stream of blood, the goings and comings of a warm life, like the exultant health of a new generation and that, when in a sweat she jumped on her horse, covered her in a healthy odor of wheat and warm bread."[66] Unlike the two brothers, Giani and Nello, whose bodies are "compromised" by fatigue and by the "perpetual occupation of their minds," Thompkins shows no signs of deterioration or of sensitivity to the world she works in. She is the emblem of a generation that would outlive the Goncourts as well: her impure, hybrid race makes her more powerful than, and hence a danger to, the aristocratic artists whose nervous refinement, evinced by physical exhaustion, makes them unfit for the modern world.[67]

MORAL MOUNTS: AMAZONS AT THE FIN DE SIÈCLE

Whereas for Zola the amazon is a cause and symptom of the degeneration of the French race, for Edmond de Goncourt she becomes emblematic of the ways a woman's body is able to adapt to or combat its physical effects, if at the expense of her aesthetic and moral sense.[68] The amazon's health, in other words, is a sign of her depravity. Here it is likely that Edmond de Goncourt is responding to and criticizing, at least for women, the physical culture movement that had begun in France after the Franco-Prussian War of 1870 and that saw physical weakness and ill health as major factors in France's defeat. As Robert Nye has demonstrated, the movement embodied nothing less than a hope for the regeneration of the French race. Unlike Goncourt, moreover, members of this movement saw sport as a means of both physical and moral regeneration. Indeed, in essays written at the turn of the century the father of the sports movement, Pierre de Coubertin, articulated the relation between body and mind in a metaphor of horsemanship: "The soul is a rider who straddles the body, an animal stronger than he and at whose mercy he would be if he did not control him with sufficient art to direct and tame that force."[69] Coubertin insisted on a correlation between physical training and psychology, an opinion repeated by a large number of riding enthusiasts toward the end of the century, hoping to restore both horses and France to their former chivalric glory. But as one of these rider-writers made clear, not all forms of riding would have a beneficial psychological effect. A prolific author on all aspects of the horse, the Baron De Vaux noted that the riding schools that were once the envy of the world had fallen into disrepute because riding was no longer practiced as an art. Repeating the by now decades-old lament that riding had become a "frivolous pleasure" done above all for the "image" (*la question du tableau passe avant tout*), he argues that with renewed support of the riding schools by the Republic, French equitation could become again the envy of other nations while imparting a knowledge (*savoir*) that was crucial for revitalizing France and its citizens.[70] De Vaux calls on the popular medical discourse of degeneration to emphasize the political significance of proper equitation. "Seen from another point of view that we have forgotten in our day, equitation is not only a luxury, a fashion, a pleasure, but is, of all the bodily exercises, the most noble, the best one for developing the physiological state of man, for diminishing the hereditary flaws engendered by tuberculosis, alcoholism, the impairment of children's development in large cities, the degeneration of the race."[71]

Those for whom riding could have the greatest benefits, the Baron continues, are those who suffer from intellectual exhaustion, those who work indoors, and those of "nervous and delicate constitutions," in particular women. Women offer evidence of the way riding can turn a fear into both a pleasure and a "passion": "by a sort of reaction the most, timid woman becomes, with barely a transition, an intrepid amazon."[72]

Curiously, the Baron offers no further comment on this amazon. I say curiously because, as should be clear by now, such "passion" between women and horses was what most writers and sports enthusiasts hoped to tame, if not suppress. Whereas sports like riding were promoted, in the words of Coubertin, as "the art of virilizing bodies and souls" and therefore as what would make real men out of the French, it was unclear what they would do for or to women.[73] And for this reason many preferred to see women interested in horses for the image rather than the passion. In his *La femme à cheval* of 1884, the Vicomte de Hédouville begins by assuring his readers of the difference between the mythological battle of the Amazons and the present-day amazon's struggle to find the correct color of corsage or angora for her riding habit. He then reminds them that "woman is not made, like a man, for riding horses."[74] Yet while much of the writing on the amazons of the fin de siècle is geared toward affirming this clear sexual difference even in the saddle, others are not so reassured. The conservative poet Catulle Mendès asserts his own reservations about the role of physical activity for women in a letter that acts as a second preface to the Baron De Vaux's *Les femmes de sport*:

> And who could foresee just how far this virilization of woman will be taken? What remorse would be yours, my dear fellow, if by virtue of weapons and of fighting strong horses, of muscling their bodies and hearts as well, the Parisian women of 1885 or 1886 made themselves similar to that extraordinary actress from Marseille whose name was immortalized by Théophile Gautier, to that fanatic Maupin, always dressed as a man, always defiance on her lips as long as she didn't have a kiss, always a sword out of its sheath, and how in the same night, during a ball, would abscond with two beautiful damsels, having killed two jealous suitors between the two abductions?[75]

Mendès reminds his reader of the hermaphroditic title character of Théophile Gautier's *Mademoiselle de Maupin* (1834) not so much as a warning against her celebrated transvestism as against her cultivation of the body that is actualized by wearing pants. In Gautier's novel Maupin is quite clear about the gender distinctions of exercise: "I was determined to have those successes as a cavalier which I could not aspire to as a woman . . . , for courage and skill in bodily exercises are the means by which a man most easily makes his reputation."[76] Maupin's name is frequently mentioned in connection with the growing popularity of women's sports at the fin de siècle. In a chapter of 1884 titled "Sportswomen and Gynanders," the writer and observer of French society Octave Uzanne refers to "attitudes à la Maupin" (attitudes can refer to both mental and physical positions) as one way for women to shake off the "already sleepy romanticism" of their suitors."[77] Mendès's letter goes even further as he explains just where Maupin's virilization will lead: not only to a confusion of gender, but also to alternative practices of sexual seduction and orientation: "I leave you to consider the pitiable face the men would make around the rare women who had kept the preciousness of their sex, if they had to enter into battle with strange rivals, no less men, and far prettier."[78]

By the end of the century it was quite clear that women and horses together stirred contradictory emotions in the fascinated men who watched them. On the one hand were the titled amazons ("la Duchesse d'Uzès, la Baronne Rothwiller, la Comtesse Billet-Will . . .") observed if not instructed by horsemen whose names contained partitives (de Montigny, de Vaux, de Hédouville). These women were identified as the thoroughbreds of French society, fulfilling their feminine role of supplying inherited elegance and beauty. According to de Montigny, they are the epitome of grace not by virtue of training, but "by nature. . . . They can make one appreciate, in equitation as in everything else, the gracious and beautiful, because they possess intuition and feeling and because they are themselves its living expression."[79] For these amazons, in other words, riding brought out their very "nature" as women of good breeding. Indeed, that nature was strengthened by it such that through her exercise the amazon would, according to the Baron De Vaux, help "the upper class refresh its impoverished blood."[80]

On the other hand, there were those amazons (often but not exclusively literary) whose riding and association with horses were seen to be compensation for a lack in nature, who were seen to be denatured by their equestrianism, becoming either more like a man or more like an animal (and here we may remember the criticisms raised against Menken and the *femmes phénomènes*). These *amazones* constituted a new "race" of women, a mixed or impure race, like the French horse known as the *demi-sang* (half-breed). They were part woman, part man; part human, part animal; in Uzanne's words, "a lovely centauress."[81]

But the real difficulty in reading the amazon was whether one could distinguish between these two types or tell which was the more desirable. For Goncourt, purity was linked to weakness and decline, impurity to strength, health, and longevity. As for the horse, it was unclear whether it was a symptom, a cause, or a cure for the aura of decadence that surrounded the amazon and for the decline of the French population, both in race and in numbers, with which she was associated.[82] This uncertainty was particularly worrisome at the fin de siècle, when it was clear that the horse's days as a means of transport were numbered and horses were soon to be replaced by bicycles and automobiles. Was this "end of the horse," as in the title of Pierre Giffard's book, *La fin du cheval* of 1899, to be welcomed or lamented? And what of the passion between women and horses?

In 1905 Hachette published a cutout book for children titled *Amazones d'hier et d'aujourd'hui* (Amazons of yesterday and today).[83] Here were paper dolls of women riders from Joan of Arc to Adah Menken and of two types of horses: Arabian and French Normand. The book signaled that at least for some people the combination of women and horses no longer seemed threatening and that the amazon's past was worthy of being told. As girls cut out the various pictures of body parts, equipment, and riding clothes, they could read about each woman's exploits from the narrative as well as learn what type of horses, what costumes, and what tack and accessories would be historically correct for each—or so the author suggested. Of course one can only imagine the historical mistakes as well as the lovely centauresses to be conjured up by young readers interchanging limbs and heads between women and horses, not to mention the escapades planned for these exceptional women, who had only an occasional groom to stop them. With the end of the horse in sight, the bond between women and horse was drawn all the tighter into an enduring fantasy, one now packaged as playtime for little girls.

Plate 1. Théodore Géricault, *The Head of a White Horse*, 1815. Image courtesy of RMN-Grand Palais/Art Resource, New York. Photo by Thierry Le Mage.

Plate 2. Jacques-Louis David, *Bonaparte Crossing the Alps at Mount St. Bernard, May 20, 1800*, 1803. Image courtesy of the RMN-Grand Palais/Art Resource, New York. Photo by Thomas Garnier.

Plate 3. Théodore Géricault, *The Charging Chasseur, or Officer of the Imperial Guard on Horseback*, 1812. Image courtesy of Erich Lessing/Art Resource, New York.

Plate 4. Rosa Bonheur, *The Horse Fair*, 1853–55. Image courtesy of the Metropolitan Museum of Art/Art Resource, New York.

CHAPTER SIX

"The Man on Horseback": From Military Might to Circus Sports

At the center of one of the many posters advertising Buffalo Bill's "Wild West" show in Europe we find Rosa Bonheur seated at her easel. She is shown between two horsemen: to the left is Napoleon I; to the right is William Cody, known as Buffalo Bill.[1]

Beneath each figure is a banner: under Napoleon we read, "The Man on Horse of 1796, from the Seine to the Neva, from the Pyramids to Waterloo." To the right, under Buffalo Bill, we read: "The Man on Horse of 1898; from the Yellow Stone to the Danube, from Vesuvius to Ben Nevis." And between the two, under Bonheur: "Art Perpetuating Fame; Rosa Bonheur Painting Buffalo Bill, Paris, 1889." Bonheur is facing Cody and painting the portrait she made that year when he visited her at her chateau in By. As in the actual portrait, Cody sits straight and tall on the horse, the image of strength, manliness, and foresight as he gazes beyond the painting. Napoleon, by contrast, sits slumped in the saddle, his belly protruding, his eyes furtive, and his mouth turned down in an expression of disgruntled disappointment. The image is reminiscent, if not a copy, of Ernest Meissonier's 1862 portrait *Napoleon in 1814* that shows the emperor on his horse shortly before his exile from France. Almost forty years later, Napoleon's exploits throughout Europe to Russia and Europe are in the distant past, and the figure of the French military horseman has been overshadowed by the immense popularity of the American entertainer who has captivated Europe with his fabricated spectacles about the American frontier.

Even without reference to a woman rider or to Bonheur's own travels on horseback, the poster is a vivid sign of the new meaning of the horseman at the end of the century. Absent, however, is the person who was known as the "Man on Horseback" of the 1880s, General Georges Boulanger. Having cut a striking and charismatic figure on his beautiful black horse named

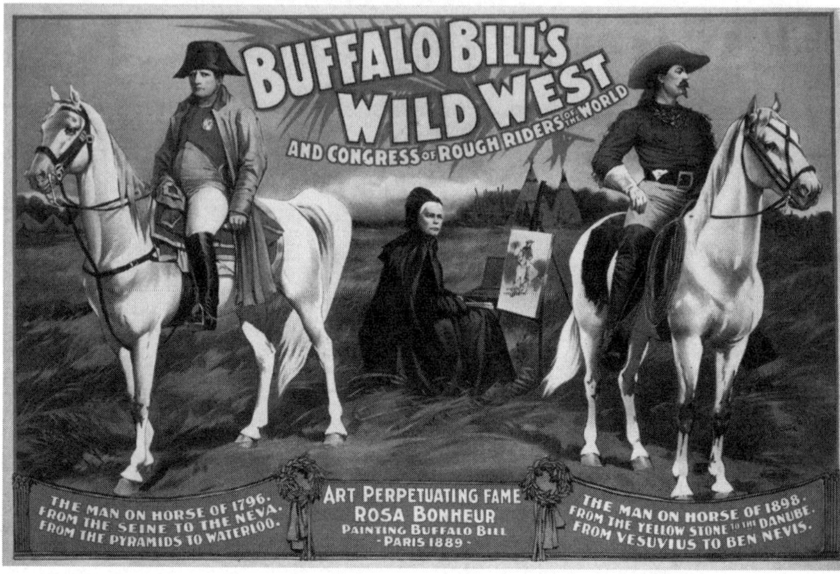

Figure 6.1. Poster for "Buffalo Bill's Wild West" 1896 show in Paris.

(in colonialist fashion) Tunis, Boulanger captivated the French imagination in the aftermath of the Franco-Prussian War as he called for avenging that defeat along with the affront to French manhood. Those hopes were quickly dashed, however, as Boulanger met his own defeat in the race for deputy in 1889. Issued a warrant for treason because of his attempts to contest the election, he fled Paris in shame and in 1891 committed suicide on his mistress's grave.

If Buffalo Bill offered any hope for the return of the man on horseback as an image of virility and national strength, it would be through the separation of this figure from any military connections and by virtue of the new glorification of riding as sport. Indeed, the democratizing of riding is central to changes in the status of equestrianism and of horses during this century, as these in turn changed the images and ideals of manhood.

Image was crucial in an age of rising print, press, and poster culture, where new forms of sport and entertainment were advertised publicly. We saw in chapter 5 how the particular partnership of women and horses was often perverted in the press to warn of the dangerous "virilization" of women that riding could produce and, more frightening (for men), of what might happen when women directed their affections, if not their erotic passions, toward their mounts. In this chapter we will see how men sought to take back the virility of the horseman and of the horse, both by desexualizing the partnership of women and horses and by reclaiming the equine's physical and sexual potency for themselves. Horses often resisted their claims, as is made clear in a short story of Maupassant's, but in the enclosed ring of the fin-de-siècle circus, the will and even the physical presence of the horse would be visibly subdued and subjected to transformed images of femininity and, curiously, of aristocratic masculinity.

HORSEMANSHIP: FROM ARISTOCRATIC SPECTACLE TO BOURGEOIS SPECTATOR SPORT

The rise of equestrianism in the nineteenth century can be counted as one of the indicators of the bourgeoisie's ambivalent attitude toward the aristocracy. In France, as Robert Nye and others have noted, an aristocratic code of honor held prestige for successive generations of bourgeois families despite their promotion of talent over blood as the determining force behind individual worth.[2] Even as horsemanship functioned as a symbol of aristocratic habits and bodily comportment, riding and driving horses became both sign and metaphor of bourgeois ascendance and savoir faire. Maupassant's "À cheval" (which can be translated as "On Horseback" or metaphorically as "Straddling") casts an ironic glance at the impotence of a new generation of "Sunday riders," men of noble blood who have fallen from their mounted position. In the story, Hector de Gribelin is a poor man of noble ancestry, married to a woman both poor and noble like himself. Despite the "misery" of his life, he "wishes still to maintain his rank," and with this objective in mind, he proposes a Sunday family outing to the Bois de Boulogne.[3] He will rent a carriage for his wife and children while he accompanies them on a saddle horse. The image he musters of himself in the saddle becomes something of an idée fixe for the entire family. Every night he places his son "astride" his leg, and every day the son, in turn, straddles chairs crying, "C'est Papa à Dada" (705), a term that (as we saw with Adah Menken) also translates, with intended irony, as "It's Papa on his hobbyhorse." For Hector this exploit is to be confirmation of his paternal and social status. "What a picture we'll be. I wouldn't mind meeting somebody from the ministry. You need nothing else to earn the respect of one's bosses" (705–6). Respect, however turns to mockery as Hector's English method of posting the trot exaggerates the precariousness of his position. "Powerless to master his horse" (707), who takes off at a gallop through Champs-Élysées traffic, the two charge into an elderly working woman. The streetwise woman capitalizes on the situation by making Hector financially responsible for what will be her unending convalescence, thus doubling the initial misery of the de Gribelin family.

Unlike riding a bicycle, riding a horse in this story is not something the body remembers, and this compromises that body's inbred nobility. In similar fashion, a noble past is not necessarily helpful in the modern city, which, the narrator declares, necessitates "special aptitudes . . . [and] a fierce energy for battle" (704). Whereas for Hector the mobility horses offer is a ticket to social mobility, Maupassant pokes fun at the speed with which one can both mount and be knocked off one's high horse, falling to a position of social castration. Mobility in the story is characterized as a "folly of movement" and "drunkenness of life," stirring the mad desires of those who don't know where or why they're going. The frenzy of "that crowd of people, carriages, and beasts," moreover, offers a stark contrast to the immobile "obelisk [that] stood erect in a golden mist" (707). Ironically, it is the old woman, Madame Simon, whose convalescent state most approximates the phallic immobility of the golden monument.

> Eight days passed by, then fifteen, then a month. Madame Simon did not leave her armchair. She ate from morning till night, got fat, chatted gaily with the other sick people, seemed accustomed to immobility as if it were the rest she had earned after fifty years of going up and down stairs, of turning mattresses, of carrying coal from floor to floor, of sweeping and polishing.
>
> "I can't move anymore, my poor Monsieur, I just can't anymore." (709–10)

In "Le Horla," Maupassant's widely read tale of human impotence before inexplicable forces, a horse and a steer are referred to as animals that man has made into "his thing, his servant, his food."[4] In this horror story, however, the horse is uncontrollable and like the invisible Horla in that he feeds off human fragility instead of providing food to strengthen it (perhaps an ironic comment on the legalizing of hippophagy).[5]

Contradictory as a marker of class, the meaning of horsemanship would also become more volatile in its gendered connotations. The rise of the Sunday rider, coupled with the growing prominence of skilled women riders, feminized a domain that was once dominated by men and brought new fears of a world of women on top.[6] With the annexation of the Bois de Boulogne as a horse playground for *le tout Paris*, the question of who was mounting whom became the focus of gossip that cut across class lines as it also threatened male supremacy. Despite (or because of) the strictly gendered rules of equitation, equestrian metaphors carried an erotic charge that linked fears about changing class relations to fears concerning changes in the gendered behavior and sexual relations of men and women. Equestrian practice and its representation bring to light the instability of what were deemed to be basic bodily distinctions of class and gender.

The ambiguous connotations of riding were also a function of the rising popularity of sports that merged bourgeois and aristocratic worlds. As Eugen Weber has noted, the very word "sport" came to have an "equivocal sound" in late nineteenth-century France owing to its associations not only with riding but also increasingly with the more vulgar practices of horse racing and betting.[7] The modern domain of sport put pressure on class and gender relations and their corporeal manifestations, and equestrianism underscores the ways this domain developed from but also clashed with fundamental principles and markers of aristocratic behavior. This is essentially because sport was regarded as a means to show (if not show off) one's physical, and by extension, moral capacities. Indeed, sport was said to inculcate those very moral properties that had been identified with the ruling classes and with horsemanship: will, courage, and virility. And yet to show off these qualities was a sign that one was not noble and was merely imitating nobility. How then, given the growing popularity of sport by the end of the century, and also its politicizing, was it possible to lay claim to that "centaur ideal" without demeaning oneself through exhibitionist behavior?[8]

What becomes clear in the fin de siècle is that efforts to restore the symbolic value of the horse and of horsemanship as a noble and masculine ideal also changed the meaning of show to allow for and promote a noble spectacle of the male body. Horses were called on by both a flaccid aristocracy and a flagging bourgeoisie as an image for virilizing and rejuvenating French manhood. This was the intent behind the new and growing field of sport science at the turn of the century, culminating in the reinstatement of the Olympic Games. It was also the aim behind the strange institution of the Cirque Molier that was established in 1880, a circus where the male performers were aristocrats. Sport science and aristocratic circus were joined in their attempts to revitalize riding as a means of fashioning and exhibiting ideal masculinity as itself a kind of thoroughbred. What it meant to be a thoroughbred or *pur-sang*, however, was itself contested terrain, since it could refer at once to a protofascist notion of the pure race and to a superior race engineered through scientific breeding and training. Indeed, whereas for much of the century women were regarded as the bearers of blood, family, and the persistence of breeding (and the ones to be punished when they transgressed), the idea of the "thoroughbred human," as one book title announced, was something men of both "noble" and mixed blood could lay claim to and exhibit in their bodies. And yet, as I argue below, the very showiness of this new breed of masculinity and the riding associated with it worked against the normative masculinity it was said to promote, tainting (in bourgeois terms) both the noble and the bourgeois horseman with the feminizing effects of spectacle and the homoerotic possibilities of being a male object of the male gaze.

THE DECLINE OF VISIBLE VIRILITY AND THE RISE OF FEMININE SPECTACLE

Already in the 1830s, Stendhal pointed to the changing symbolic function of riding. Whereas in our post-Freudian century we tend to think it is little girls who dream of a horse between their legs, Stendhal makes it clear that in Napoleonic France this was the dream of adolescent boys. Julien Sorel is one such cavalier who is "at the height of joy" when allowed to ride in the king's *garde d'honneur*. His mastery of the horse as it bolts out of line and rears immediately brings him to imagine himself a hero of the Napoleonic army—"he was an officer by decree of Napoleon and was leading the charge against a battery."[9] Mounting a horse is both a sign of Julien's (social) mobility, taking him out of the dung where he was born, and a sign of his virility, confirmed by the women who turn their heads to watch him on horseback. "He saw in the women's eyes that it was him they were looking at."[10] Riding, in other words, makes him into a spectacle of virility. But as Maya Longstaffe has pointed out, in the nineteenth century "heroes start falling off their horses in French literature," and Julien is no exception.[11] A subsequent fall while riding with the Count Norbert makes Julien realize he might better impress Norbert's sister Mathilde with his humor than his riding. More important, the novel makes it clear that in the years following Napoleon's defeat and retreat, the hero on horseback is no longer born or made in battle but is produced in riding lessons. The only heroism that can't be bought, as Mathilde claims, is the death penalty.[12]

The same gendered distinction between riding and watching occurs in *Le rose et le vert* (1837) (The pink and the green), written seven years later. Here Prussian men reveal their pleasure in parading up and down the streets of Königsberg on horseback as they know that women are watching their every movement from behind covered windows but appear not to notice.

> The curiosity of the women is aided by an accessory resource: in each reputable house, on either side of the ground floor windows, elevated four feet above the street, one finds foot-high mirrors attached to a small iron

> arm and slightly inclined toward the inside. By the reflection of these inclined mirrors, the women see the passersby who arrive at the end of the road; at the same time, as we have said, the curious eyes of these men are not allowed to penetrate into the apartment because of the metallic sheets that cover the bottom of the windows. But if they don't see, they know that they are seen, and that certitude gives a particular rapidity to all the small novels that animate the societies of Berlin and Königsberg.[13]

In this unfinished novel Stendhal makes it clear that under the July Monarchy in France riding has come to have different meanings than it does in Prussia, and the difference between those two nations is presented in terms of the idea of spectacle and its relation to knowledge-power. In Prussia, being a spectacle is still an honorable and satisfying distinction for a man. Even without seeing into the windows, Prussian men could strut their stuff with the "certitude" of being both watched and desired, the very certitude that also animates their novels. Such certainty was harder to come by in Paris, where the incipient commodification of the horse created unexpected changes in class and gender codes. Indeed, by the time Stendhal wrote *Le rose et le vert*, the upper classes of Paris had all but abandoned the once obligatory parade down the Champs-Élysées so as not to mix with the hordes now crowding the streets. In 1847 the French author Delphine de Girardin claimed it was now *la mode* not to join the promenades.[14] Stendhal's novel opens with a Prussian general who has returned from Paris and complains that the only Frenchman he could strike up a friendship with was one "whose role, or 'individuality' as they say, is to shine by virtue of his carriage horses."[15] But while the Frenchman appeared to hold on to certain ideals of love and beauty, he was also ready to gamble them away: "In fact those horses that he loved so well, into whose stable he went to breakfast almost every morning, he was ready to lose."[16] Unlike Prussia, Paris is a place where ideals can be bought and sold and where noble masculinity is no longer situated in the body and blood. Consequently it can as easily be gained as lost. Whereas equestrianism in Prussia is still a sign of heroic, virile undertakings, in Paris the horse has become a sign of the surrender to idle wealth, *la vie de café*.[17] The physical mastery represented by the spectacle of the horseman has ceded pride of place to the economic mastery represented by the gambler or horse breeder.

For Stendhal, Julien Sorel's loss of ideals comes with a compensatory gain in ironic vision that presages changes in the representation of male bodies more generally. Whereas Prussian customs celebrate what D. A. Miller refers to as the "pleasurable visibility of the male body as such," Julien's situation represents a shift in the role of the Romantic hero after the Revolution and the fall of Napoleon. The Parisian male body disappears as spectacular object and increasingly finds its power in a disembodied gaze upon others—the gaze that in Prussia is held by the women behind the shutters.[18] Riding, in other words, may be one of the last desires to succumb to the "great masculine renunciation" described by the psychoanalyst J. C. Flugel:

> Thus we can see that, in the case of the exhibitionistic desires connected with self-display, a particularly easy form of conversion may be found in a change from (passive) exhibitionism to (active) scoptophilia (erotic pleasure in the use of vision)—the desire to be seen being transformed into the desire to see. This desire to see may itself remain unsublimated and find its appropriate satisfaction in the contemplation of the other sex, or it may be sublimated and find its expression in the more general desire to see and know.[19]

The rise of riding as a spectator sport in nineteenth-century France may be explained in part by what Flugel describes as its compensatory pleasures for exhibitionism and narcissism. In the course of the century such pleasures were projected onto the *amazone* or *écuyère* as a rising specular object of desire, but also onto the horse, allowing the Frenchman, as Stendhal suggested, to "shine by means of his horses."[20] The result was a certain feminizing of the horse (in particular the thoroughbred) and of riding, especially as practiced in its more relaxed English manner. Whereas the French school of riding had been dominated by haute école dressage as developed by and for the military, a more forward and relaxed style of riding imported from England became increasingly popular, especially among women. "Anglomania" was thus blamed for everything from men's losing control of their horses to the masses attempting to "seize the reins" of the state.[21] A "real man," moreover, no longer had to ride in order to "know" horses. The eye of the *véritable amateur*, as Charles Baudelaire suggests in his poem "A Thorough-bred" ("Un cheval de race"), could recognize the still "delicious" thoroughbred "even when harnessed to a hired hack or lumbering coach."[22] The "Society for the Encouragement of the Betterment of the Races of Horses in France and the Jockey Club, founded in 1833 and 1834, gave distinction to men who had a passion for horses, albeit often with a preference for judging their conformation and betting on them rather than riding them. According to Anne Martin-Fugier, with the Jockey Club high society took its place on the Boulevard. By promoting a life composed principally of horses and entertainment, the club functioned as the link between high society and the world of spectacle.[23] Horse racing, especially, turned watching into an activity privileged over riding, transforming more and more horse enthusiasts into spectators and making the thoroughbred into the privileged object of their gaze. Racehorses, as Thorstein Veblen remarks in *The Theory of the Leisure Class*, become the ultimate objects of "wasteful display" through commodified "exhibitions of force and facility of motion that gratify the popular aesthetic sense.[24] By 1880 this spectatorship itself is figured as pathological. As we saw in chapter 5, Zola's Nana, both courtesan and racehorse, mesmerizes all who set eyes on her, enticing them to mount her and spread her unnamed disease.

Adah Menken's brief stage appearance on horseback in 1866 thus marked the beginning of new forms of entertainment starring horses and women together as objects of spectacle. The circus and hippodromes, originally developed for the aristocratic display of military maneuvers on horseback and haute école dressage, were becoming chic entertainment for a rising middle class. Increasing competition from the music hall and cabaret during the latter decades of the century meant that equestrian performances of haute école riding had to make way for clowns, jugglers, and acrobats who, when they did perform with a horse, did so to show off their own physical agility and bodily mastery (or exaggerated lack of it), rather than the horse's. Such acrobatic numbers on horseback increasingly became the particular province of a special type of *écuyère* who, instead of mastering the horse with her thighs, used the animal as a stage on which to display her agility and femininity. For many, the popularity of the *écuyère* whose image appeared on posters all over fin-de-siècle Paris marked a clear decline in the classical, heroic ideal the circus was founded on, and a decline of the horse, its original raison d'être. In 1874 Victor Franconi, the last of the great *écuyers* of the nineteenth century and founder of the hippodrome of the place de l'Étoile, bemoaned the fact that a certain mule named Rigolo, whose "dressage" consisted of throwing off anyone who tried to ride him, had become the hit of his circus. "A mule fills my hall while the horse is no longer the winning ticket."[25]

If the circus's replacement of haute école dressage with the *écuyère*'s acrobatics can be seen as the logical outcome of a century that put women in the role of spectacular object, the replacement of horsemanship by the burlesque spectacle of a mule throwing its rider can be read as both social-sexual and political satire: the nightly reenactment of France's military defeat by its suddenly more modern German foe. Here it is important to remember the tight association between military glory and the horse around which the circus was built. The point is not only that the haute école was derived from military maneuvers, but also that it produced an erotic identification between man and horse that gave proof of the rider's virile mastery. As Henry Thétard, horse trainer and historian of the French circus, explains, "Haute école is the ultimate dressage because the rider is one with his student and can, by his permanent contact, not only use pressure and violent force, but also transmit to him his dominating fluid."[26] Continuing, Thétard describes the moment every horseman works toward, when he is one with his horse, who submits to his will: "The man, kneads with his legs that powerful and warm mass that seeks to escape his orders by any means, to flee the hold over her will that she fears. When finally the beast abdicates, gives in, half weary, half confident, what an intoxicating triumph, what joyous pride for the victor who has conquered the empire of a being."[27] Even as more and more women performed dressage with great success, fin-de-siècle representations of *écuyères* rarely show them straddling their mounts except as comic mockery of the noble equestrian (like the star of Félicien Champsaur's *Lulu: A Pantomime in One Act* (1888), who would be represented in posters dancing on her pig). On the contrary, they are largely desexualized or etherealized, as in Georges Seurat's phantomlike circus girls or Tissot's *Ladies of the Cars* (fig. 6.2) from his series on the Parisienne, finished in 1885.

Here the scaled and mermaidlike drivers are robbed of their genitals, as also of their will. Their vacant stares and marblelike skin turn them into statues, an image completed by their liberty headdresses. Dominance is visible only in the horses, who threaten at any moment to run over the audience. For these horses, as for Franconi's mule, there is no abdication of the beast: they have absorbed the ladies' life force as the mule absorbs his rider's, rendering him sterile through his own degenerative impotence as a mule.

Having previously celebrated France's military might, the circus appeared now to be an arena for the parodic display of masculine impotence, feminine sterility, and animal domination. Franconi's mule, like Tissot's mermaids, illustrates these changes in the gendered and eroticized aesthetics of the circus performance, since both also implicate the circus in the psychosexual maladies of the French nation that were diagnosed after the defeat in 1870 and on into the Third Republic. How then are we to interpret the fact that, at the same moment when the circus had become a form of entertainment for the display of feminine (and feminized) bodies and of human impotence in the face of the animal other, it also became the provenance of a new breed of performer—the aristocrat?

Figure 6.2. James Jacques Joseph Tissot, *The Ladies of the Cars*, 1883–85.

THE ARISTOCRATIC CIRCUS

In March 1880, Ernest Molier founded his amateur circus, the Cirque Molier, in a wing of his *hôtel particulier* where he had previously housed his riding school. He claimed to have had a lifelong "passion" for horses.[28] The performers were chosen from among his friends: members of the French aristocracy including such notables as the Comte de la Rochefoucauld and Baron de Bizy, and the audience was also selected by personal invitation. Thus, in the place of mules and women this circus presented aristocratic men who aimed to take back a display of mastery that had once been theirs. It was a risky business. Many saw the circus as a further symptom of aristocratic ennui and indolence. Such bodily display, they argued, threatened to further feminize, if not mongrelize, the aristocracy and thus compound its image as the segment of society most weakened by modern life.

The apprehensive response to Molier's circus was drawn largely from bourgeois concerns about masculine display and about the physical body as sign not only of individual health and potency but also of the health of class and nation. Drawing on Foucault's statement that the bourgeoisie's "blood" was its sex (referring to the capacity to produce heirs), Robert Nye explains that "a man's sexual identity was thus revealed in his physical sex and manly character, a view that for a number of reasons may have been more deeply rooted in France than elsewhere in the West."[29] On the one hand, the demanding physical exercises of the circus offered the aristocracy the possibility of rehabilitating its body, thereby proving its "sex" and its capacity to govern. On the other hand, the desires and pleasures solicited by the circus are symptomatic of the physical and psychological maladies of the fin de siècle and of minds and bodies said to be overdeveloped at the expense of morality. Such is the implication behind the title of Daniel Lesueur's 1892 novel *Névrosée*, where the culminating scene at the amateur circus precipitates the heroine's physical and moral degeneration.

Oddly, the amateur circus was regarded both as symptom of and cure for such maladies. Molier reports in his own history that the press set high stakes by representing the circus as either "the regeneration of the human race or its demoralization."[30] Taking the latter position, *Le radical* (May 25, 1886) claimed that this is what the aristocracy does when it fails at everything else; it was "the beginning of the end." A letter printed in *La tribune* bemoaned in political terms the "humiliation" of a duke proving himself on the trapeze or a count doing so on horseback: "Here are the supports of the throne and the altar! Here they are! And that is why I can't stay serious when I read, the day after an Orléanist evening, that . . . all is ready and that we have only to breathe on the Republic. The sympathizers of Orléans are on the assault of our institutions with a troupe of titled clowns!" (191).[31] One of the more sustained criticisms came from an article in *Le Figaro* of 1886 in which the journalist Henry Fouquier railed against Molier's assault on the "moral health" of the country. "What in effect dominates the endless representations, which have nothing in common with the national training in ancient times, is the desire to be seen, the desire to be seen with which Agrippa d'Aubigne already reproached the nobility of his time" (186). For nobles to put on leotards and perform for fashionable girls (*les filles à la mode*) was, according to Fouquier, democracy taken to extremes and the abdication of their sense of duty to the people. In fact, he adds, referring to the ways France's victories have led to its own (moral) downfall, "It is the number one French disease that spoils the best things, that gives even to patriotism the allure of showing off; from this have greatly suffered those who, in history, came after the severe regeneration of Prussia after Iena" (186). In the aftermath of the war, that pleasure in male spectacle that for Stendhal had previously distinguished Prussia now invaded France as a disease.

Enthusiasts, by contrast, saw Molier's circus as a means for men of the aristocracy to prove themselves not through the number and elegance of their homes, but by the force and agility of their bodies. "Charmed by the resurrection of muscle in the ruling classes," wrote Henri de Pène of the *Paris-journal* (1881), they saw the exercises as renewing an old tradition of aristocratic sportsmanship (186). As another writer from the *Figaro* contested, even if there should be a "a grain of vanity in this need to show oneself, to be applauded, that spurs these amateur riders and improvised clowns, . . . it is an *idéal* like any other, which one should not pooh-pooh." Indeed, physical exercise, as one writer for *Le temps* extolled, was what the present generation had wrongly abandoned and precisely what it and the country needed:

> The same pens that condemn the degeneration of modern society do wrong to stigmatize sports that put that idea to the test, at least physically. With all due respect to those malcontents who are afflicted with that bilious attitude we consider to be the privilege of old maids jaundiced by celibacy, the spectacle of hotly disputed assaults of arms, of the work of haute école, of jumping courses, of gymnastic exercises, of swimming contests, of all that requires an expenditure of moral energy and material vigor, is otherwise salutary for the spectators than the idiotic songs of the café concerts and the plastic, plunging necklines of fairies; by fortifying those who do it, they propagate the attraction of those virile pastimes that make the kind of solid men our country needs. (189–90)

The amateur circus thus played into conflicting views about the propriety of the body that were both class- and gender-based. While its equestrian focus promised to restore chivalric relations between men and women, its presentation of half-dressed male bodies (the maillot and leotard were insisted on even over Molier's own skepticism) seemed to offer a scandalous reversal of class and gender decorum. Though it was originally planned as a performance of men before their male friends and their lower-class mistresses, the question of roles for women presented itself almost immediately. As Molier explained, the performance of aristocratic men in tights would be acceptable only if women joined in. "Since we were determined to present a veritable circus show, we needed women. Some even said that without women we would seem silly: maybe they went a bit far. In any case, the feminine element having been judged indispensable, it was left to resolve the frightful question, From which world would we find our female colleagues?" (7).

Understanding that respectable men would not allow their wives to parade themselves, they hired professional women from among Molier's students and the Cirque d'été. In doing so they earned a sense of professionalism for their work even as they proved their own disdain for the professions. The women performers, moreover, like the well-heeled women in the audience, often displaced the men as objects of attention, helping them to disavow any pleasure gained through men's gazing upon male bodies. That the homoerotic gaze was part of the pleasure is suggested by the fact that it was only in response to the demands made by the upper-class women, or *femmes du monde*, that women were even permitted in the audience, and then only in a special second performance added for "respectable" couples.[32] Whereas aristocratic men were thus permitted to move between the worlds of high society and of entertainment, if not of hetero- and homoeroticism, their wives were restricted to the former, as if they were to maintain the increasingly untenable separation of those worlds.

The gender dynamics of the circus and the way it responded to the increasing importance of a certain exhibitionism and delight in appearance across genders and class boundaries is at the core of Tissot's series on Parisian women, which Tamar Garb has called a "taxonomy of contemporary femininity."[33] Tissot had returned to Paris in the 1880s after ten years of success on the London art scene documenting fashionable women in various settings of everyday life. The Parisian women he paints are of different class origins and walks of life, but all are seen to attract and hold the gaze of the men who watch from the background. Recent commentary on the artist has stressed that his "female subjects are not what they appear to be" and that viewers must learn to decode their dress and gestures in order to read their identities.[34] A subversive artist, as Katharine Lochnan and others argue, Tissot "mocks the people to whom his works are visually most appealing." Indeed, it is not simply fashion that Tissot documents, but the allure of appearing and being seen; hence his interest in the aristocratic circus. Here, moreover, men's fashion was situated in more than their attire.

The ambivalent dynamic of the viewer's gaze during Molier's mixed performances is ironically rendered in a second painting from Tissot's *Femmes à Paris* series titled *The Circus Lover* (1883–85) (fig. 6.3).

At the center of his composition are seemingly nonprofessional male performers, including a trapezist listed in the original catalog as the Duc de

Figure 6.3. James Jacques Joseph Tissot, *Women of Paris: The Circus Lover*, 1885.

la R (presumably the Duc or Comte de la Rochefoucauld). His monocle and the handkerchief tucked into his leotard are mocking reminders of his class, otherwise difficult to hold on to in his precarious situation. He seems to enjoy himself in his position of spectacular object, which nevertheless has little response. The men in top hats talk to each other or look beyond in a bored daze; the women above them are looking right and left into the boxes. The most "brazen" gaze, as Garb describes it, picked up by other ladies to the right, is that of the woman in pink in the foreground who stares right at the viewer, bringing us in as the newcomers.[35] Her position reinforces the ambiguous boundaries between spectacle and spectator, as between class and gender. As Garb suggests, she is not the "exclusive object of display," and if she is a privileged object, she is also a privileged subject, an active status emphasized by the title of the painting. Although "De la R" has a bird's-eye view, his monocle and his wandering eye point to his impoverished gaze, exacerbated by his position as object and his desire to be looked at. The precariousness of his position is exaggerated by his widely spread legs and the illegible gender of his crotch, to which the viewer is directed. The only male gaze with any weight is that of the gentleman to the right whose line of vision takes the viewer to the buttocks of the second trapezist, who in effect acts as a mirror image of La Rochfoucauld. In this "(be)hindsight" can be read the aristocracy's apparent, if disavowed, investment in sodomitic fantasy.[36] For the men, the pleasure in being looked at may be what the contemporary horseman and historian Baron De Vaux called the "pretext of decadence" through which the *vie élégante* passed each year, but it is also a means to retrieve the status of spectacular object renounced by aristocratic men at the time of the Revolution.[37]

The meaning of such objectification in this context is unclear. De Vaux's notion of pretext hints that such decadent display paradoxically secures the aristocrat's social position by distinguishing him from the bourgeoisie's fearful avoidance of such decadence. In *The Politics and Poetics of Transgression*, Peter Stallybrass and Allon White demonstrate how elements of the carnivalesque—defined as spectacles of the body, the animal, the grotesque—persisted into the nineteenth century in certain "liminoid" or "low" practices from which the bourgeoisie distanced themselves, claiming to be different. Such distancing, however, necessarily produced that low as "a primary eroticized constituent of [the bourgeoisie's] own fantasy life, thereby incorporating it, however clandestinely, into bourgeois identity."[38] That possibility is revealed in the opening pages of Molier's account of his passion for the circus, where, "damning the fate that made me be born into a bourgeois family," he explains that he "would have preferred to spring from a big drum and have been nursed by one of those vigorous women who jump through paper-covered hoops while making energetic hop-hops" (1). Molier's circus offered a strategy for subject formation different from the apparently "degenerating" aristocracy of the fin de siècle, attempting to rehabilitate or produce a new form of carnival in which the upper classes (or at least upper-class men) could participate with impunity while still offering the kinds of symbolic release and bodily expression of earlier carnival forms—the almost-bared chest, the bits of fat hanging over the trapeze, the clown. This is carnival as Marcus Verhagen has described it, an expression not so much of revolt as of "social promiscuity," though in this instance a controlled promiscuity, limited by the "by invitation only" audience.[39]

Condemnation of such promiscuity and disdain for bourgeois propriety is the inspiration behind Daniel Lesueur's novel *Névrosée*, written during the twelfth year of Molier's performances. Lesueur (pen name for Jeanne

Loiseau) shows, moreover, how the acceptability of promiscuous display is inflected by gender. Warned against any flirtation with carnivalesque outlets, aristocratic women faced a particular danger that their male counterparts were spared.[40] At the core of the novel is a critique of the atrophied state of the aristocracy, whose talents are no longer productive or reproductive. Étiennette, the main character, called Nénette, suffers a miscarriage owing to her misguided intellectual pursuits and neglect of her body. The penultimate scene takes place at the Cirque Laurencie (modeled on Molier's circus), where the Vicomte Norbert d'Epeuilles is an equestrian performer who uses his talents to seduce the women "who forgot themselves to the extent that they clapped their hands" (255). Among these is Étiennette, his married cousin. Untrained in the passions, she begins to succumb to his advances even as she is equally drawn by "a fierce and unhealthy curiosity" toward a female performer wearing boy's clothes: "That girl, with her boyish clothes, her thin and pale face, her perverse and sad eyes, her tired voice, pouring forth cynical couplets with a horrible erudition, exercised a kind of fascination on the young woman. Nénette, who didn't understand the half of what she sang, didn't understand herself, but felt overtaken, in the face of that bizarre scene, by an acrid and unhealthy curiosity" (204).

Lesueur's misogynistic and homophobic didacticism warns female readers against women who stray from their domestic duties, putting the circus at the center of a novel about degeneration, education, and breeding—subjects linked through an equestrian theme. Étiennette, like her cousin, shows unmistakable signs of her aristocratic heritage and is said to be a thoroughbred or pureblood d'Epeuilles—a d'Epeuilles *pur-sang* (53). But that heritage is useless to her in the modern world, much as Norbert has no use for the glorious military skills he inherited from the family and now uses in the circus. Norbert, in fact, not only rides, he is a painter and sculptor of horses (his work is said to be chic but show little talent), and his cousin's downfall begins when she poses for him in a riding habit, though she has no intention of riding.[41] Nénette and Norbert are figures of a degenerate aristocracy whose showy exteriors mask the neurosis of the novel's title and a moral vacuum that is exteriorized in their taste for the circus. Even if women are barred from performing, the novel suggests, the risks of the circus are as great, if not greater, for such women. Lured into this world by their men, they come to know the "the anguish of passions without knowing their appeasement" and, unlike their male counterparts, are either forbidden from or punished for taking part in its pleasures. Disgusted (like Molier himself), with "boring, bourgeois customs," Nénette is torn between the desire to see and the desire to separate herself from the women riders, "those women who, at least, know change, spontaneity, caprice and sometimes, danger" (259). In this she incarnates the female bourgeois subject theorized by Stallybrass and White who, when "placed on the outside of a grotesque carnival body which is articulated as social pleasure and celebration . . . introjects the spectacle both as the pathos of exclusion (Why can't that be me?) and as a negative representation which becomes phobic precisely through the law of her exclusion, the interdiction which defines her difference (You must not be *that*)."[42] The result for Nénette is a particularly modern neurosis that is terminated only by her suicide.

HORSE TRAINING AND PHYSICAL EDUCATION: BUILDING AND BREEDING STRONG BODIES, MINDS, AND NATIONS

In linking degeneration and horsemanship, Lesueur shows the influence of her lover and longtime companion the popular scientist Gustave Le Bon. Known most widely for his writings on crowd psychology that were taken up by Freud, Le Bon also wrote extensively on matters of education, race, and, perhaps surprisingly, horse training or dressage. As I will discuss further in chapter 7, for Le Bon riding was not simply a sport. For him the correct, scientific training of horses offered a model of education that had application to the modern world; under the influence of crowds and the wrong kinds of education, individuals were increasingly dominated by their animal instincts. According to Le Bon, some men and most women were like horses that required moral rather than intellectual training. Indeed, their "natures," he warned, could be destroyed by higher learning. This is the case with Étiennette, whose suicide offers support to Le Bon's admonitions regarding the growing opportunities for higher education for women during the Third Republic.[43] "What are these women doing here?" asks Maxime, a distinguished professor and Nénette's eventual husband, when she and other women show up in his classroom. "It was impossible that they understood. They could understand the words, the establishment of certain facts; but to penetrate to the bottom of things was forbidden by the organization of their brains as well as well as by their primary education" (26). Women, Maxime concludes, in words that echo Le Bon, "are not made for reasoning" (197). In an article titled "Women's Education Today," Le Bon writes that "by the laws of heredity, the civilized human brain continues to evolve after childhood, while the Negro's and the woman's are condemned to remain at a certain level."[44] To give such inferior beings more than basic moral training, whether they be animals, women, or people of color, is to put at risk that training and the moral judgment it enforces. In the case of women it turns them into neurotics, *névrosées*. What they require instead is training like that given to horses.

By the end of the century metaphors of the horse and horsemanship resurfaced in relation to the new sports and hygiene movement that was critical of the French educational system's emphasis on the intellect, which produced, as Robert Nye has cited, "only rhetoricians and dilettantes and so few men of character, will and action."[45] References to riding as the most noble of sports (and to Buffon's statement that the horse is the most noble conquest of man) helped advance the idea of horse sports as a means to combat the ills of modern democratic and industrialized life. Similarly, in an essay titled "Equitation in France," published in 1896, the riding enthusiast Baron De Vaux reminded his readers that of all types of bodily exercise, "equitation is the most noble, the most suited to develop the physiological state of man, to diminish hereditary defects engendered by tuberculosis, alcoholism, the imperfect development of children in large cities, the degeneration of the race. . . . In addition, is it not the best antidote against the ills that attack men who sit in offices, the bureaucrats, against the intellectual overload of our young generations . . . against the degeneration of the race?"[46]

In a publication of 1908, the founders of the physical culture or hygiene movement, Drs. Rouhet and Desbonnet, shifted attention from riding to the horse itself with the publication of their controversial *L'art de créer le pur-sang humain* (The art of creating a thoroughbred human; fig. 6.4). The appeal of the title, which Pierre de Coubertin, the founder of the modern Olympics, called "appetizing," belied its ambiguity.[47] What is a thoroughbred human? Is it made or born? Evoking a Darwinian notion of the thoroughbred as the "fittest" for survival, the title played into both the hopes and the fears of the aristocracy, who defined themselves by their blood but looked down on the notion of sport. Rouhet and Desbonnet reminded their readers that there was only one pureblood race of horse, the Arabian, but that the English had succeeded "in truly creating a new race of thoroughbred horse."[48] The same method, they argued, could be applied to humans: "If we want to obtain a race of thoroughbred humans, we must use the procedures undertaken to obtain a thoroughbred horse. Let us first create strong and robust individuals who will be, if current prudishness will pardon the term—the stallions of the future" (lxviii).

In the hygiene movement, the thoroughbred was emptied of its associations with women and transgendered into a poster boy for a cult of youthful masculinity, beauty, and health. Turning the body into an object of rigorous scientific investigation through the analysis of the function and potential of each muscle group, Rouhet and Desbonnet's book presented a rehabilitated

Fig. 31
Un pur-sang humain.
L'amateur Forestier, produit de la méthode Desbonnet.

Figure 6.4. "Un pur-sang humain," from Georges Rouhet and Edmond Desbonnet, *L'art de créer le pur-sang humain* (Paris: Berger-Levrault, 1908). Image courtesy of the New York Medical Academy.

image of the thoroughbred by transforming its showiness, now cleansed of erotic and lascivious potential, into a kind of mechanical motor, the mark of efficiency and productivity. In this Rouhet and Desbonnet were heirs of Étienne-Jules Marey, who put the horse at the center of the newly emerging conception of the body as an "animal machine," the title he gave to his studies of human and animal motion, published in 1873. In the animal machine, Anson Rabinbach explains, life becomes a "field of forces to be investigated and measured by medical technologies rather than praised for its unknowable vitalism."[49] By studying the horse as a motor, Marey intended to determine its optimum use. Rouhet and Desbonnet's thoroughbred men were also designed for efficiency of movement with the least amount of fatigue, illustrating what had become a neo-Lamarckian belief that race is the result of function, not environment or breeding. Breeding would of course have a role in the race, but it was seen to follow from the normative aesthetic function of the thoroughbred: "Handsome and strong men, by virtue of a natural affinity which only a false, irrational, and harmful morality could cause to go astray, would go toward beautiful and strong women, as the bee turns to the flower and the flower to the sun."[50] Natural selection, for Rouhet and Desbonnet, is helped along by beautiful bodies, perfected through rigorous training in the method of "logical sport and of certain fecundity."[51]

The metaphorical associations of the thoroughbred horse inflected visual representations of thoroughbred humans. Photographs of successful male bodybuilders worked in tandem with photographs of classical statuary that were included in the book, as in the journal *La culture physique* (Physical culture) founded by Rouhet and Desbonnet. Together, aristocratic and classical codes of aesthetic purity and authenticity redeemed the spectacle of the male body and opened its availability to a larger, democratic audience. The representatives of the physical culture movement were photographed in poses of classical sculpture not only to prove the effectiveness of their method but also to ensure the nobility of their athletic bodies. This classical ideal was already in place in Molier's circus history, moreover, which includes a snapshot of La Rochefoucauld in the pose of a classical athlete, frontally lit according to the convention for photographing classical sculpture (fig. 6.5).[52]

Unlike Tissot's painting that accentuates the flesh and its inadequate covering, the snapshot turns flesh to stone in an idealizing light. Like the image of the thoroughbred, whose animal body is mechanized through its photographic representations, the Greek athlete stands in opposition to the weakened, degenerative state of the contemporary Frenchman, whom Rouhet and Desbonnet describe as a "limousin donkey," and offers an image of what the Frenchman could become through the proper hygiene.

For the physical culture movement of the end of the century, nobility, like race, was not given by birth. Rather, it was a product of culture, the result of a system of physical education (including riding) and breeding for which there was no replacement. Understandably, Rouhet and Desbonnet's method was strongly criticized by more conservative sports enthusiasts like Pierre de Coubertin, and in an essay titled "L'homme et l'animal" (Man and animal), Coubertin took a stance against the notion of the thoroughbred human, which epitomized for him a contemporary tendency to focus exclusively on the (animal) body and neglect the moral and psychological capacities that distinguish man from animals. "After having neglected the human animal in man, we have come to neglect the very significant fact that in the

Figure 6.5. *Le Comte Hubert de La Rochefoucauld.* Image from Ernest Molier, *Cirque Molier, 1880–1904* (Paris: P. Dupont, 1905), 26. Image courtesy of the Archives and Special Collections of the Thomas J. Dodd Research Center at the University of Connecticut.

human animal, there is man."[53] But Coubertin's objection also has much to do with his resistance to the thoroughbred as signifier of the possibility of creating a new, pure race. While paying lip service to neo-Lamarckian ideas by suggesting that certain sports, "practiced by former generations, imprint themselves on the race," he declared himself a colonial fanatic who believed in the inequality of races and found the idea of the thoroughbred human contrary to his faith in "colonial progress."[54] The issue of healthy masculinity nevertheless was central to Coubertin's overriding concern with sport as a means of strengthening the French race and building its resistance to the forces of degeneration. As distinguished from body training, sports like equestrianism produced a healthy nervous system by training body and mind together, reaching to their psychological interaction. Rejecting the analogy between man and horse, Coubertin puts the rider back on top and begins his *Essays on Sport Psychology* with a metaphor of horsemanship reminiscent of Socrates's good horseman in Plato's *Phaedrus*. "Consider the equestrian sport and see how it gives an image of life," he writes in 1906; "the 'soul'—mind and character—is a cavalier who straddles the body, an animal stronger than he and at whose mercy he would find himself if he did not control it with an art sufficient to direct and tame that force."[55] Indeed, in a series of essays—"Equitation and Life," "Spurs," and "Dressage"—Coubertin repeatedly returns to horse and rider as a metaphor for the perfect, "moral" governance of mind over body and to riding as the ideal sport for regenerating the will and shaping real men. "There is nothing more virilizing for man than contact with a horse."[56]

The new political significance that sport attained in the years before the First World War thus came down to a politics of the body—its legitimacy and its legitimate use. As a training ground for building the moral and manly character of future leaders, the notion of sport that Coubertin promoted instituted an aristocratic ethic that had links both to the aristocratic circus and to Le Bon's educational methods, even as it assimilated a growing bourgeois understanding of the body as a form of sexual and social capital, evident in Rouhet and Desbonnet. Bourdieu's theories in "Sport and Social Class" are pertinent here. Coubertin's promotion of the Olympic Games, like Molier's circus, draws on a theory of amateurism that, as Bourdieu writes,

> is in fact one dimension of an aristocratic philosophy of sport as a disinterested practice, a finality without an end, analogous to artistic practice, but even more suitable than art (there is always something residually feminine about art . . .) for affirming the manly virtues of future leaders: sport is conceived as training in courage and manliness, "forming the character" and inculcating the "will to win" which is the mark of the true leader, but a will to win within the rules.[57]

Indeed, amateurism is a means of asserting a hierarchy of birthright over any academic achievements, as if those who know and play by the rules, or those who ride horses, do so by virtue of heredity rather than through learning. As Coubertin writes, "Every healthy boy must feel a keen desire to mount a horse, and even if this happens to him only two or three times, he will have discovered and felt something at once new and ancestral, which will make him grow, if one may dare to put it in this way, both muscularly and even mentally."[58]

According to Bourdieu, the philosophy of amateurism goes hand in hand with a form of anti-intellectualism; an observation seconded both in Lesueur's novel and even to a certain extent in Le Bon, whereby "energy, courage, and willpower" are valued above "knowledge and erudition," at least for most students. Of course, Le Bon considered himself among those men for whom intellectual pursuits were to be encouraged. He was a scientist who marshaled the terms of psychology and the instruments of Muybridge and Marey to calculate, photograph, and explain the minds and movements of horses, but he warned of the moral dangers that can occur when "inferior" minds are given higher education. Thus he professed that it is because France has ignored the psychological principles of education—whether for horses or for humans—that it is "incontestably the country in the world where horses and children are the most poorly trained."[59]

If sport is basic to education for Le Bon, then, it is not because it engages what distinguishes man and animal, but because it exercises the kinds of "nonrational forms of logic" that both share.[60] Le Bon demonstrates little of Coubertin's concern for safeguarding man's exceptionalism and builds on a human-animal continuum to distinguish between "superior" and "inferior" human mentalities and, by extension, races. "Horses are a bit like peoples and children" and thus "the basic principles of dressage or education apply to all three."[61] Where Coubertin opposed women's participation in sport, fearing it might unnaturally virilize them, Le Bon opposed women's intellectual education: "That education threatens them with profound physical decadence and, as a result, threatens us in our descendants."[62] In the end both ideas come down to the notion that women's best qualities are those that are natural to them, not those they acquire. Hence their education should concentrate on exercising those essential characteristics.

If the concept of the thoroughbred human is anathema to both Coubertin and Le Bon, it is not simply because it foregrounds the body and bodybuilding but, more important, because it promotes the possibility of mixing and fixing races to create a new, pure one. Coubertin and Le Bon offer a conservative notion of the purebred in their view of woman as the embodiment of racial stability and the guarantor of "natural" evolution—a view echoed by one of the first sporting magazines for women, *La femme française* (The French woman), published from 1902 to 1904. Its goal was to find and promote those physical activities that would "teach women how to remain what they are so well: French women of race, that is to say, the naturally noble woman."[63] For Coubertin and Le Bon, if not also for Rouhet and Desbonnet, women were the born, not made, thoroughbreds of French society. As women should encourage men's progress by "rewarding them with their applause" (so said

Coubertin),[64] so women's stability and imperfectability were what allowed men to cultivate and perfect themselves.

In a passage often cited by theorists of gender, John Berger describes the conventions used to distinguish between the social standing of men and of women: "men act and women appear."[65] By the beginning of the Third Republic, one might also have written the statement in terms of class: men of the bourgeoisie act and aristocrats appear—thereby admitting the risks of feminization attendant on the aristocracy's showy exterior. I suggest, however, that Molier's aristocratic circus and the eager participation of the upper classes in the physical education movement of the turn of the century worked to undo the gendered and classed distinctions between action and appearance. Appearances, such performers would come to profess, like the sleek lines of the thoroughbred, are the result not only of bloodlines but also of training and hard work. Amateur training, whether for the circus or for the Olympics, may not be productive in a strictly utilitarian sense, but it could be said to produce a race of potent, or potentially useful, bodies. Through discipline and hygiene the spectacle of the male body, whether on horseback or in the gymnasium, would no longer be sign of idle wealth but would be an indication of the physical and moral virility needed to govern both self and others. Whereas military might and aristocratic honor could no longer compete with the seductive charms of Buffalo Bill and a growing entertainment industry, nevertheless there was something to be celebrated in the recognition that heredity is no determinant of individual worth. Indeed, as indicated by the image this chapter began with, and with all due respect to Berger, by the turn of the century it is increasingly men who appear and women who act. Like Rosa Bonheur, women act not only as fellow performers but also as observers, authors, and painters who will document and judge the changing appearance of men for generations to come.

CHAPTER SEVEN

Animal Magnetism, Affective Influence, and Moral Dressage

The idea of a "thoroughbred human," as we saw in chapter 6, was inspired by a growing physical education movement that sought to train the body so that its developed lines, taut and sleek, would bear witness to the force of the (masculine) mind behind and within it. The idea of the "embodied mind" is implied in the emphasis on physical endurance at the end of the century and in the image of bodily strength that, as we have seen, the men's circus and the physical education movement of the end of the century were meant to promote and to produce through training. The "embodied mind" was also central for the Idéologues at the very beginning of the century and their promotion of the interdependence of *physique et moral*, or physical and mental well-being.[1] What newly emerged in the Third Republic, concurrent with the training of muscular bodies at the gym and the circus, was a new medical and cultural concern about the effects of heredity and memory on the body, or about how forces of the past (in addition to environmental forces) might influence body and mind together in ways that had little to do with conscious, intentional thought. Nervous diseases like that diagnosed in Lesueur's novel were understood to result from the reflexive function of the brain, confirming the separation of *psychisme et conscience* that would culminate in notions of the Freudian unconscious.[2] Marcel Gauchet calls the work done to prove the material functioning of the brain the "Trojan horse" that was mobilized against the citadel of Freud's unbelievers.[3] As we shall see in this chapter, psychologists and writers often turned to horses to test or illustrate aspects of subjectivity that could escape conscience or consciousness and to enmesh human and animal alike in a material *oeconomie animale*, animal economy, that stripped both of autonomy and self-sovereignty. The dark horse of Plato's *Phaedrus* gains a new symbolic force in this regard to warn of those beastly forces, shared by horses and humans alike, that neither reason nor the will can control. Human beastliness, moreover, would be of far greater magnitude and consequence than its manifestation in horses, whose capacity for training, whether or not they were "well bred," would offer a new model for shaping animality.

FROM ANIMAL ECONOMY TO AFFECT THEORY

The term animal economy dates back to the Enlightenment, when it was used to emphasize the integration of *physique et moral* within human life. To be a "good moralist," concludes the entry on animal economy in the *Encyclopédie*, "one must be an excellent doctor."[4] The implication was that the source of human movement or activity is to be found not in the mind or soul, which was understood only to obscure the question, but rather in the entire system of nerves and fluids that regulate the circulation of impressions and affections. As Philippe Huneman explains, "Animal economy was both a medical and a psychological concept because it dealt with the human organism as a whole, with a psychic as well as an organic life."[5] In its insistence on the interdependence and inseparability of organic and psychic life, the idea of the animal economy can be seen as a precursor to contemporary investigations into the workings of affect, understood as those forces that move us independent of language and conscious intention. Affect works through and on bodies and minds, passing from one to another in ways that reveal our essential porosity to others. Recent affect theory from Teresa Brennan to Brian Massumi surmounts a challenge to the idea of the sovereign and bounded individual by showing how subjectivities are penetrated by and thus subject to the emotions and physical expressions of other bodies.[6] Affect is a kind of influence, but one that may be independent of or prior to apprehended meaning. As such, affect underscores the so-called animality of the human as it also challenges humanist understandings of subjectivity as sovereign and linguistically determined.

Recent debates concerning affect and whether it is or is not wholly physical and independent of mind can be traced back to eighteenth-century considerations of animal magnetism, a concept that similarly threatened accepted boundaries between humans and between humans and other animals. In *The Transmission of Affect*, Teresa Brennan suggests that notions of animal magnetism "led to the subsequent decline of interest in the transmission of affect," but it might be more correct to say that ideas of affective transfer were resisted and suppressed during the course of the nineteenth century, only to resurface in what Gustave Le Bon referred to as "the affective revolution" at the end of the century.[7] The resistance to animal magnetism was tied to negative reactions to eighteenth-century materialist views of those who wished to bring back the influence of the church and reinstate clear hierarchies of the human spirit over the animal body. Animal magnetism challenged man's place in the great chain of being, threatening his pronounced spiritual proximity to God as the human slipped closer to the status of an animal ruled by bodily reflexes and instinct. Darwinian evolution would eventually contribute to growing anxiety over human animality, but such anxieties were already provoked by Enlightenment *philosophes* who stressed the importance of the senses (rather than soul) as the source of knowledge and saw sensibility as a natural and physical basis for moral behavior (as we saw in chapter 1). Efforts to respiritualize the human were a reaction to Enlightenment materialism, whether of a religious right or through the "eclectic spiritualism" that developed from Maine de Biran to Victor Cousin and eventually took hold in the Academy. This effort to respiritualize was extended even to the nonhuman world, as seen in the philosophy of Lamennais, in the poetry of Victor Hugo and Alphonse de Lamartine, or, as we saw in chapter 3, in Rosa Bonheur's painting *The Horse Fair*, where horses emerge from the darkness of the Salpêtrière hospital to enter the light at the center of the canvas.

By the end of the eighteenth century, the Salpêtrière was already well known for its "humane" treatment of the insane and the practice of "moral medicine" developed by Philippe Pinel. In the nineteenth century it would become the birthplace of modern psychiatry, taking over from the priesthood the role of counseling and consoling the mentally ill.[8] As such, the hospital became symbolic of medical contestation against the primacy of the spiritual in human nature and the role religion might play in healing. Whereas priests believed psychiatry to be acting in defiance of the "way of the Lord" because of its focus on the body instead of the soul, psychiatrists saw themselves as *médecins-philosophes* and paid keen attention to physiology and the interactions between mind and body.[9] For them, moreover, religious healing was viewed as another form of charlatanism that was ill equipped to deal with psychological problems. By midcentury such a view was widespread, as Flaubert illustrates in a telling episode in *Madame Bovary*. When Emma finds her way to the curé so that he might "cure her soul," he reports that she must be suffering from digestive problems and prescribes tea. Then, in an implicit comparison, he complains about the cows he was brought to examine that morning for having been put "under a spell." In fact, he consoles, they were only bloated, the result merely of digestive issues.[10]

Whereas the priest's blind focus on the body takes the brunt of Flaubert's irony, the reference to a spell or *sort* placed on the cow hints at the continuing interest in occult practices despite efforts to repress and outlaw them. Of these, animal magnetism was perhaps the most prominent. Many have drawn the line from animal magnetism (first called mesmerism) as a form of healing that put patients in a somnambulist state to hypnosis and other forms of psychological healing that gained recognition toward the end of the century. Little attention has been paid to the status or meaning of the "animal" in animal magnetism, however, whether at its inception or in its various manifestations during the century. And yet, as I will suggest in what follows, it was because magnetism brought human and animal closer together as bodies subject to gravitational as well as unconscious or affective forces that the practice became suspect and threatening to the church and humanists alike. From Balzac's "Passion in the Desert" to Maupassant's 1882 short story "Crazy?" (*Fou?*), men, but more frequently women, are seen to fall under the "spell" of an animal, lending metaphorical support to the perversions of magnetism and its bestial undercurrents. The occult status of magnetism, moreover, and the impossibility of proving or locating the magnetic "fluids" involved were reasons behind its rejection by the Academy of Sciences in 1784 and again in 1840.[11] In his *Introduction to Experimental Medicine* of 1865, Claude Bernard wrote that scientific reason "cannot admit the indeterminable, for this would be only to admit the marvelous, the occult, the supernatural, which must be absolutely banished from all experimental science."[12] Toward the end of the century, however, animal magnetism would once again become worthy of medical consideration, especially in connection with growing interest in hypnosis within the French psychiatric establishment.[13] It was at this point, moreover, that theories of magnetic or hypnotic influence would contribute to new understandings of crowd theory (also known as herd theory), emphasizing the instinctive or reflex-driven animality of human nature in order to lend support to new forms of political control over the unruly and brutish masses. It was in this regard that the writings of Gustave Le Bon were of central importance. And whereas the first animal to be magnetized was a horse (in Lyon in 1784), horses figure prominently for Le Bon as a means for showing the importance of a scientific understanding of unconscious or affective influence and of how that influence can be turned to a means for educating the masses in the service of the state.[14]

The tradition linking animal magnetism to affective influence and hypnosis holds particular relevance for the potential connections between contemporary affect theory and understandings of human animality. "If man shares the capacity to be hypnotized with the animal, could it be because of their common quality of being subjects?" writes the French neurobiologist

Jean-Didier Vincent.[15] The subjectivity that hypnosis and magnetism reveal, like that of the "animal economy," is neither sovereign nor autonomous because the subject *is*, by virtue of being under the influence. That is not to say that the subject is merely reflexive or unknowing, however. Rather, as Vincent writes, "I am because I am moved and because you know it."[16] In what follows, I want briefly to consider the mesmerist movement in order to better understand the place of the animal within animal magnetism and its affective legacies.

MESMER AND THE MATTER OF MAGNETISM

The term animal magnetism was coined in 1773 by the German physician Anton Mesmer to describe invisible forces that act on living bodies. It was to be distinguished from "mineral magnetism" that acts on inorganic matter. Mesmer posited a magnetic, if unseen, fluid whose flow within and between bodies was vital for health. Its blockage was said to be the cause of a range of physical and emotional ills that could be cured by "magnetic passes" by hands held near the locus of injury and believed to transmit energy to unblock the fluid, bringing the body back to health and into harmony with nature and even the cosmos. As François Roustang explains, Mesmer extended the history and understanding of astronomical influence and the gravitational pull between planets to relations between humans as "animal bodies." Indeed, Mesmer first named this force of influence "animal gravitation," only to replace it afterward with "animal magnetism."[17] Such ideas were quickly rejected by the scientific community, and Mesmer's methods were mocked and scorned in the press, in part because of their illicit potential. A cartoon from the period pictures Mesmer with the head of an ass, standing in a contemporary salon while raising his hands in a "pass" that brings a woman to swoon and submit before him (fig. 7.1). Women in particular were seen as compromised victims of his treatments.

At its inception this view of the human at the mercy of natural and material forces found favor with Enlightenment materialism and, as Robert Darnton writes, in the years before the French Revolution there was a frenzy of interest in mesmerism from the academies to the salons and from the queen to the local café.[18] Animal magnetism held particular interest for followers of Condillac, who believed the senses to be the pathway of ideas. Rousseau's writings on the natural sympathy we share with animals (discussed in chapter 1) were also influential for Mesmer's disciple Nicolas Bergasse, who, according to Darnton, turned magnetic theory into a theory of education. As explained by Bergasse, "The action of mesmerist fluid determined the devel-

Figure 7.1. *Le doigt magique, ou Le magnétisme animal.* Engraving in Cornelis Veth, *De arts in de caricatuur* (Amsterdam: Van Munster, ca. 1925). Image courtesy of the Cushing Center, Harvey Cushing/John Hay Whitney Medical Library, Yale University.

opment of children in two ways: through the direct influence of other beings, and indirectly through the transmission of sensations from which children build ideas."[19] A moral education would thus begin by surrounding children with the "right sort of people." Conversely, we will find that at the end of the century moral education will be especially concerned with gatherings of the wrong sort of people, whose transmissions build immoral mobs.

Sensationalism would also be the focus of the group of Idéologues formed under the leadership of Destutt de Tracy in 1795 who, according to George Boas, "emphasized the animality of the human mind."[20] Perhaps this is why, as we saw in chapter 1, the Idéologues were the first to propose animal welfare as a public concern. Indeed, Destutt de Tracy wrote in his preface to the *Éléments d'idéologie* that ideology (the study of ideas), "is a branch of zoology."[21] But as Boas adds, this text may account for the negative reaction to "ideology" and its materialist basis: "For the people during the Empire were no longer willing to admit that they were on a level with the brutes. They had a more lofty conception of the human spirit."[22]

Despite the rejection of magnetism from the standpoints of science and of religion, the practice infiltrated popular culture and literature. As it did so, its meanings and animal associations shifted to lend support to Romantic and mystical understandings of the human spirit rather than giving evidence for the priority of the senses.[23] Balzac is a case in point. His novel *Ursule Mirouët* is a commentary on magnetism and its affiliation with physiognomy, calling attention to the "imperceptible fluid, the base of the phenomena of human will from which result the passions, the habits, and the form of the face and skull."[24] Chris Rivers writes that for Balzac the major significance of this fluid is the link it creates between human and animal physiologies. This is the link Balzac articulates in his preface where, we might remember, he admits to constructing *The Human Comedy* according to a model of zoology and to the "comparison between humanity and animality" that culminated in the debates between the natural historians Georges Cuvier and Étienne Geoffroy Saint-Hilaire. As Balzac explains, one finds in the mystical writings of Swedenborg and Saint Martin, as in the naturalist writings of Leibnitz, Buffon, and Bonnet, the law of *soi pour soi*, or that innate property of matter that underlies the idea of "the unity of composition."[25]

Balzac refers to zoology to call attention to the influence of *milieu* or exterior forces on individual development and form, but clearly this is not the materialist zoology promoted by Destutt de Tracy. For Balzac life originates with the Creator—whether in its human form or its animal form—and both forms are subject to their environments. But whereas for animals milieu is "a geographical, climatic, and ecological phenomenon," human society is also influenced at a secondary level by history, economy, and sociological groups.[26] For him, this is the level where ideas are formed, written, and exchanged.

Balzac himself was a convert to the healing powers of magnetism, which he referred to as his "favorite science," and he would even offer his services as a magnetizer to help heal his friends.[27] But what becomes apparent in Balzac is that the success of magnetic healing depends less, if at all, on that affective and bodily "sympathy" described by Bergasse and Deleuze and more on the will of the magnetizer, an effective force that is regarded as foremost a function of the *esprit* or spirit. Thus, in *Louis Lambert* (a novel that was described as "a protest against materialism"), magnetism is associated with electricity, heat, and light, but only insofar as these are all endowed with that uniform substance of the Creator understood alternatively as energy, spirit, and the Word.[28] Will as directed energy and spirit is what operates on other, weaker wills and also on inorganic matter (not vice versa). This understanding of the vital fluid as a function of volition that precedes and "commands" sensation will be emphasized by Edgar Allen Poe in his *Philosophy of Animal Magnetism*. Since the will acts as the intermediary between body and soul and keeps the body under the soul's control, animal magnetism, Poe writes, "is a powerful support of true religion."[29] Balzac understood animals to also have volition, but not of the same magnitude as man's. In this he perpetuates a line of reasoning expressed by the influential Catholic and mystical thinker Pierre-Simon Ballanche, who professed that animal domestication was achieved by virtue of the magnetic power that men hold over animals and through which they share in their passions and projects. "The horse is a part of his noble master and is ignited by his passions."[30]

If magnetizers were men of superior will, the question thus arose of how far those who were magnetized were creatures whose wills were diseased or at least naturally weaker, like those of animals, indigents, or even women. Susceptibility to magnetism was thus claimed to be either a universal trait or a sign of inferiority, whether of the mind or the body—the same question that would divide two schools of thought surrounding the practice of hypnosis toward the end of the century. On the one hand, the school of Nancy believed that hypnotism worked because of the brain's physiological suggestibility. Anyone, healthy or sick, could be hypnotized. On the other side of the debate was Jean-Martin Charcot, director of the Salpêtrière, who claimed that the capacity to be hypnotized was a function of hysteria and proof of an abnormal neurological condition.

Whether as a function of disease or of a natural physiological process, mental contagion and its hysterical effects would lend their weight to explain the series of popular uprisings in France from the Revolution to the Commune. Such theories increasingly turned to metaphors of the brute or herd behavior especially evident in crowds. It was the critic Hippolyte Taine who suggested that men and women in crowds "revert to a state of nature," a state controlled not by Rousseau's instinct of pity, but by Hobbes's wolfish aggression. Natural man, for Taine, is a brutal beast, a baboon controlled by appetite.[31] Taine suggested that the working classes revolted for "animal" reasons of poverty or hunger, but he also advanced the idea of mental contagion as a naturalized weakness, prevalent especially among the lower classes and women. Women especially were regarded as susceptible to the "infectious malady" of the crowd because they are most controlled by their appetites.[32] Many of Taine's ideas find their literary counterpart in the writings of naturalists like Zola, but in his work horses also offer a counterpoint to, rather than an illustration of, the herd mentality of human crowds.

HORSES AND HYSTERIA IN *GERMINAL*

In *Germinal*, Zola's 1885 novel about a miners' strike in the prefecture of Lille, the miners' bedrooms are said to "reek of the human herd," women are seen with their breasts exposed like udders to suck on, and a young girl working "down on all fours with her backside in the air" is held responsible for the "whiff of animal lust" in the air.[33] Humans and animals are seen to share a manifest susceptibility to milieu, where milieu is both the material environment and the others within it. The effects are both physical and mental, turning the miners' saliva black and hastening a kind of hysteria even in the horses. Permanently enslaved within the darkness of the underground, it is the horses who go mad from searching for the light they once knew.

At the center of the novel is the Maheu family, miners for generations past and, with seven children, for generations to come. The toll of heredity and environment is most visible in the ten-year-old son Jeanlin, described as having the "instinctual intelligence and quick dexterity of some freakish human runt which had reverted to its original state" (188). But as these several children prove, heredity and environment have different effects on different individuals, and Jeanlin's sadistic tendencies find their contrast in his sister Catherine, who is hardworking, responsible, and clearly a victim of sexual assault.[34] Indeed, in Catherine one sees also that herd mentality is above all a matter of blind obedience to the "deity" of the mine, on whom they depend for their food and livelihood. "Animals they no doubt were," thinks the owner of one of the mines shortly before the strike, "but animals who could not read and were starving to death" (329).

Zola's mention of reading is significant. Taine saw the origins of the crowd in a horde whose leaders would be drawn from its own lowest elements.[35] Étienne Lantier, the mechanic who instigates the miners' strike, is distinguished from the others by his reading, and more generally by his intellect and education. "He'd had more of an education than the rest of them, which meant he didn't share their herd-like sense of resignation, and he'd only end up strangling the life out of one boss or another" (63). It is Étienne who inspires the workers' revolt, not by rousing their animal appetites, but rather by speaking dreamily about an "age of equality" where sunshine swept away the deprivation and wretchedness and where "justice, as if by some dazzling enchantment, came down from above" (171). It is with these ideas that one by one the miners fall "under the spell" and "enter the fairyland of hope" (171) he conjures up. Having roused their desire for that better world, however, Étienne is unable to control the passions he has unleashed, passions that strike out with vengeance against everything and everyone that might stand in the way of achieving the dream. Jeanlin's atavistic savagery is the most accurate portrait of these. In one scene toward the end of the novel Étienne himself feels a certain "repugnance" toward the "wretched people lying on top of each other. . . . They might as well be animals." And as he sets himself apart from and above them, he realizes that his thinking is "lending him the soul of one of those bourgeois he so despised" (381). Opposed in their methods yet alike in their desires, brutes and bourgeois reveal the inadequacy and potential violence wrought by oppositions between us and them, human and animal.

Many have understood Zola's crowds through the lenses of Taine's and Le Bon's theories of mental contagion and the brutish behavior it is said to produce. But the meaning of the brute is complicated by the presence in the novel of the horses, whose labor is both symbolic and real. On the one hand Monsieur Hennebeau, director and part owner of the central mine operation called Le Voreux, is frequently seen astride his mare with "his coat buttoned up like a uniform" (268), much like General Boulanger, who was already well known as a military leader. Boulanger's unparalleled popularity during the Third Republic was often connected to the magnetic attraction of his image on horseback, but as his attraction and his bid for political power were quickly extinguished by his retreat in shame, so Hennebeau is revealed to be a pathetic figure, pining for love and cuckolded by his wife.

Most horses in *Germinal*, however, are the workhorses of the mines. They are even more enslaved than the workers because, as one miner suggests, "at least a person can decide if they want to go down there or not" (427). These are creatures for whom daylight is only a memory, who spend their days hauling heavy cartloads through dank, narrow underground tunnels. Their different reactions to their work and environment, importantly, attest to their individuality and their unique psychologies.[36]

Battle, a white horse who had already "served" ten years in the mine, is referred to as "an elder statesman" (59). He knows his routine, is described as "clever" in opening doors with his head or in remembering where to stoop because of low ceilings. He also knows when it is quitting time and refuses to start another turn (60). When a newcomer named Trumpet arrives, Battle welcomes him with a whinny and a "sob of tender pity . . . sadness at the sight of yet another prisoner who would never return to the surface alive" (61). The friendship between Battle and Trumpet is by far the most genuine and selfless of the novel. Battle, with the "warm compassion of an elderly philosopher," attempts to comfort Trumpet at every chance he gets but is unable to help the younger horse adapt to the life of the mine. Toward the end of the novel he finds him lying in the straw, dying of his misery.

> He had never been able to accustom himself to life underground. He had always looked miserable and never wanted to work, as though tormented by longing for the daylight he had lost. Battle, the doyen of the pit horses, had tried in vain to pass on some of his ten years' accumulated compliance by rubbing up against him in a friendly way and nibbling at his neck. . . . Each time they met and exchanged a snort, they both seemed to be uttering a lament, the older horse because he could no longer remember, the younger because he could not yet forget. (426)

With tropes of enlightenment used to describe the hunger for bodily nourishment, Zola echoes Victor Hugo's description of a "a soul dying from hunger for the light," as Trumpet also exposes the power that memories of the past hold over the present.[37] Much as Freud says of hysterics, Trumpet's illness and death are caused by reminiscences, in this case reminiscences of what would not be repeated: of the light he was prevented from ever seeing again.

Of the many murders and killings and deaths of workers and children in *Germinal*, the deaths described most movingly are those of the horses.[38] The deaths of both Trumpet and, following him, Battle are heart-wrenching. We witness Battle's desperate but ultimately vain efforts to nuzzle and comfort his new friend, and when he also dies we are reminded only of his innate goodwill and good sense. The intimately described details of his horrific drowning in the floodwaters that overtake the mines can only be read as tragic. Unlike the attitude earlier in the century, for Zola pity or empathy for the horse and between horses has become a worthy subject of literature.[39] In the juxtaposition of animal empathy and human brutality, moreover, he challenges simple oppositions between human and animal. Whereas Jeanlin's brutality is said to be caused by degeneration and the reversion to an "original state," that original state bears no similarity to the horses in the novel, whose only evidence of destructiveness is the torment Trumpet enacts on himself.

What humans and horses share in the novel is hunger—hunger for food, for companionship, or for the light. It is hunger, not weakness, that turns the obedient herd into a destructive pack simply through the power of suggestion, by feeding images or memories of a better life. Gilles Deleuze and Félix

Guattari promoted the pack as leading to creative forms of involution that work against capitalist injustice. Packs, they suggested, could "proliferate by contagion, epidemics, battlefields and catastrophes," and their proliferation led to creative forms of "involution" that work against capitalist injustice.[40] But whereas Zola's pack is also the product of a protest that causes catastrophes and minefields of destruction, there is no creative outcome. Out of necessity, the miners return to the herd. We see the injustice and subjection wrought on the herd as "state" or corporate animals, but the protesting pack was never innocent or transformative in its destructive involution.

The novel closes with the question of what, if anything, could have been done to ensure that contagion would be productive and creative rather than simply destructive. This is the question Étienne ponders as he thinks back over what went wrong and tries to imagine how it might be righted, how a "new dawn of truth and justice" could break so that the workers would take power and become the masters" (532). As Étienne takes his leave of Montsou and the ruined mines, the narrator turns to the signs of spring: the April sun, the budding trees, and the fields bursting with new life. This is the time of "Germinal," the seventh month of the Revolutionary calendar, and faith in nature must take over from faith in God, the human and nonhuman worlds working in concert. New life there will be—the strongest will survive, so science tells us—but it is unclear whether the strongest will be new masters who change the shape of history or whether they will be like Battle, merely adapting to revolution as a natural and historical cycle over which they have little power, like the Earth revolving around the sun. The last line of the novel offers little hope: "New men were starting into life, a black army of vengeance slowly germinating in the furrows, growing for the harvests of the century to come; and soon this germination would tear the earth apart" (532).

GUSTAVE LE BON, ZOOPSYCHOLOGY, AND MORAL DRESSAGE

"I believe that the crowd, the common herd will always be hateful. The only important thing is a little group of minds—always the same—which passed the torch from one to another." So wrote Gustave Flaubert to George Sand in September 1871, adding that for France's rebirth "she must pass from Inspiration to Science, she must abandon all metaphysics in favor of objective inquiry—that is, the examination of reality."[41] Flaubert's statement is premonitory of Third Republic efforts to move away from metaphysical explanations for human and nonhuman nature and to observe and discover the biological and physical laws for why and how things are what (or who) they are. Memory, like that which killed Trumpet, is proof that horses (and other animals) share a psychology with humans, leading to the founding of the first Institute for Zoological Psychology in Paris at the turn of the century. But as memory was increasingly regarded as a biological phenomenon affecting and affected by heredity and evolution, there were also different schools of thought about how far memories and the habits or "instincts" they produced in the body were intractable and to what extent they could, perhaps in Lamarckian fashion, be changed by a change in milieu and the behaviors it enacted.

According to the French psychologist Théodule-Armand Ribot, instinct "is a sum of hereditary habits."[42] Ribot's writings on the "maladies of memory" had a strong influence on Zola's works, where memory infects the body much like Étienne's inherited alcoholism. As Laura Otis writes, "Zola was the writer of heredity and memory par excellence: in his hands, organic memory became a tragedy, a mythology, an uncontrolled biomechanical force driving the narrative."[43] The question for Zola, as for psychology, was not only whether inherited diseases can be overcome, but also whether and how new habits and instincts can be learned and passed on. Why was Trumpet never able to acquire the habits needed to survive? Was temperament or training what distinguished him from Battle? Ribot and other zoological psychologists understood that the most powerful force behind instinct was milieu, and for Zola milieu included everything from working conditions to education. It was the latter that protected Étienne from the mental contagion of the other workers and that he hoped—rightly or wrongly—would eventually act as an evolutionary force to implement the conditions for a different world order. As Étienne wonders "whether all the violence had really helped their cause," he represents Zola's progressive views and looks forward to the day when "the law might provide a more terrible and powerful weapon" (531).

Ten years after the writing of *Germinal*, Gustave Le Bon responds negatively to Étienne's hopes by insisting that neither reason nor laws can change character. Crowds are to be led not with rules or institutions, he writes, "but by seeking what produces an impression on them, and what seduces them."[44] Impression, seduction, magnetism, these would be key notions in Le Bon's 1895 study *The Crowd* (*Psychologie des foules*), a text dedicated to Ribot and influential both for Freud's understanding of herd theory and for the establishment of the first zoological institute of psychology. For Le Bon, neither laws nor education, neither bodybuilding nor breeding, could counteract the insurmountable forces of heredity that determined personality. A conservative Republican, Le Bon believed there was no use trying to change what he regarded as inborn characteristics of race, sex, and class, those characteristics that are exaggerated by the "feminine" behavior of crowds. The effect of crowds is to swamp conscious and individual capabilities with the homogeneous and unconscious effects of heredity, or what he calls "historical race." Race, for Le Bon, refers not to the body per se but to the hereditary forces stored in the body and unleashed by a form of emotional contagion to which intelligence offers little resistance. It is less a matter of morphophysiological differences than the sum of qualities acquired over time, including those moral, religious, and political convictions that "become so fixed in the soul that everybody accepts them without discussion."[45] Such racial domination is especially unleashed in crowds, which function regressively to return men to what Herbert Spencer described as a homogeneous past, if not to a state that is closer to animals. Certain "inferior" races and individuals are more susceptible to such domination because of their biological inheritance. Women in particular, Le Bon argued, have cranial structures closer to gorillas than to men, with the result that their brains are "condemned" not to evolve past childhood. Consequently, higher education of the intellect is dangerous for women, as Daniel Lesueur's novel confirmed.

While one cannot erase one's race, Le Bon argues that one can "train" the unconscious to strengthen its resistance to crowds and the dangerous influences of heredity. What inferior beings and races need is affective, moral training that works by turning conscious responses to stimuli into unconscious habits. This is training that he has learned with and from horses, as he underscores in his article on the psychology of dressage, originally published in the *Revue psychologique de France* in 1894 and in his book-length work on equitation, published two years before his work on crowd theory. "From the point of view of psychology and education, on the means of penetrating the brain of inferior beings, on the manner of transforming conscious movements into unconscious ones, on the mechanisms of persuasion and of obedience, the horse has taught me a lot."[46] Horses take the place of students as Le Bon professes that "all education must have as its goal the transformation of conscious acts into unconscious acts. . . . Morality itself is created in the same way. . . . Whether it is a question of training a horse or his rider, the method is always the same: repeat the associations until the presence of one signal fatally provokes the act associated with that signal."[47] Indeed, he says such education is usually more quickly accomplished in an animal than in humans, where reason too often intervenes to thwart the accumulation of hereditary reflexes that allows for morality to become unconscious. Correct equitation, *équitation savante*, must be based on scientific principles—principles, moreover, that cannot be explained by riders—for they, like their horses, have already turned these principles into habits and thus have forgotten them. If the same principles are to be applied to establishing moral behavior in the nation, it will, for such reasons, be up to educated scientists like Le Bon, beyond mere trainers, to articulate them.

On one hand Le Bon illustrates the distance animal science has traveled since Descartes, acknowledging that horses, like humans, have a psychology that must be considered in training. As the chief trainer for the Saumur Cavalry School writes in his preface to the book, "For the first time I saw someone isolate and put the horse's personality on par with man's and speak of shared responsibilities."[48] On the other hand, as he emphasizes a psychological continuum between man and horse, so does he naturalize divisions among humans and between the born leaders/scientists who can understand the principles of moral education and those who must merely undergo those principles. Horses may be "like the common people [*le peuple*] and children" in their susceptibility to training, but unlike horses and common people, some can grow out of their animal-like state: those who, born of a superior and we can assume European race, have the capacity for higher-level reasoning. Le Bon implies that these men of science are the born leaders of France and must be recognized as such if France is to prepare itself for the modern world.

Le Bon went further than most thinkers in his analogy of education to animal training, but he was not alone in connecting the horse to notions of moral citizenship. As we saw in chapter 6, by the end of the century metaphors of the horse and horsemanship resurfaced in relation to the new sports and hygiene movement that was critical of the French educational system's intellectual emphasis. Le Bon's criticisms of France's educational system bear echoes of Nietzsche's disdain for the "herd morality" and his expression of the need for leaders and scientists like himself who know how to dominate and control the herd. Both Nietzsche and Le Bon saw themselves as psychologists of sorts, philosopher-scientists who understood the mind as embodied, material, and as such susceptible to suggestion. "One will see that under mind I include foresight, patience, dissimulation, great self-control, and all that is mimicry," wrote Nietzsche.[49] For both Le Bon and Nietzsche, mimicry and suggestibility were behaviors of "inferior" and weak humans. But whereas for Nietzsche weakness showed itself especially in expressions of self-denial, for Le Bon and a nation still reeling after a century of upheavals from the Terror to the Commune, mimicry and suggestibility were associated with the dangers of the people's revolt and thus warranted political and psychological control. Training, for Le Bon, was a viable political and psychological means of controlling the herd.

Unlike either the eighteenth-century revolution in sensibility that resulted in Rousseau's praise of sympathy as a natural and moral state or Mesmer's view of sympathy as the basis for affective healing, the later affective revolution would appear to condemn sympathy as the physical and instinctive cause of mimicry and contagion, what Nietzsche condemned as "anti-nature." "Strong ages, noble cultures, see in pity, in 'love of one's neighbor,' in a lack of self and self-reliance, something contemptible," writes Nietzsche, for whom pity and sympathy are responsible for a negatively tame and "gelded society."[50] The prevalence of animal metaphors and references in Nietzsche lends all the more support to his celebration of a virile bodily instinct. But in comparing contemporary psychologists to horses, he betrays a self-conscious caution. "There are times when we are like horses, we psychologists, and grow restive: we see our shadow moving up and down before us. The psychologist has to look away from *himself*, to see at all."[51]

Psychologists, like horses, must look away from themselves so that their own passions—whether fears or desires—do not interfere with the training or healing process. Horses may be trained to respond to the learned, repeated stimuli proposed by Le Bon—this is the education of dressage. But they cannot always be counted on to ignore other, unanticipated signals. In this, moreover, they may reveal aspects of our human selves that we prefer not to see. *Twilight of the Idols* was written during the last year of Nietzsche's "sane" life, just before the alleged Turin episode where, in response to witnessing the hideous beating of a horse, he is said to have thrown his arms around the animal's neck and collapsed into madness. According to Roland Barthes, Nietzsche had "gone mad for pity's sake," succumbing to the very "moral" and mimetic sympathy he so often assailed.[52]

As psychologists, Le Bon and Nietzsche are committed to a particular notion of what it is to be human and of who they are as human males of a certain breed or race. Why does the psychologist study men? Nietzsche asks. "He wants to gain little advantages over them, or big ones too—he is a politician." At least the politician-psychologist "involves" himself with others, unlike the "impersonal" psychologist who wants "an even worse advantage: to feel himself superior to men, to have the right to look down on them, no longer to confuse himself with them."[53] In Nietzsche's mind, we might assume, only an impersonal psychologist would deign to study women and nonhuman animals.

AFFECTIVE TRAINING AND/AS COEDUCATION

With his emphasis on training as moral education, Le Bon's foray into the principles of equitation would mark the beginning of a new field of zoological psychology that spread throughout Europe. Less than ten years after the publication of his text (and before its second edition), the German comparative biologist-psychologist Oskar Pfungst would carry out his formal investigation of the horse who became known as Clever Hans. Hans was reported to have superior intellectual skills and to perform an array of mathematical computations. Pfungst discovered, however, that Hans had no such skills, and the "Clever Hans effect" became a cautionary warning to animal scientists of the dangers of anthropomorphism. What Pfungst did discover, and what the "hoax" obscured, was that Hans was responding to subtle cues that his trainers didn't know they were giving. Unlike the cues Le Bon writes about, Pfungst's cues were never consciously planned. As historian of science Vincianne Despret writes, "Yes, it was a beautiful case of influence, but it was moreover a wonderful opportunity to explore a fascinating question. Indeed, the horse could not count, but he could make human bodies be moved and affected, and move and affect other beings and perform things without their owners' knowledge." Hans was able to make his examiners talk to him without realizing they were doing so, through a body language that he could read and respond to. In this way, Despret concludes, "both, human and horse, are cause and effect of each other's movements such that who influences whom has no clear answer."[54] Nietzsche's impersonal psychologist must thus stand ready to be threatened by horses, because as Stanley Cavell also surmised, horses stand as "a rebuke to our unreadiness to be understood . . . our will to remain obscure."[55]

It is a short step and moral leap from Zola and Le Bon's horses to Hans. "A beautiful case of influence": Despret's rhetoric signals how far we have come in understanding that affective transfer happens not only between humans, but also between humans and nonhumans. "I am because I am moved and because you know it," even if I don't.[56] We might see Hans as an evolved Mesmer, once a donkey and now a horse who is in such sympathetic attunement with his human as to make him readable. Perhaps it took distance from the quackery and sexual abuse associated with Mesmer and animal magnetism to enable a new appreciation of the animal side of the story and to recognize not only the "sensibility" of nonhuman animals but also the extent of their capacity for psychological attunement to others, including humans. Such attunement is one reason equine-assisted therapy is so effective and has become so popular today.

The point is not, moreover, that suggestibility and attunement are mere bodily reflexes that bypass cognitive faculties. Such a view merely reinstates a Cartesian dichotomy between mind and body, much like recent theories that focus on mirror neurons and empathy as an automatic, sympathetic response to another's face or pain. This is a view supported by neuroscience, whereby Frans de Waal writes, "We activate neural representations of motor actions in our own brain similar to the ones we perceive or expect in the other. That we do so unconsciously has been tested with facial expressions on a computer screen."[57] Historian of science Ruth Leys has questioned the incentives behind focusing on empathy as an automatic and reflexive force and wonders to what extent this trend is due to efforts to overcome the human-animal divide. But, she adds, "there is nothing about the cognitive or intentionalist position that limits the capacity for cognition and intentionality to human animals. Nor is there anything about the cognitive position that is opposed to the idea that humans and nonhuman animals are emotionally embodied creatures and that this fact is of the highest importance."[58]

As psychologists, ethologists, or literary critics, we are still looking for the best language to express the ways species are porous to each other physically, emotionally, and intellectually. We are affected by them, done and "undone" by them emotionally and through evolution, which is why Donna Haraway writes that we, as subjects or as partners, do not "precede our relatings."[59] Rather, we become in and through our relations with other creatures. Such becoming is quite different from that of Deleuze, moreover, which he proudly presents as an escape from the past. For Haraway, rather, even if the legacies of the past will not be the sole determinants of the future, they must be acknowledged. Only in coming to terms with a past can it be rewritten or redirected toward a different future.[60]

This is a becoming that Gustave Le Bon tried to guard against, that we can be changed by our relationships—that the body and race are not the sole determinants of who we are. His understanding is very different from more recent views of what training and education can do or be, such as that of the late philosopher and animal trainer Vicki Hearne. Whereas for Le Bon training was a process of learning to control bodily reflex so as to keep instinct at bay, for Hearne training is a means of developing a language that both parties can speak and so learn to say something new. "If we describe the integrity of a language as the physical, intellectual and spiritual distance talking enables the speakers of that language to travel together, then it looks very much as though the dog and the horse have a greater command of language than chimpanzees do."[61] For Hearne training is a means of entering a relationship and developing a language shared by horse and rider (or dog and handler) with which each can be said to speak, not merely to react.

The training relationship reveals how far animals and humans both act and are acted on so as to produce a jointly constituted language and subjectivity. Language in this regard is not merely spoken language, since it is a function of bodily signification and desire as well as words. Referencing the age-old opposition of mind and body, Judith Butler reminds us that "it is one of the great contributions of feminist philosophy to call those dichotomies into question and so to ask as well whether in sensing, something called thinking is already at work, whether in acting, we are also acted upon."[62] This susceptibility to the other—human and nonhuman alike—was the very theory behind animal magnetism, a theory that was resisted and criticized during the course of the nineteenth century because of its threat to the priority of a humanist subject defined by reason and language. It was also threatening, if less manifestly so, because it acknowledged nonhuman animals as subjects in their own right, subjects who are also capable of affecting humans.

In training, horse and rider enter into a history through which each is transformed by the other. Our habits are not what they were when we began. This is true for our ontological histories and for our evolutionary histories, both products of our entangled and changing relations with others—human and nonhuman. The effects of such training can lead us to think of evolution less in terms of species or individuals than of interspecies *ménages* or *manèges*—households and riding schools that account for our entangled ontologies. Such a notion has been raised in other terms by the contemporary French philosopher-ethologist Dominique Lestel, who writes that "what is important is not only to think the evolution of organisms, but to think together the evolution and history of organisms as they are intertwined. Ecology does that very well at the level of behavior," he adds, "but I want to do it at the ontological level: how the nature of organisms . . . evolves as a function of other organisms.[63] Writing about experiments where a researcher wants to intrude as little as possible so as not to "perturb" the animal he or she is observing, Lestel writes, "The interesting question is not how NOT to perturb the animal (which is important, we must be clear on this point), but to understand why an animal is so easily perturbed by a human."[64]

Reading Despret, we might want to change the question Lestel poses to animals from Why are you perturbed? to Why do you care? or Why are you so attuned to me and to other humans as to be affected by us? It is not a bad question, although one that may lead to endless arguments over origins or nature. A better question may be to ask the horse, Can I engage your interest and affection in ways that will do justice to them? What counts as a proper response to this question will, of course, be controversial. Some animal "abolitionists" will claim that any form of training is a form of enslavement and a means of subordinating other animals to humans.[65] Susceptibility, the capacity to be affected, however, as Butler also claims, is not the same as subjugation, even if it can lead to exploitation. Indeed, I suggest that exploitation cannot be acknowledged without also acknowledging susceptibility, which is to say sensibility or being sensitive to another. If the exploitation of horses became especially visible over the course of the nineteenth century, whether in the horrid conditions of the mines or on the streets, it was in part because of the growing awareness of horses' susceptibility to others, of their willingness to participate and learn a job, if also to resist. Le Bon acknowledged these capacities only to exploit them for his own ends.

Any effort at communication can be manipulative, but it can also be mutually inspiring as intellectual, physical, and moral capacities are excited and expanded for horse and human alike. That training may change the nature of a horse is no more argument against it than saying that education can change the nature of a child. Instead, we should underscore the possibilities for mutual training, horse and human each effecting habitual responses in the other by learning to read the other and make the other readable.

The resistance to ideas of animal magnetism during much of the nineteenth century was effectively a refusal to recognize a different Enlightenment subject, one defined as much by material and affective forces as by the rational mind. It was a refusal to acknowledge our human animality, our susceptibility to being affected by others—human and animal—in ways we cannot always know or control. How much horses have figured in the many ways we have tried to understand the forces of influence, will, and sympathy is as much a function of the many partnerships between humans and horses as of how we come to recognize susceptibility itself as a productive capacity that makes possible training and education, and indeed mutual affection. Recognizing this in ourselves as in the horses and other animals we live with is a step toward making our own training and education more open to discovery, to generosity, and ultimately to justice.[66]

AFTERWORD

As I was completing the manuscript for this book I made a trip to New York City for the Delacroix retrospective on view at the Metropolitan Museum of Art. I had read Peter Schjeldahl's review in the *New Yorker* and knew I had to see it. Even as he belittles what he describes as Delacroix's tendency to show off, Schjeldahl is won over by one feature in his works: "But the horses! Like movie stars, they register as at once archetypal and particular—obliging but slightly aloof in their violent roles."[1] According to Schjeldahl, it is in the horses that Delacroix reveals the deepest feelings and instincts of life. I knew, of course, that horses figure frequently in his works (and I've included brief mention of one of them in chapter 2), but because they typically appear in more fantastical scenes of Arabian life and warfare ("cultural booty of imperialism" as Schjeldahl points out) than in local scenes of France, his horses held less interest for my purposes in this book. As I walked through the exhibition, however, I was struck by the central roles they play. Indeed, I found them to be fantastically indicative of the ubiquity of horses in the nineteenth century and of their literal and symbolic importance at that time. Delacroix's horses are partners to his humans in every sense, carrying them through distant lands, aiding them in battle, but also joining them in offering peace and sustenance. Thus one painting shows a mare being milked as she turns to look acceptingly at her human. Delacroix's horses, however, are also victims of that partnership, withstanding violent attacks by humans and lions alike. And what was especially telling, and newly apparent to me in these works, was the way Delacroix paints the horse as witness, figured with one eye on the violence of the scene and one on the viewer who is pulled in by his (or her) often terrified look. The lateral placement of horses' eyes perfectly positions them to allow for such a range of vision. As historical actors in these scenes, the horses also solicit the viewers' gaze and implore them to notice and respond to the lives and suffering shared by human and nonhuman animals alike. They remind us that horses and other animals have a point of view with regard to the action, one we would do well to consider, to the extent that we can know it.

Horses' eyes are no longer upon us as they were for Delacroix and others for much of the nineteenth century, when they were an integral part of daily life. Their beauty and power are no longer seen on the streets or in the parks (the last mounted policeman in New York City just announced his retirement), and neither are we faced with the many ways they labor for us and trust in us, often right up to the time of slaughter. Only those who work closely with horses are aware of how sensitive their bodies are to our touch and our voices—a sensitivity that is all too easy to exploit and abuse. Horses have perhaps been replaced in this regard by dogs and cats and other pets who are largely confined to the home. To be sure, some working dogs may remind us of some of the varied and important roles horses once held in our public lives, but they cannot compete with that inescapable presence and significance.

In our Anthropocene age, we would do well to remember the horse as witness, to take heed of that nonhuman eye upon us in our battles, our travels, and our daily escapades through city streets or country fields. We should ask ourselves how that eye might regard and respond to our current modes of travel and transport—whether cars, trucks, or planes—and what that eye might be seeing that we miss. We should remind ourselves of the effects our lives and lifestyles have on the many creatures whose lives depend on us as we remember how our lives once depended on horses.

ACKNOWLEDGMENTS

First I thank the editors of the Animal Lives series at the University of Chicago Press. I could not have hoped for sager or more enthusiastic advice than I received from the series editor, Jane Desmond, and her associate editor, Kim Marra, was the perfect partner who set a high bar in equine expertise. Dylan Joseph Montanari at the press attended to a myriad of details with surprising speed and precision, and I am grateful to Alice Bennett for her careful copyediting. I am also indebted to Douglas Mitchell, former executive editor at Chicago, for initially spurring the project forward and keeping it steady in harness through to his retirement; he was a master of equestrian puns. His death was a shock, and he will be greatly missed.

Because I began research related to this book so long ago, I fear I have forgotten some of the people who gave input along the way, and to them I apologize. I do remember—it may have been twenty years ago—sitting and discussing horses in nineteenth-century France with Margaret (Peggy) Waller, who then began to map out chapter possibilities, proving to me that this could be a book. Thank you, Peggy. Early versions of chapters were presented to astute audiences at nineteenth-century French studies meetings and shared with my Nineteenth-Century French Studies colleague (and longtime friend) Mary Harper, who has been an endless fount of insight and enthusiasm for my work. As I moved more and more into animal studies, the Society for Literature, Science, and the Arts (SLSA) became an increasingly important venue for my work, and Richard Nash, Ron Broglio, Karen Raber, and more recently Lynn Turner have been especially helpful interlocutors. The initial meeting of the Living with Horses conference of 2013 at Eastern Kentucky University was also timely for my research, and I thank Gala Argent and Angela Hofstetter for inviting me and indulging me in horse talk at the highest levels. I also thank Stephen Houston and Susan Curry for inviting me to participate in the 2013 Mellon Foundation Sawyer Seminar on Animal Magnetism and the Emotional Bond at Brown University. I owe credit to that seminar for bringing me to rethink the history of "magnetic attraction." Thanks are also due to the newly formed Faculty in Animal Studies Working Group at Brown, including Nancy Jacobs, Thalia Field, Thangam Ravindranathan, and Connie Crawford, for inviting me back to Brown in 2017 to present more recent research. Their thoughtful questions continue to engage my own thinking, as does their own work with and writing on animals. Thanks also to Chiara Mengozzi for her invitation and warm welcome to the Human-Animal Line conference at the Centre français de recherche en sciences sociales (CEFRES) in Prague.

At Wesleyan University, members of the Eighteenth-Century Group were kind enough to extend their focus into the next century and invite me to present work from the book. Deep thanks go to Andy Curran, Courtney Weiss-Smith, Roger Grant, and Stephanie Weiner for ongoing conversations and inspiration. And I could not have gotten through the labyrinth of image permissions without the help of our art librarian, Susanne Javorski. Thank you for your speedy and thorough research, Susanne.

My final thanks are to my husband, Michael Roth, our daughter Sophie, and the horses who have carried me over the years: Cacahuète, Cash, Bay Knight, and Ender. Michael not only was a discerning reader of many of the chapters but also has indulged me in my equine partnerships. And though I no longer have the pleasure of watching Sophie on horseback as I did when she was younger, I am gratified that she regards my riding as a healthy habit and encourages me to continue.

This book is dedicated to the memory of Holly Rothschild, my friend from childhood and self-elected godsister. Holly and I went to horse camp together outside Chicago where we grew up and spent many enchanting summer afternoons of our youth riding through the woods of northern Michigan. I thank Holly for teaching me to love horses, even as I always wondered if I could live up to the skill, ease, and beauty she rode with. May she be cantering comfortably atop the clouds.

Some of the material here has previously appeared in publications that have graciously granted permission to reproduce my work.

Parts of chapter 1 appeared as "Heads or Tails: Géricault's Horses and the Painting of (Natural) History," *Antennae: The Journal of Nature in Visual Culture* 25 (Summer 2013): 66–82.

Parts of chapter 2 appeared in "La guerre au sujet de la pitié: De Rousseau à Derrida," in *Zoopoétique: Des animaux en littérature moderne de langue française*, ed. André Benhaïm and Anne Simon, special issue of *La revue des sciences humaines* 328 (April 2017): 165–81, and in my essay "Empathy," in *The Edinburgh Companion to Animal Studies*, ed. Lynn Turner, Undine Sellbach, and Ron Broglio (Edinburgh: Edinburgh University Press, 2018), 126–39.

Parts of chapter 4 appeared as "They Eat Horses, Don't They?," *Gastronomica: The Journal of Critical Food Studies* 7, no. 2 (Spring 2007): 44–51.

Part of chapter 5 appeared first as "Purebreds and *Amazones*: Saying Things with Horses in Nineteenth-Century France," *Differences: A Journal of Feminist Cultural Studies* 11, no. 1 (Spring 1999): 1–37, and later as "Miss Mazeppa and the Horse with No Name," in *Performing Animals: History, Agency, Theater*, ed. Karen Raber and Monica Mattfeld (University Park: Pennsylvania State University Press, 2017), 141–53.

Parts of chapter 6 appeared first as "Men and Horses: Circus Studs, Sporting Males and the Performance of Purity in Fin-de-Siècle France," *French Cultural Studies* 17, no. 1 (Winter 2006): 87–105, and later as "Circus Studs and Equestrian Sports in Turn-of-the-Century France," in *Equestrian Cultures: Horses, Human Society, and the Discourse of Modernity*, ed. Kristen Guest and Monica Mattfeld (Chicago: University of Chicago Press, 2019), 179–200.

NOTES

PREFACE

1. Donna Haraway, *The Companion Species Manifesto: Dogs, People, and Significant Otherness* (Chicago: Prickly Paradigm Press, 2003).

2. Jean-Jacques Rousseau, *Discourse on the Origins of Inequality*, part 2, n. 39.

3. Kari Weil, *Thinking Animals: Why Animal Studies Now?* (New York: Columbia University Press, 2012), chapter 8.

4. Claire Hansen, "Bucking Critics, U of Wyoming OKs Controversial 'Cowboys' Slogan," *Chronicle of Higher Education*, July 13, 2018, https://www.chronicle.com/article/Bucking-Critics-U-of-Wyoming/243929.

5. Troy Duster, "What to Do with a Man on Horseback," was the title of a related article in the *Chronicle of Higher Education*, August 14, 2017, https://www.chronicle.com/article/what-to-do-with-a-man-on-horseback/240923.

6. Colin Coyle, "Stormy Daniels Opens Heart for an Irish Stud," *Times UK*, April 1, 2018, https://www.thetimes.co.uk/article/stormy-daniels-opens-heart-for-an-irish-stud-wr273p2r8. See also Matt Flegenheimer, Rebecca R. Ruiz, and Katie Van Syckle, "Stormy Daniels, Porn Star Suing Trump Is Known for Her Ambition: She's the Boss," *New York Times*, March 2, 2018, https://www.nytimes.com/2018/03/24/style/stormy-daniels.html.

7. Melissa Stusinski, "Romney's Dressage Horse a New Source of Political Criticism," *Inquisitr*, November 7, 2017, https://www.inquisitr.com/287442/romneys-dressage-horse-a-new-source-of-political-criticism/.

8. Natasha Brooks, "U.S. Government Releases Plan to Cull and Slaughter 100,000 Wild Horses and Burros," *One Green Planet*, April 27, 2018, http://www.onegreenplanet.org/news/u-s-government-releases-plan-cull-slaughter-wild-horses-burros/.

9. Susanna Forrest, "The Troubled History of Horsemeat in America," *Atlantic*, June 8, 2017, https://www.theatlantic.com/technology/archive/2017/06/horse-meat/529665/.

INTRODUCTION

1. Georges-Louis LeClerc, Comte de Buffon, "Le cheval," in *Histoire naturelle des quadrupèdes: Oeuvres* (Paris: Gallimard, 2007), 503.

2. Albert Cler, *La comédie à cheval, ou Manies et travers du monde équestre* (Paris: Ernest Boudin, 1842), 1.

3. Thomas Couture, *Méthode et entretien d'atelier* (Paris: Guérin, 1867), 257–58.

4. Cited in Pierre Serna, *L'animal en République, 1789–1802: Genèse du droit des bêtes* (Paris: Anacharsis, 2016), 7–8.

5. Serna, 9.

6. Daniel Roche, *La culture équestre de l'Occident, XVIème–XIXème siècle: L'ombre du cheval*, vol. 2, *La gloire et la puissance* (Paris: Fayard, 2011), 10. On the importance of the horse in the nineteenth century see also Étienne Saurel, *Histoire de l'équitation* (Paris: Stock, 1971).

7. I am borrowing the idea of an "emotional regime" or prescribed displays (and speech acts) of emotion from William Reddy, *The Navigation of Feeling: A Framework for the History of Emotions* (Cambridge: Cambridge University Press, 2001).

8. Gustave Flaubert, *Madame Bovary*, trans. Lydia Davis (New York: Penguin, 2011), 50.

9. Saurel, *Histoire de l'équitation*, 370, 369. According to Saurel, two tendencies dominated equitation in France at this time: "democratization" and Anglomania. On the debates and contest between French dressage, represented by the school of François Baucher, and the English style promoted among the well-to-do by the Comte d'Aure, see Roche, *Culture équestre*, 238–43.

10. See, for instance, chapter 17 of Balzac's *Mémoires de deux jeunes mariées*.

11. Interestingly, eighteenth-century dictionaries make clear distinctions of race for men and for women. The expression *chasser de race*—literally to hunt race, but translated as showing characteristics of one's parents—was usually positive for a man but always negative for a woman, such as indicating that she's just like her mother, who was also a *coquette*, or a tease. See "race" in the *Dictionnaire de l'Académie française*, 5th ed.

12. See Alain Corbin, *The Foul and the Fragrant: Odor and the French Social Imagination* (Cambridge, MA: Harvard University Press, 1986).

13. Gustave Flaubert, *Éducation sentimentale*, part 2, chap. 4.

14. Émile Zola, *La curée* (Paris: Éditions Gallimard, 1981), 40–41.

15. Cited in Ghislaine Bouchet, *Le cheval à Paris de 1850–1914* (Geneva: Librairie Droz, 1993), 262.

16. Honoré Balzac, "The sportsman parisien," in *Les Français peints par eux-mêmes: Encyclopédie morale du dix-neuvième siècle*, vol. 2 (Paris: L. Curmer, 1840), 280.

17. Buffon, "Le cheval" in *Oeuvres* (Paris: Gallimard, 2007), 503, and see Jacques Roger and Jacques-Louis Binet, *Un autre Buffon* (Paris: Hermann, 1977), 177–79.

18. Plato, *Phaedrus*, trans. Alexander Nehamas and Paul Woodruff (Indianapolis: Hackett, 1995), 44.

19. Cler, *Comédie*, 56.

20. Christopher Prendergast, *Napoleon and History Painting: Antoine-Jean Gros's "La bataille d'Eylau"* (New York: Oxford University Press, 1997), 188.

21. On this point see Walter Leidtke, *The Royal Horse and Rider: Painting, Sculpture and Horsemanship, 1500–1800* (New York: Abaris Books/Metropolitan Museum of Art, 1989), 320.

22. On the tradition of representing women as allegory, see Marina Warner, *Monu-*

ments and Maidens: The Allegory of the Female Form (Berkeley: University of California Press, 2000).

23. Devorah Lauter, "Women in Paris Finally Allowed to Wear Trousers," *Telegraph*, February 3, 2013, https://www.telegraph.co.uk/news/worldnews/europe/france/9845545/Women-in-Paris-finally-allowed-to-wear-trousers.html.

24. Gabrielle Houbre, "L'âge des amazones," in *L'éducation des filles au temps de George Sand* (Arras: Artois Presses Université, 1998), 85–99.

25. François Baucher, *Dictionnaire raisonée d'équitation*, in *Oeuvres complètes*, 11th ed. (Paris: Dumaine, 1959), 394–96. Note that Baucher's methods were greatly contested, and he would be replaced as the chief trainer at Saumur by the Comte d'Aure, who promoted a more forward frame and a looser style of riding that was more sympathetic to the horse.

26. Jules Pellier, *La selle et le costume de l'amazone* (Paris: Rothschild, 1897), 7; Baucher, *Dictionnaire raisonée*, 156–67.

27. Théophile Gautier, *Mademoiselle de Maupin* (Paris: Garnier Flammarion, 1966), 46.

28. Anna Klumpke, *Rosa Bonheur, sa vie, son oeuvre* (Paris: Flammarion, 1909), 203–4.

29. Saurel, *Histoire de l'équitation*, 375. On "Astley's Amphitheater," see Monica Mattfeld, *Becoming Centaur: Eighteenth-Century Masculinity and English Horsemanship* (University Park: Pennsylvania State University Press, 2017), chap. 4.

30. Henri Thétard, *La merveilleuse histoire du cirque* (Paris: Prisma, 1947), 2:165.

31. Cler, *Comédie*, 115.

32. See Ulrich Raulff, *Farewell to the Horse: The Final Century of Our Relationship*, trans. Ruth Ahmedzai Kemp (London: Penguin Books UK, 2017), 23–24.

33. Rifa'a al-Tahtawi, *An Imam in Paris: Al-Tahtawi's Visit to France, 1826–1831* (London: Saqi Books, 2011), 185.

34. The use of horses in mines began in 1821.

35. Buffon, "Cheval," 503–4.

36. Cf. Roger and Binet, *Autre Buffon*, 178.

37. P. Leroux and J. Reynaud, "Le cheval," in *Encyclopédie nouvelle, ou Dictionnaire philosophique scientifique, littéraire et industriel, offrant le tableau des connaissances humaines au XIXe siècle*, ed. Pierre Leroux and Jean Reynaud (Paris: Librairie de Charles Gosselin, 1836–42), 3:505–10; gallica.bnf.fr/Bibliothèque nationale de France.

38. Leroux and Reynaud, "Cheval."

39. Maurice Agulhon, "Le sang des bêtes: Le problème de la protection des animaux en France au XIXème siècle," *Romantisme* 11, no. 31 (1981): 81–110.

40. On this point and for connections between race and slavery in the eighteenth century, see Andrew Curran, *The Anatomy of Blackness: Science and Slavery in an Age of Enlightenment* (Baltimore: Johns Hopkins University Press, 2011), 168.

41. Jeremy Bentham, *Introduction to the Principles of Morals and Legislation* (Oxford: Clarendon Press, 1907), 17n22.

42. Karl Marx, *The Communist Manifesto* (London: Pluto Press, 1996). On this point see also Tim Ingold, *The Perception of the Environment: Essays on Livelihood, Dwelling and Skill* (New York: Routledge, 2011), 74, and Kathleen Kete, "Animals and Ideology:

The Politics of Animal Protection in Europe," in *Representing Animals*, ed. Nigel Rothfels (Bloomington: Indiana University Press, 2002), 251.

43. Leo Spitzer, "Wortgeschictliches," *Zeitschrift für romanische Philologie* 53 (July 1933): 300–301. See also Sandra Swart, *Riding High: Horses, Humans and History in South Africa* (Johannesburg: Wits University Press, 2001), chap. 3, and Margaret Derry, *Bred for Perfection: Shorthorn Cattle, Collies, and Arabian Horses since 1800* (Baltimore: Johns Hopkins University Press, 2003).

44. Charles Du Haÿs, *Le cheval percheron* (Paris: Librairie agricole de la Maison rustique, 1866).

45. Michel Foucault, *Security, Territory, Population*, trans. Graham Burchell (New York: Palgrave, 2009), 1.

46. Buffon, "L'àne," 557.

47. Buffon, 558–59.

48. Buffon, 561. Ed Cohen emphasizes the newly secular nature of Buffon's understanding of species as a product of sex and sexual difference, adding that "individualism thus constitutes a logical, bio-logical and historical precondition for the conceptualization of the human species as a species." See Ed Cohen, "Human Tendencies," in *E-misférica* 10. 1 BIO/ZOO, http://hemisphericinstitute.org/hemi/en/e-misferica-101/cohen.

49. Leroux and Reynaud, "Cheval," in *Encyclopédie nouvelle*, 504–10.

50. Gayle Rubin, "The Traffic in Women: Notes on the 'Political Economy' of Sex," in *Toward an Anthropology of Women*, ed. Rayna R. Reiter (New York: Monthly Review Press, 1975), 157–210.

51. Donna Landry, *Noble Brutes: How Eastern Horses Transformed English Culture* (Baltimore: Johns Hopkins University Press, 2009), 25.

52. See B. Ricardo Brown, *Until Darwin: Science, Human Variety, and the Origins of Race* (London: Routledge, 2015), and Toby Appel, *The Cuvier-Geoffroy Debate: French Biology in the Decades before Darwin* (Oxford: Oxford University Press, 1987).

53. "Race," in Larousse, *Grand dictionnaire universel du XIXe siècle* (Paris: Larousse, 1866–77), 13:595–600.

54. Landry, *Noble Brutes*, 75.

55. Landry, chap. 3. Richard Nash, "'Honest English Breed': The Thoroughbred as Cultural Metaphor," in *The Culture of the Horse*, ed. Karen Raber and Treva Tucker (Ithaca, NY: Cornell University Press, 2004), 245–27.

56. On degeneration see Daniel Pick, *Faces of Degeneration* (Cambridge: Cambridge University Press, 1989), and Robert Nye, "Degeneration, Neurasthenia and the Culture of Sport in Belle Époque France," *Journal of Contemporary History* 17 (January 1982): 51–68.

57. This was also advocated by the natural historian Jacques-Christophe Valmont de Bomare in his *Dictionnaire raisonné universel d'histoire naturelle*, 6 vols. (Paris: Lacombe, 1764–68).

58. Georges Rouhet and Edmond Desbonnet, *L'art de créer un pur-sang humain* (Paris: Berger-Levrault, 1908), lxviii.

59. Michel Foucault, *Security, Territory, Population: Lectures at the Collège de France, 1977–78* (Basingstoke, UK: Palgrave Macmillan, 2007), 1–4.

60. Raulff, *Farewell to the Horse*, 10.

61. Donna Haraway, *When Species Meet* (Minneapolis: University of Minnesota Press, 2008), 3.

CHAPTER ONE

1. See Daniel Roche, "Equestrian Culture in France," *Past and Present* 199 (May 2008): 120.

2. Roche, 120.

3. Gary Shaw, ed., "Does History Need Animals?" special issue of *History and Theory* 52, no. 4 (2013).

4. On the continuity of the Cartesian notion of animal machines and its importance for labor in nineteenth-century US history, see Clay McShane and Joel Tarr, *The Horse in the City: Living Machines in the Nineteenth Century* (Baltimore: Johns Hopkins University Press, 2007). For another perspective on animal agency as resistance in Géricault and in eighteenth-century British visual art, see Stephen F. Eisenman, "The Real 'Swinish Multitude,'" *Critical Inquiry* 42 (Winter 2016): 339–73.

5. Donna Landry, *Noble Brutes: How Eastern Horses Transformed British Culture* (Baltimore: Johns Hopkins University Press, 2009).

6. Landry, 154–55.

7. Walter Leidtke, *The Royal Horse and Rider: Painting, Sculpture, and Horsemanship, 1500–1800* (New York: Abaris Books/Metropolitan Museum of Art, 1989), 83, 320.

8. See Karen Raber and Treva Tucker, "Introduction," in *The Culture of the Horse: Status, Discipline and Identity in the Early Modern World* (New York: Palgrave Macmillan, 2005), 16.

9. Harriet Ritvo, *The Animal Estate: The English and Other Creatures in Victorian England* (Cambridge, MA: Harvard University Press, 1989), 14–18.

10. Buffon, "Le cheval" in *Histoire naturelle des quadrupèdes: Oeuvres* (Paris: Gallimard, 2007), 503.

11. Buffon, 503.

12. Leidtke, *Royal Horse and Rider*, 85.

13. Raber and Tucker, "Introduction," 16–17. On the growing "expectations" of rationality among horses, or what she often describes as Houyhnhnmizing under the influence of Swift's *Gulliver's Travels*, see also Landry, *Noble Brutes*. Landry suggests that the "blood horse" in particular was given powers of rationality and intelligence, but distinctions by breed are less apparent in Géricault.

14. Linda Nochlin, "Géricault, or the Absence of Women," *October* 68 (Spring 1994): 45–59.

15. Catriona Mortimer-Sandilands and Bruce Erickson, eds., *Queer Ecologies* (Bloomington: Indiana University Press, 2010).

16. Timothy Morton, "Queer Ecology," *PMLA* 125 (March 2010): 273, 275.

17. Régis Michel, *Géricault: L'invention du réel* (Paris: Découvertes Gallimard, 1992), 144 (this and all following translations are my own unless otherwise specified).

18. Alex Potts, "Natural Order and the Call of the Wild: The Politics of Animal Picturing," *Oxford Art Journal* 13, no. 1 (1990): 12.

19. Martin Heidegger, "The Age of the World Picture," in *"The Question concerning Technology" and Other Essays* (New York: Harper Colophon, 1977), 129.

20. Ritvo, *Animal Estate*, 14.

21. "If one only describes one or several parts of each object, without taking into account its totality, one only presents a defective and fanciful picture." Cited in Potts, "Natural Order," 22.

22. Cited in Potts, "Natural Order," 23.

23. Potts, 29.

24. Stefan Germer, "Pleasurable Fear: Géricault and Uncanny Trends at the Opening of the Nineteenth Century," *Art History* 22 (June 1999): 170.

25. Walter Kaufmann, *Hegel: A Reinterpretation* (Notre Dame, IN: University of Notre Dame Press, 1978), 318–19, cited in Christopher Prendergast, *Napoleon and History Painting* (Oxford: Clarendon Press, 1977), 188.

26. Napoleon also instructed David in the rules of classical "picturing," suggesting that "it is not the exact reflection of features, warts on the nose, that makes a likeness; it's the character and what animates the physiognomy, that needs to be painted." Cited in Albert Elsen, *Purposes of Art* (New York: Holt, Rinehart and Winston, 1962), 242.

27. On Napoleon's riding and on the levade in classical portraiture see Leidtke, *Royal Horse and Rider*, 14–16 and 85. See also the discussion of the levade in Raber and Tucker, "Introduction," 18.

28. Cf. Lorenz Eitner, *Géricault: Sa vie, son oeuvre* (Paris: Gallimard, 1991), 36.

29. One may be reminded of the portrait of Louis XIV by Hyacinthe Rigaud in which the king's head is framed by a red silk canopy.

30. On the body's weakness, see Thomas Crow, "The Heroic Single Figure," in *Géricault*, ed. Régis Michel (Paris: Documentation française, 1996), 1:48.

31. On genre bending in Géricault, see Michael Marrinan, "Narrative Space and Heroic Form: Géricault and the Painting of History," and Henri Zerner, "Le portrait, plus ou moins," both in Michel, *Géricault*, and Abigail Solomon-Godeau, "Gender, Genre and Géricault," in *Théodore Géricault, the Alien Body: Tradition in Chaos*, ed. Serge Guilbault, Maureen Ryan, and Scott Watson, exhibition catalog (Vancouver, BC: Morris and Helen Belkin Art Gallery, 1997).

32. Régis Michel, "Le nom de Géricault," in Michel, *Géricault*, 1:5.

33. According to Heidegger, the subject as "representer of all representing" is rendered "safe and secure" through the "certainty of his representations." Heidegger, "World Picture," 50.

34. Crow, "Heroic Single Figure," 50–51.

35. On Camper and the role of the facial angle, see Elfed Huw Price, "Do Brains Think? Comparative Anatomy and the End of the Great Chain of Being in Nineteenth-Century Britain," *History of the Human Sciences* 25, no. 3 (2012): 41.

36. Jacques Derrida, *The Animal That Therefore I Am*, trans. David Wills (New York: Fordham University Press, 2008), 11.

37. Emmanuel Levinas, "Ethics as First Philosophy," in *The Levinas Reader*, ed. Sean Hand (Oxford: Blackwell, 1989), 83. For Levinas, of course, only the face of the "other man" could summon me to my ethical responsibility to the other. For Géricault that summons comes, at least potentially, from the horse.

38. I am thinking of Michael Fried, *Absorption and Theatricality: Painting and Beholder in the Age of Diderot* (Berkeley: University of California Press, 1980).

39. The popularity of *War Horse*—both on stage and in film—seems to attest to a current fascination with horses as sacrificial victims (if not erotic partners) as well.

40. Stefan Germer has written of the common "symptomatic character" of the fears triggered by Géricault's portraits of the living dead, not-to-be domesticated pets, and sexualized children. "They involve a confusion between and erasure of what, within that social context, was considered to be 'alive,' 'animal,' or 'childlike' respectively" (Germer, "Pleasurable Fear," 160).

41. Solomon-Godeau, "Gender, Genre, Gericault," 94–114.

42. Nochlin, "Géricault," 56.

43. In this, Géricault's horses are very different from the focus on racehorses in works by Stubbs and other eighteenth-century British depictions of horses discussed by Donna Landry.

44. The biographical details of Géricault's retreat to Italy are not without relevance here. Italy was an escape from the depleted heroics of the Restoration if also a reminder of his brief stint with the Gray Musketeers—an elite body of the Royal Cavalry who rode magnificent gray horses.

45. Lorenz Eitner, *Géricault: His Life and Work* (London: Orbis, 1983), 119–20.

46. Eitner, 159, 153.

47. Sigmund Freud, "An Infantile Neurosis," in *The Standard Edition of the Complete Psychological Works* (London: Hogarth Press, 1955), 17:57.

48. Lee Edelman, "Seeing Things: Representation, the Scene of Surveillance, and the Spectacle of Gay Male Sex," in *Inside/Out: Lesbian Theories, Gay Theories*, ed. Diana Fuss (New York: Routledge, 1991), 95.

49. Cited in Eitner, *Géricault*, 177.

50. Émile Zola, *Nana* (Paris: Éditions Gallimard, 1977), 374.

51. Cited in Philippe Bordes, "*L'écurie dont je ne sortiai que cousu d'or*: Painters and Printmaking from David to Géricault," in Guilbault et al., *Théodore Géricault*, 130.

52. See also the suggestive description of this print in Guilbault et al., *Théodore Géricault*, 246.

CHAPTER TWO

1. See the introduction, 2–3.

2. Eugène Sue, *Godolphin Arabian, or The History of a Thorough-bred* (London: Chapman and Elcoate, 1845), 9–10 (future references will be cited parenthetically in the text).

3. Maurice Agulhon, "Le sang des bêtes: Le problème de la protection des animaux en France au XIXème siècle," *Romantisme* 31 (1981): 81–110.

4. Keith Thomas, *Man and the Natural World* (New York: Penguin, 1984), 303.

5. Thomas, 303.

6. Jean-Jacques Rousseau, "Discourse on the Origin and Foundation of Inequality among Men," in *Rousseau: The Discourses and Other Early Political Writings*, ed. Victor Gourevitch (Cambridge: Cambridge University Press, 1997), 152. Jean-Jacques Rousseau,

"Discours sur l'origine et les fondements de l'inégalité parmi les hommes," in *Oeuvres complètes* (Paris: Éditions du Seuil, 1971), 223 (future references to these editions will be cited parenthetically in the text). Note that Buffon also agreed that animals shared in a natural sense of pity: "L'âme a moins de part que le corps à ce sentiment de pitié naturelle, et les animaux en sont susceptibles comme l'homme" (The soul plays less of a role than the body in the sentiment of natural pity, and animals are just as susceptible as man). *Histoire naturelle*, 7:6–7.

7. Derrida, *Animal That Therefore I Am*, 29.

8. "Any enduring political regime must establish as an essential element a normative order for emotions, an 'emotional regime.'" William M. Reddy, *The Navigation of Feeling: A Framework for the History of Emotions* (Cambridge: Cambridge University Press, 2001), 124.

9. W. J. Gordon, *The Horse World of London* (London: Religious Tract Society, 1893), 16, cited in McShane and Tarr, "Horse as Technology," 366.

10. "The suffering we see is an infection, pity is an infection." Friedrich Nietzsche, *The Will to Power*, trans. Walter Kaufmann (New York: Vintage, 1968), 199. See also Hannah Arendt, *On Revolution* (New York: Penguin, 2006), where she blames compassion and pity for the failures of the French Revolution.

11. "Empathy," first used in English in a publication of 1909 (and in French only a few years earlier), is said to be a loose translation of the German word *Einfülung*—literally "in-feeling"—which was coined in the late nineteenth century to theorize how one's emotions are projected onto a work of art and allow one to feel oneself into it. See "Introduction," in *Empathy, Form and Space: Problems in German Aesthetics, 1873–1893*, ed. and trans. Harry F. Mallgrave (Santa Monica, CA: Getty Center, 1994), 22 and 71n64. See also Juliet Koss, "On the Limits of Empathy," *Art Bulletin* 88 (March 2006): 139–57.

12. Louis, Chevalier de Jaucourt, "Pitié," in *Encyclopédie, ou Dictionnaire raisonné des sciences, des arts et des métiers*, ed. Denis Diderot and Jean le Rond d'Alembert, 12:663, https://artflsrvo3uchicagoedu.ezproxy.wesleyan.edu/philologic4/encyclopedie 1117/navigate/12/2969/.

13. Jacques Derrida, "L'animal que donc je suis," in *L'animal autobiographique: Autour de Jacques Derrida*, ed. Marie-Louise Mallet (Paris: Galilée, 1999), 279.

14. Tobias Menely, *The Animal Claim: Sensibility and the Creaturely Voice* (Chicago: University of Chicago Press, 2015), 2.

15. Anne Vila, *Enlightenment and Pathology: Sensibility in the Literature and Medicine of Eighteenth-Century France* (Baltimore: Johns Hopkins University Press, 1998), 2.

16. Reddy, *Navigation of Feeling*, 108.

17. Reddy, 3.

18. "They seek to stir our pity, soon we will be purchasing tears as is done at funerals in Rome." Cited in Anne Vincent Buffault, *History of Tears*, trans. Teresa Bridgeman (New York: St. Martin's Press, 1991), 92. In her critique of the Jacobin Revolution and Robespierre's "virtuous" goals, Hannah Arendt writes that "pity, taken as the spring of virtue, has proved to possess a greater capacity for cruelty than cruelty itself." "Par pitié, par amour pour l'humanité, soyez inhumains," she asserts, was the battle cry. Even Michelet, who believed in their cause, decried the "pitilessness" of the Jacobins

and blamed the failures of the Revolution on lack of regard for the person of the king as separate from his political position. Buffault notes Michelet's concern when he writes, "The day when pity became mockery began an age of barbarity" (92), and as Saint-Just's statement about tears suggests, it was the monarchists who would eventually confiscate the power of pity for the Restoration. On the role of the dog, see Reddy, *Navigation of Feeling*, 195. See also Gonzolo Sanchez, *Pity in Fin de Siècle French Culture: Liberté, Égalité, Pitié* (Westport, CT: Praeger, 2004), and Katharine MacDonogh, "Prison Pets in the French Revolution," *History Today* 46 (August 1996): 36–42.

19. Reddy, *Navigation of Feeling*, 142–43.

20. Menely, *Animal Claim*, 17.

21. Jan Plamper, "The History of Emotions: Interview with William Reddy, Barbara Wosenwein and Peter Stearns," *History and Theory* 49 (May 2010): 237–65, 239.

22. Plamper, 240.

23. Plamper, 240.

24. On the association of the sentimental with women in the nineteenth century see, for instance, Margaret Cohen, *The Sentimental Education of the Novel* (Princeton, NJ: Princeton University Press, 1999).

25. Valentin Pelosse, "Imaginaire social et protection de l'animal," *L'homme* 21 (October–December 1981): 5–33. Just recently the revolutionary historian Pierre Serna has made the essays digitally available and offered his own analysis in Pierre Serna, *L'animal en République, 1789–1802: Genèse du droit des bêtes* (Paris: Anacharsis, 2016).

26. Jacques Delille, *La pitié, poëme* (Paris: Giguet et Michaud, 1803), 18.

27. Charles Augustin Sainte-Beuve, "Delille," *Revue des deux mondes*, August 1837, 18–30.

28. Pelosse, "Imaginaire social," 8.

29. Pelosse, 40–41.

30. "L'effet d'une impression sur le sentiment intérieur, qui prend sa source dans un acte d'intelligence et n'appartient qu'au sentiment moral" (Pelosse, 8–9). For slight shifts in Rousseau's understanding of pity as having a reflective component, see Kari Weil, "La guerre su sujet la pitié," *Zoopoétique: Revue des sciences humaines* 328, no. 4 (2017): 165–81. Visible in Rousseau as in these early nineteenth-century texts are ongoing questions regarding what in the eighteenth century was referred to as the "animal economy" that governed man's physical and moral constitution.

31. Rousseau, *Émile*, book 2, 80.

32. On the Grammont Law see Agulhon, "Sang des bêtes," and Éric Pierre, "Réformer les relations entre les hommes et les animaux: Function et usages de la loi Grammont en France (1850–1914)," *Déviance et Société* 31, no. 1 (2007): 65–76.

33. Peter Singer, *The Expanding Circle: Ethics, Evolution and Moral Progress* (Princeton, NJ: Princeton University Press, 2011).

34. Jeremy Rivkin, *The Empathic Civilization: The Race to Global Consciousness in a World in Crisis* (New York: Penguin, 2009); Elaine Scary, "Poetry, Injury and the Ethics of Reading," in *The Humanities and Public Life*, ed. Peter Brooks and Hilary Jewett (New York: Fordham University Press, 2014).

35. Balzac, "Préface à Pierrette," and cited in Pierre Laubriet, "L'intelligence de l'art chez Balzac," 97.

36. For more on this see Cary Wolfe, *Before the Law: Humans and Others in a Biopolitical Frame* (Chicago: University of Chicago Press, 2013).

37. Zoe and bios are the categories that Agamben, following Aristotle, used to distinguish between bare or animal life and a human life of the polis. Giorgio Agamben, *The Open: Man and Animal*, trans. Kevin Attell (Stanford, CA: Stanford University Press), 2004. Note that from the Enlightenment on is when we might consider the modern and premodern forms of the anthropological machine to coexist, if not to complement each other.

38. Pelosse, "Imaginaire social," 36.

39. Kathleen Kete, *The Beast in the Boudoir: Petkeeping in Nineteenth-Century France* (Berkeley: University of California Press, 1994), chap. 1, and Harriet Ritvo, *The Animal Estate: The English and Other Creatures in Victorian England* (Cambridge, MA: Harvard University Press, 1987), chap. 3.

40. See Agulhon, "Sang des bêtes." Also see Suzanne Keen, *Empathy and the Novel* (New York: Oxford University Press, 2010), which discusses the way "sympathy becomes tainted with a sense of social as well as moral superiority, and the suspicion that it exists only to shore up middle-class identity" (47). Keen adds that recent readers see the representations of suffering slaves as pornographic, appealing to sadomasochistic appetites. But fiction in the Victorian period attests to novelists' belief in their ability to move feelings and convictions.

41. Karl Marx, *The Communist Manifesto* (New York: International Publishers, 1948), chap. 3.

42. This outpouring of grief for over the horse, "l'ami, le compagnon, la gloire de son maître," can be contrasted with the horse in Balzac's "Passion dans le désert," who is immediately abandoned upon being killed.

43. Donna Landry, *Noble Brutes: How Eastern Horses Transformed English Culture* (Baltimore: Johns Hopkins University Press, 2009), 25.

44. Agulhon, "Sang des bêtes," 81, 92.

45. Charles Baudelaire, "Counterfeit," in *Paris Spleen*, trans. Louise Varèse (New York: New Directions, 1970), 58–59.

46. Derrida, "Animal que donc je suis," 255.

47. See, for instance, his poem "Beat Up the Poor" (101–3) in *Paris Spleen*.

48. For Levinas it is the vulnerable expressivity of the face that interrupts my egoism and brings me to acknowledge my responsibility to the other, over and above myself. See Emmanuel Levinas, *Totality and Infinity: An Essay on Exteriority*, trans. Alphonos Lingis (Pittsburgh, PA: Duquesne University Press, 1969), 64–70.

49. Emmanuel Levinas, "The Paradox of Morality," portions reprinted in *Animal Philosophy: Essential Readings in Continental Thought*, ed. Matthew Calarco and Peter Atterton (New York: Continuum, 2004), 50.

50. Reddy, *Navigation of Feeling*, 212.

51. This notion of the "duty of thinking . . . to suffer our exposure to the world," as Cary Wolfe phrases it in his introduction to *Philosophy and Animal Life* (New York: Columbia University Press, 2008), 8, is at the forefront of the essays in that book, including those by Wolfe, Cora Diamond, and Stanley Cavell.

52. Nietzsche, *Will to Power*, 199.

53. Baudelaire, "The Faithful Dog" (104–7), in *Paris Spleen*, 104.

54. Derrida, *Animal*, 7.

55. Derrida, 11.

56. On philosophy's fear of anthropomorphism, see Vicki Hearne, *Adam's Task: Calling Animals by Name* (Pleasantville, NY: Common Reader Editions, 2000). See also Frans de Waal, "Appendix A: Anthropomorphism and Anthropodenial," in *Primates and Philosophers: How Morality Evolved*, 59–68 (Princeton, NJ: Princeton University Press, 2006).

57. Jacques Derrida, *The Beast and the Sovereign*, vol. 1, trans. Geoffrey Bennington (Chicago: University of Chicago Press, 2009), 336.

58. Derrida, "Des Tours de Babel," trans. Joseph Graham, in *Psyche: Inventions of the Other* (Stanford, CA: Stanford University Press, 2007), 1:196. And in *Psyche: Inventions de l'autre*, vols. 1 and 2 (Paris: Galilée, 1987).

59. Menely, *Animal Claim*, 79.

60. See Vincianne Despret, "The Body We Care For: Figures of Anthropo-zoo-genesis," *Body and Society* 10, no. 2–3 (2004): 111–34.

61. Judith Butler, *Parting Ways: Jewishness and the Critique of Zionism* (New York: Columbia University Press, 2012), 17.

62. Vicki Hearne, "Job's Animals," in *Animal Happiness: A Moving Exploration of Animals and Their Emotions* (New York: Skyhorse, 1994), 237.

CHAPTER THREE

1. See Dore Ashton, *Rosa Bonheur: A Life and Legend* (New York: Viking Press, 1981), 161.

2. Anna Klumpke, *Rosa Bonheur: The Artist's (Auto)biography*, trans. Gretchen Van Slyke (Ann Arbor: University of Michigan Press, 1997), chap. 3, 20. Further references to Klumpke, *Rosa Bonheur*, are to this translation.

3. See especially James Saslow, "'Disagreeably Hidden': Construction and Constriction of the Lesbian Body in Rosa Bonheur's *Horse Fair*," in *The Expanding Discourse: Feminism and Art History*, ed. Norma Broude and Mary D. Garrard (New York: HarperCollins, 1992), 187–206; Gretchen Van Slyke, "The Sexual and Textual Politics of Dress: Rosa Bonheur and her Cross-Dressing Permits," *Nineteenth-Century French Studies* 26 (Spring-Summer 1998): 321–35; and Albert Boime, "The Case of Rosa Bonheur: Why Should a Woman Want to Be More Like a Man?," *Art History* 4 (December 1981): 384–409. Boime discusses the importance of animals but still privileges the gender anomalies of Bonheur's methods and style.

4. Bruce Bagemihl, *Biological Exuberance: Animal Homosexuality and Natural Diversity* (New York: Stonewall Inn Editions, 2000).

5. Leidtke, *Royal Horse and Rider*, 85.

6. On agency in Stubbs's painting of *Whistlejacket*, "a portrait of a horse completely free of human contact or control," see Donna Landry, *Noble Brutes: How Eastern Horses Transformed English Culture* (Baltimore: Johns Hopkins University Press, 2009), 148–61.

7. "Rosa Bonheur Ploughing in Nevers," Musée d'Orsay, Jean-François Millet, *The Angelus*, February 4, 2009, https://www.musee-orsay.fr/en/collections/works-in-focus/painting/commentaire_id/ploughing-in-nevers-2040.html?tx_commentaire_pi1%5BpidLi%5D=509&tx_commentaire_pi1%5Bfrom%5D=841&cHash=60f905d6af; accessed June 1, 2019.

8. Boime, *Case of Rosa Bonheur*, 393.

9. Vincianne Despret, "Do Animals Work? Creating Pragmatic Narratives," in *Animots: Postanimality in French Thought*, ed. Matthew Senior, David L. Clark, and Carla Freccero, Yale French Studies 127 (New Haven, CT: Yale University Press, 2015), 124–42.

10. On the origin of representation as animal, see John Berger, "Why Look at Animals?," in *About Looking* (New York: Pantheon Books, 1980), 1–28.

11. Mary Lou Roberts, "Out of Their Orbit: Celebrities and Eccentrics in Nineteenth-Century France," in *The Question of Gender: Joan W. Scott's Critical Feminism*, ed. Judith Butler and Elizabeth Weed (Bloomington: Indiana University Press, 2011), 50–79.

12. "The illegibility of Bonheur's and Bernhardt's images rested in their androgynous and therianthropic qualities, that is their ability to visually merge male and female, human and animal forms." Roberts, 59.

13. Saslow, "Disagreeably Hidden," 187.

14. Building on Whitney Chadwick, "The Fine Art of Gentling: Horses, Women, and Rosa Bonheur in Victorian England," in *The Body Imaged: The Human Form and Visual Representation since the Renaissance*, ed. Kathleen Adler and Marcia Pointon (Cambridge: Cambridge University Press, 1993), Saslow writes that the key to understanding human-animal relations in the painting is through "the animals' freedom and uncorrupted nature" (Saslow, 197).

15. Donna Haraway, *When Species Meet* (Minneapolis: University of Minnesota Press, 2007).

16. Klumpke, *Rosa Bonheur*, 122.

17. Theodore Stanton, *Reminiscences of Rosa Bonheur* (New York: Hacker Art Books, 1976), chap. 11.

18. Quoted in Stanton, 341.

19. Quoted in Stanton, 343.

20. On Lamennais's influence, see *Atelier Rosa Bonheur*, vol. 1, *Tableaux* (Paris: Imprimerie Georges Petit, 1900), xi–xii.

21. Quoted in Léon Roger-Milès, *Rosa Bonheur: Sa vie, son oeuvre* (Paris: Société d'édition artistique, 1900), and cited by Cristina Portell, "The Bonheur Family," in *Rosa Bonheur: All Nature's Children* (New York: Dahesh Museum, 1998), 84. See also Claude Carcopino, *Les doctrines sociales de Lamennais* (Geneva: Slatkine Reprints, 1968), 180.

22. Stanton, *Reminiscences of Rosa Bonheur*, 9. Bonheur recognized and described the toll this retreat took on her mother, who died of exhaustion from caring for her children and whose neglect by Raymond mirrors the fate of many of the women involved in or related to the movement, despite its pro-woman pronouncements. As Gretchen Van Slyke comments, Rosa "recalled the grievous discrepancy between her mother's lonely hardships and her father's sublime enthusiasms . . . about saving the human race." Introduction to Klumpke, *Rosa Bonheur*, xvi.

23. On the role of art and the artist in Saint-Simonianism, see Ralph P. Locke, *Music, Musicians and the Saint-Simonians* (Chicago: University of Chicago Press, 1986), chap. 6.

24. Locke, 45. On Halévy see F. A. Hayek and Bruce Caldwell, eds., *Studies on the Abuse and Decline of Reason: Text and Documents* (Chicago: University of Chicago Press, 2010), 220.

25. On the situation of Saint-Simonian women, see Kari Weil, "Spectacular Bodies: Women in the Discourse of the Saint-Simonians," *Nineteenth-Century Contexts* 16, no. 1 (1992): 33–45, and Weil, "A Woman's Place in the Utopian Home, 'The New Paris' and the Saint-Simoniennes," in *Homelessness and the Poetics of Dislocation in Nineteenth-Century France*, ed. Suzanne Nash (New York: SUNY Press, 1993), 231–45.

26. Klumpke, *Rosa Bonheur*, 206. Note that Raymond is said to have designed the costume for men. See Theodore Stanton, "The Brotherhood of Saint-Simon," in *The Open Court*, vol. 24 (Chicago: Open Court, 1910), 545–52.

27. Klumpke, *Rosa Bonheur*, 147.

28. Balzac, *L'avant-propos à la Comédie humaine*, http://visualiseur.bnf.fr/CadresFenetre?O=NUMM-101394&M=imageseule; my translation.

29. Toby A. Appel, *The Cuvier-Geoffroy Debate* (Oxford: Oxford University Press, 1987), chap. 8.

30. Appel, chap. 8.

31. Kari Weil, *Androgyny and the Denial of Difference* (Charlottesville: University of Virginia Press, 1992).

32. Stanton, *Reminiscences of Rosa Bonheur*, 41.

33. See the Joconde catalog entry "Portail des collections des musées de France," http://www.culture.gouv.fr/public/mistral/joconde_fr?ACTION=CHERCHER&FIELD_1=REF&VALUE_1=000PE011439. In a related comment, Boime reminds his readers of Bonheur's remark about bulls and men: "The fact is, in the way of males, I like only the bulls that I paint" (386).

34. Klumpke, *Rosa Bonheur*, 133.

35. Klumpke, 122.

36. On Isidore Geoffroy Saint-Hilaire's theories of domestication see Ceri Crossley, *Consumable Metaphors: Attitudes towards Animals and Vegetarianism in Nineteenth-Century France* (Bern: Peter Lang, 2005), chap. 5; Claude Blanckaert, "Les animaux 'utiles' chez Isidore Geoffroy Saint-Hilaire," *Revue de synthèse*, July-December 1992, 347–82, and Dorothee Brantz, "The Domestication of Empire: Human-Animal Relations at the Intersection of Civilization, Evolution and Acclimatization in the Nineteenth Century," in *A Cultural History of Animals in the Age of Empire*, ed. Kathleen Kete (Oxford: Berg, 2007), 73–94.

37. Buffon, "Les animaux domestiques," in *Oeuvres* (Paris: Gallimard, 2007), 499.

38. On the differences between Isidore Geoffroy Saint-Hilaire and Buffon, see Blanckaert, "Animaux 'utiles.'" Note also that progress in the understanding of animals as feeling, intelligent beings who could still be justifiably "enslaved" created considerable difficulties for the abolitionist cause.

39. Isidore Geoffroy Saint-Hilaire, "Domestication des animaux," in *Encyclopédie nouvelle, ou Dictionnaire philosophique, scientifique, littéraire et industriel*, ed. Pierre Leroux and Jean Reynaud, vol. 4 (Paris: Libraire de Ch. Gosselin, A. Pougin libraire, Hector Bossange et Cie, libraires, 1836).

40. Note that Isidore would be the prime mover behind legalizing horsemeat for human consumption, as I discuss in chapter 4.

41. Jules Michelet refers to the "great work of the education of animals" as the "veritable rehabilitation of inferior life" in Michelet, *Le peuple* (Paris: Flammarion, 1974), 181–82. On this point see also Blanckaert, "Animaux 'utiles,'" 361.

42. Isidore Geoffroy Saint-Hilaire, *Acclimatation et domestication des animaux utiles*, 4th ed. (Paris: Librairie agricole de la Maison rustique, 1861), 281.

43. With the advent of realism and the increasing influence of the art market during the Empire, art and literature were seen to lose their "divine" inspiration. See Ashton, *Rosa Bonheur*, chap. 9.

44. Klumpke, *Rosa Bonheur*, 149.

45. Klumpke, 150.

46. "Eccentric" relations with animals were understood or represented as related to being Jewish. See Roberts, "Out of Their Orbit," and Ashton, *Rosa Bonheur*, 171.

47. Klumpke, *Rosa Bonheur*, 204.

48. Klumpke, 203.

49. "On trouvera sur tous les animaux esclaves les stigmates de leur captivité et l'empreinte de leurs fers; on verra que ces plaies sont d'autant plus grandes, d'autant plus incurables, qu'elles sont plus anciennes, et que dans l'état ou nous les avons réduits, il ne seroit peut-être plus possible de les réhabiliter, ni de leur rendre leur forme primitive, et les autres attributs de Nature que nous leur avons enlevés" (44). Cited in Blanckaert, "Animaux 'utiles,'" 357.

50. Jan Goldstein, *Console and Classify: The French Psychiatric Profession in the Nineteenth Century* (Cambridge: Cambridge University Press, 1987), 233.

51. Michel Foucault, *Histories de la folie à l'âge classique* (Paris: Gallimard, 1972), 165, cited in Matthew Senior, "Introduction," in *A Cultural History of Animals in the Age of Enlightenment*, ed. Matthew Senior (Oxford: Berg, 2007).

52. Senior, "Introduction," 16.

53. The Idéologues, as discussed in chapter 2, stressed the intimate connections between body and mind (*physique et moral*) and between physical and mental well-being. At the juncture between the two domains, moreover, was the imagination—a capacity regarded as shared between humans and animals and that often must be treated and healed.

54. Goldstein, *Console and Classify*, 45–55. On Pinel, see also Dora Weiner, *Comprendre et soigner: Philippe Pinel (1745–1826); La médecine de l'esprit* (Paris: Fayard, 1999).

55. Weiner, *Comprendre et soigner*, 240.

56. Weiner, 19.

57. Pierre Serna, *L'animal en République, 1789–1802: Genèse du droit des bêtes* (Toulouse: Anacharsis, 2016), 18.

58. Serna, 20.

59. Weiner indicates that Pariset was one of Pinel's "privileged students," along with Jean-Étienne Dominique Esquirol and, interestingly, Jean-Marc Gaspard Itard, who was responsible for educating the *enfant sauvage* or "wild child." Weiner, *Comprendre et soigner*, 179–80.

60. Although the connection between Pariset's work with Pinel and his work with the SPA seems obvious, I have found no sources that deal with it. On Pariset's role in the founding of the SPA see Georges Fleury, *La belle histoire de la S.P.A. de 1845 à nos jours* (Paris: Bernard Grasset, 1995), 20–22.

61. Fleury, 22.

62. Erica Fudge, "Farmyard Choreographies in Early Modern England," in *Renaissance Posthumanism*, ed. Joseph Campana and Scott Maisano (New York: Fordham University Press, 2016), 145–66.

63. Donna Haraway, *The Companion Species Manifesto* (Chicago: Prickly Paradigm Press, 2003), 60.

64. Kelly Oliver, *Animal Lessons: How They Teach Us to Be Human* (New York: Columbia University Press, 2009), 216–17.

65. In its size it recalls Géricault's almost life-size scenes of soldiers on horseback.

66. Ashton, *Rosa Bonheur*, 86.

67. On the painting as self-portrait, see Saslow, "Disagreeably Hidden."

68. Ashton, *Rosa Bonheur*, 135.

69. Chadwick, "Fine Art of Gentling," 95.

70. Ashton, *Rosa Bonheur*, 143.

71. This parallel of heads might also recall a statement Pinel made in his early "Memoir on the Head of an Elephant," which Isidore Geoffroy Saint-Hilaire cites to include him among the precursors for the idea of the unity of composition: "Quand on a soigneusement passé par divers intermédiaires, en s'élevant de la tête des Quadrupèdes et en partant de celle de l'Homme, il s'agit toujours d'y reconnaître le type primitive, de voir comment les os qui se correspondent offrent des variétés plus ou moins subordonnées." Isidore Geoffroy Saint-Hilaire, *Vie, travaux et doctrine scientifique d'Étienne Geoffroy Saint-Hilaire par son Fils* (Paris: Librairie de la Société géologique de France, 1847), 145.

72. Klumpke, *Rosa Bonheur*, 217.

73. Chadwick, "Fine Art of Gentling," 92.

74. Klumpke, *Rosa Bonheur*, 10.

75. Klumpke, 216.

76. "Le cheval," in *Encyclopédie nouvelle, ou Dictionnaire philosophique, scientifique, littéraire et industriel*, vol. 3, ed. M. M. P. Leroux and J. Reynaud (Paris: Librairie de Charles Gosslin, 1840), 505. For more on Meunier, see Crossley, *Consumable Metaphors*, chap. 5.

77. "Cheval," 506.

78. Michelet, *Peuple*, 175, 182.

79. Sue Donaldson and Will Kymlicka, *Zoopolis: A Political Theory of Animal Rights* (London: Oxford University Press, 2013), 73.

80. Donaldson and Kymlicka.

81. Ashton, *Rosa Bonheur*, 143.

82. Bonheur supported maintaining the purity of a breed, providing her support and the frontispiece for the first studbook of the Percheron Society in 1885. See Ashton, *Rosa Bonheur*, 146.

83. Klumpke, *Rosa Bonheur*, 123.

CHAPTER FOUR

1. Roland Barthes, *Mythologies*, trans. Annette Lavers (New York: Hill and Wang, 1983), 62–63.

2. Daniel Roche, "On mange bien les chevaux . . . ," *Huffington Post*, October 5, 2016, https://www.huffingtonpost.fr/daniel-roche/histoire-viande-cheval_b_2906018.html.

3. During the siege of Paris of 1870–71, when famine was widespread and beef practically impossible to obtain, horsemeat gained favor with all classes. From fewer than 2,000 horses butchered for meat in 1870, the number grew to 65,000 during the siege, a number almost matched again in 1912. At other times the number of horse eaters has been estimated at about one-third of the population. For the history and statistics of hippophagy in France see Daniel Gade, "Horsemeat as Human Food in France," *Ecology of Food and Nutrition* 5 (1976): 1–11, and Ghislaine Bouchet, *Le cheval à Paris, 1850–1914* (Geneva: Librairie Droz, 1993), 219–46.

4. Gade, "Horsemeat as Human Food in France," 1.

5. Jacques Derrida, "Eating Well, or The Calculation of the Subject," in *Points: Interviews, 1974–1994*, ed. Elisabeth Weber, trans. Peter Connor and Avital Ronell (Stanford, CA: Stanford University Press, 1995), 258.

6. Derrida, 282. The French version, which reads "apprendre à donner à manger à l'autre," is translated by Connor and Ronell as "learning-to-give-the-other-to-eat," but I think it would be translated more faithfully as "learning to feed the other," where the other could be both direct and indirect object, both the food and the recipient of the food.

7. On this point see, for instance, Elizabeth Guild, *Unsettling Montaigne: Poetics, Ethics, Affect in the "Essais" and Other Writings* (Cambridge: Brewer, 2014), 113–14.

8. Gade, "Horsemeat as Human Food in France," 1.

9. Alan D. Krinsky, "Let Them Eat Horsemeat: Science, Philanthropy, State and the Search for Complete Nutrition in Nineteenth-Century France" (PhD diss., University of Wisconsin, Madison, 2001), chap. 5. On the role of the SPA in the legalization of horsemeat, see Krinsky and also Éric Pierre, "Une société sous la Monarchie de Juillet: La S.P.A. formation, idéologie, sociologie," in *Histoire et animal*, ed. Alain Curet and Frédéric Ogé (Toulouse: Presses de l'Institut d'études politiques de Toulouse, 1989), 315–31, where he identifies utility as the major criterion for laws concerning slaughter.

10. Marshall Sahlins, *Culture and Practical Reason* (Chicago: University of Chicago Press, 1976), 174–75.

11. On the distinctions afforded the pet and the history of pet keeping in England, see Keith Thomas, *Man and the Natural World: Changing Attitudes in England, 1500–1800* (Oxford: Oxford University Press, 1996), part 3.

12. For a provocative discussion of the way pets advantageously transgress boundaries of kin and kind, see Mark Shell, "The Family Pet," *Representations* 15 (Summer 1986): 121–53.

13. Claude Fischler, *L'hommivore* (Paris: Éditions Odile Jacob, 1990), 132. These and all following translations are my own unless otherwise specified.

14. This is what Carol Adams calls the "absent referent." See Carol Adams, *The Sexual Politics of Meat: A Feminist-Vegetarian Critical Theory* (New York: Continuum, 1990).

15. Noélie Vialles, "De l'animal à la viande: Une mort sans cadavre," *French Cultural Studies* 6 (1995): 338.

16. Noélie Vialles, *Le sang et la chair* (Paris: Éditions de la Maison des sciences de l'homme, 1987), 19.

17. Vialles, "De l'animal à la viande," 346.

18. Albert Cler, *La comédie à cheval, ou Manies et travers du monde équestre* (Paris: Ernest Boudin, 1842), 153.

19. Maurice Agulhon, "Le sang des bêtes: Le problème de la protection des animaux en France au XIXème siècle," *Romantisme* 31 (1981): 85.

20. This is the estimate given in A. J. B. Parent-Duchâtelet, "Des chantiers d'équarrissage de la ville de Paris," in *Hygiène publique, ou Mémoires sur les questions les plus importantes de l'hygiène appliquée aux professions et aux travaux d'utilité publique*, vol. 2 (Paris: J. B. Baillière, 1836). See also M. Perrot, *Impressions de voyage: Montfaucon, son gibet, sa voirie, son écorcherie; description topographique, historique et industrielle* (Paris: Chez l'éditeur, quai des Augustins, 1840).

21. Derrida, "Eating Well," 280.

22. For more on Pinel's "moral medicine," see chapter 3 above on Rosa Bonheur.

23. A. J. B. Parent-Duchâtelet, "Préjugés sur l'hygiène," in *Hygiène publique*, vol. 1 (1836), 23.

24. Parent-Duchâtelet, "Préjugés," 17.

25. Parent-Duchâtelet, "Préjugés," 17.

26. On deanimalization see Vialles, "De l'animal à la viande," 341.

27. Perrot, *Impressions de voyage*, 85.

28. Foucault, *Les mots et les choses* (Paris: Gallimard: 1966), 144–45.

29. Théophile Gautier, *Voyages hors barrières* (Paris: Archange minotaure, 2003), 12.

30. Gautier, 13.

31. Vialles, "De l'animal à la viande," 340.

32. On this point and on the use of color see also E. S. Burt, "Limitrophic Animals, Aesthetics and Poetics in Gautier's *Voyages hors barrières*," *Dix-Neuf* 19 no. 3 (2015): 228–43.

33. Un Zoophile, *De l'hippophagie dans ses rapports avec la protection due aux animaux* (Paris: Limoges-Imprimerie Ducourtieux, 1864), 3, cited in Krinsky, "Let Them Eat Horsemeat," 190. Note that Krinsky also reminds readers that his translation of *légumiste* as "vegetarian" is anachronistic.

34. Parent-Duchâtelet, "Des chantiers d'équarrissage," 151–54.

35. Usage alimentaire de la viande de cheval, *Banquet des hippophages* (Paris: Soye et Bouchet, 1865).

36. Usage alimentaire de la viande de cheval.

37. Usage alimentaire de la viande de cheval.

38. *Le mousquetaire*, January 30, 1867.

39. *La lune*, July 15, 1866.

40. *La lune*, July 15, 1866.

41. S. J. Tambiah, "Animals Are Good to Think and Good to Prohibit," *Ethnology* 8 (1969): 423–59.

42. Paul Rozin and April E. Fallon, "A Perspective on Disgust," *Psychological Review* 94, no. 1 (1987): 29.

43. Pierre Bourdieu, *Distinction: A Social Critique of the Judgement of Taste* (London: Sage, 1979), 84.

44. On the identification between eater and eaten through cannibalism see H. Peter Steeves, "They Say Animals Can Smell Fear," in *Animal Others: On Ethics, Ontology, and Animal Life*, ed. H. Peter Steeves (Albany: State University of New York Press, 1999).

45. Parent-Duchâtelet, "Des chantiers d'équarrissage," 180.

46. Walter Benjamin, "One-Way Street," in *Reflections: Essays, Aphorisms, Autobiographical Writings* (New York: Harcourt, Brace, Jovanovich, 1978), 66–67.

47. Benjamin, 67.

48. Derrida, "Eating Well," 280.

49. William Ian Miller, *The Anatomy of Disgust* (Cambridge, MA: Harvard University Press, 1977), 49.

50. Eugène Sue, "Godolphin Arabian," in *Le cheval*, ed. Jean-Pierre Digard and Jean-Louis Gouraud (Paris: Omnibus, 1995), 51. See also Guy de Maupassant, "Coco," in the same collection.

51. Sue, "Godolphin Arabian," 100.

52. Miller, *Anatomy of Disgust*, 38.

53. On the similarities of Parent-Duchâtelet's studies of prostitution and of the horse slaughter yards, see Charles Bernheimer, *Figures of Ill Repute: Representing Prostitution in Nineteenth-Century France* (Cambridge, MA: Harvard University Press, 1989).

54. "From Horses to Horsemeat's Dreambook," http://books.dreambook.com/rocky123/gbook.html (website is no longer available).

CHAPTER FIVE

1. For a brief discussion of the Universal Exhibition, see Jill Forbes and Michael Kelly, *French Cultural Studies: An Introduction* (Oxford: Oxford University Press, 1995), 16.

2. By Hausmannization I refer to the massive renovation of Paris commissioned by Napoleon III and carried out by the prefect, Baron Haussmann. Note that using a balloon to represent the sun was common, according to Patricia Mainardi, "Edouard Manet's View of the Universal Exposition of 1867," *Arts Magazine* 54 (January 1980): 112.

3. T. J. Clark, *The Painting of Modern Life: Paris in the Art of Manet and His Followers* (Princeton, NJ: Princeton University Press, 1984), 61.

4. Clark, 64.

5. Mainardi writes of the ambivalence of the painting toward "its actual themes . . . of peace and progress," adding that it is "an accurate reflexion of the mood of Paris in 1867—a mixture of gaity and apprehension, hope and fear" (112).

6. The Cirque des Champs-Élysées, otherwise known as the Cirque de l'impératrice, Cirque d'été, and Cirque Franconi, was opened in 1852. The Hippodrome de la Porte Dauphine, currently the place Victor Hugo, ran from 1856 to 1869. On circuses in the nineteenth century see Ghislaine Bouchet, *Le cheval à Paris* (Geneva: Librairie Droz, 1993), 273–76.

7. Mainardi, "Edouard Manet's View," 111.

8. See, for instance, the preface to Baron De Vaux, *Écuyers et écuyères: Histoires des*

cirques d'Europe, 1680–1891 (Paris: Rothschild, 1893), in which Henri Meilhac reprints a letter from a woman of some standing to the Countess Soperan (once an *écuyère* herself) asking for her opinion on whether the woman's daughter should be allowed to pursue her wish to train as a rider of the haute école.

9. Clark, *Painting of Modern Life*, 63.

10. Alfred Delvau, *Les plaisirs de Paris* (Paris: Presses d'Imera, 1991), 37.

11. Delvau, 37. Delvau's book, originally published in 1867, was one of the most popular examples of a new genre of writing produced to celebrate the spectacle of contemporary life. The "parade" of horses through the Bois or on the boulevards was one of the major subjects for this genre, which lay somewhere between fiction and journalism. Other examples include Crafty (pen name for victor Eugène Géruzez), *À travers Paris* (Around Paris), 1894, and Gyp (pen name for Sybille Riquetti de Mirabeau), *Sportmanomanie* (Sport-monomania), 1898.

12. Speaking of the Jockey Club, which promoted "a lifestyle made principally of horses and entertainment," Anne Martin–Fugier suggests that it "created a link between high society and the world of spectacle." Anne Martin-Fugier, *La vie élégante, ou La formation du tout-Paris, 1815–1848* (Paris: Fayard, 1990), 340.

13. Walter Benjamin, *Illuminations: Essays and Reflections*, trans. Harry Zohn (New York: Schocken Books, 1968), 172.

14. Preface to Jean Delton, *Le tour du Bois: Photographie hippique au Bois du Boulogne* (Paris: Legoupy, n.d.), n.p.

15. See Albert Cler, *La comédie à cheval, ou Manies et travers du monde équestre* (Paris: Ernest Bourdin, 1842), 115, on the *amazone* and the *lorette*; and see the entry by Eugène Guinot on "La Lionne" (lioness) in the 1841 edition of *Les français peints par eux-mêmes: Encyclopédie morale du XIXe siècle* (Paris: L. Curmer), which describes the "indefatigable amazons . . . queens of the horse world, who have been nicknamed *the Lionesses* to pay homage to their strength and courage and the inexhaustible ardor they give proof of every day." The author writes that the *lionne* cares little about love and is difficult to please unless "one is a prince or has the most beautiful horses of Paris." http://www.bmlisieux.com/curiosa/guinot01.htm; accessed June 2019.

16. Céleste Mogador, *Mémoires de Céleste Mogador* (Paris: Librairie nouvelle, 1858), 139.

17. *Les amazones de Paris* (Paris: E. Dentu, 1866), 8.

18. *Amazones*, 6.

19. Alice A. Kuzniar, "'I Married My Dog': On Queer Canine Literature," in *Queering the Non/Human*, ed. Noreen Giffney and Myra J. Hird (Farnham, UK: Ashgate, 2008), 208.

20. George Sand, *Indiana* (Paris: Gallimard, 1984), 161–62.

21. Gustave Flaubert, *Madame Bovary* (Paris: Gallimard, 1972), 79, 234.

22. Cler, *Comédie à cheval*, 115.

23. Théophile Gautier, *Mademoiselle de Maupin*, trans. Joanna Richardson (New York: Penguin Books, 1981), 320.

24. Charles Londe, *Gymnastique médicale, ou L'exercise appliqué aux organes de l'homme* (Paris: Crouillebois, 1821), 208.

25. On the restrictive nature of the amazon position see Croqueville, *Paris à cheval*,

en voiture, aux courses, à la chasse (Paris: Librairie de la Nouvelle revue, 1892), chap. 30, and L. H. Pons d'Hostun, *L'écuyer des dames, ou Lettres sur l'équitation* (Paris: Librairie Mme Huzard, 1817), letter 10.

26. On the notion of an "equestrian sublime" see Nigel Leask, "'To Canter with the Sagitarre': Burns, Byron and the Equestrian Sublime," *Byron Journal* 39, no. 2 (2011): 117–33.

27. Victor Hugo, *Poésie*, ed. Bernard Leuillot, 3 vols. (Paris: Seuil, 1972). On the Mazeppa myth see "Many Ways to Ride a Horse: Mazeppa," in Patricia Mainardi, *Husbands, Wives and Lovers: Marriage and Its Discontents in Nineteenth-Century France* (New Haven, CT: Yale University Press, 2003), chap. 6.

28. Cler, *Comédie à cheval*, 1.

29. Henri Thétard, *La merveilleuse histoire du cirque* (Paris: Julliard, 1947), 167.

30. Frank Rich, "Review/Theater; "Gypsy Is Back on Broadway with a Vengeance," *New York Times*, November 17, 1989.

31. Cited in Bernard Falk, *The Naked Lady: A Biography of Adah Isaacs Menken* (London: Hutchison, 1952), 141.

32. Allen Lesser, *Enchanting Rebel: The Secret of Adah Isaacs Menken* (New York, Beechhurst, 1947), 192.

33. Cited in Falk, *Naked Lady*, 78. A version of the letter is reprinted in French in *Le mousquetaire*, December 31, 1866.

34. Abigail Solomon-Godeau, "The Legs of the Countess," *October* 39 (Winter 1986): 76.

35. Daphne Brooks, *Bodies in Dissent: Spectacular Performances of Race and Freedom, 1850–1910* (Durham, NC: Duke University Press, 2006), 182. Brooks's chapter is a brilliant reading of the racial politics involved in Menken's performances and their reception, especially within the American context. Beyond this one comment, however, she has little to say about the role of the horse or species identity.

36. Donna Haraway, *When Species Meet* (Minneapolis: University of Minnesota Press, 2008), 15–16.

37. On the centaur ideal see Monica Mattfeld, *Becoming Centaur: Eighteenth-Century Masculinity and English Horsemanship* (University Park, PA: Penn State University Press, 2016), and also Kim Marra, "Horses Queer the Stage and Society of Shenandoah," in *Performing Animals*, ed. Karen Raber and Monica Mattfeld (University Park, PA: Penn State University Press, 2017). Marra's essay also demonstrates how horses acted to queer conventional boundaries of sex, race, and species on the American stage.

38. "One has never seen in the theater a more perfect beauty, more elegant forms, more seductive or graceful poses," *L'univers illustré*, January 5, 1867.

39. A writer herself, Menken befriended a number of literary personalities in both France and Britain.

40. *Uncle Tom's Cabin* was first published in France in 1853.

41. Cited in Falk, *Naked Lady*, 182.

42. "The word *race* . . . has had many accepted uses. Some have used it to encompass both race and species, others have made it a division of species. We, who are polygeneticist, consider the word *race* to be too abstract a term. In fact, where does a race begin

and end?" Pierre Larousse, ed., *Dictionnaire universel du XIXe siècle*, vol. 13 (Paris, 1875), 596.

43. H. V. de Loncey, *Les races de chevaux de trait: Études hippiques, documents et pratiques* (Paris: Bureaux de l'acclimation, 1888), 187.

44. De Loncey, 5.

45. De Loncey, 353, 244.

46. See Georges Rouhet and Edmond Desbonnet, *L'art de créer le pur-sang humain* (Paris: Berger-Levrault, 1908). Belief in the degeneration of the French "race" grew in part as an explanation for the French defeat in the 1870 war with Prussia and in light of statistics showing a declining birthrate. For more on this discourse and its reported causes, whether environmental or hereditary, see especially Robert Nye, "Degeneration and the Medical Model of Cultural Crisis in the French Belle Époque," in *Political Symbolism in Modern Europe*, ed. Seymour Drescher, David Sabean, and Allan Sharlin (New Brunswick, NJ: Transaction Books, 1982).

47. In *The Theory of the Leisure Class* (New York: Modern Library, 1934), Thorstein Veblen comments on the example of the "fast horse," which "is on the whole expensive, wasteful and useless—for the industrial purpose. What productive use he may possess . . . takes the form of exhibitions of force and facility of motion that gratify the popular aesthetic sense" (144).

48. Honoré Balzac, *Le Père Goriot* (Paris: Garnier-Frères, 1963), 44.

49. In this they continue the reputation of the "Amazonian Revolution" of those unsexed women who attempted to free themselves of domestic duties around the time of the French Revolution. See Donna Landry, "Figures of the Feminine: An Amazonian Revolution in Feminist Literary History," in *The Uses of Literary History*, ed. Marshall Brown (Durham, NC: Duke University Press, 1995), 107–28.

50. Guy de Maupassant, "Fou?," in *Contes et nouvelles*, vol. 1, ed. Louis Forestier (Paris: Gallimard, 1974), 525.

51. Maupassant, 524.

52. Maupassant, 525.

53. Maupassant, 522.

54. Émile Zola, *Nana* (Paris: Éditions Gallimard, 1977), 202 (future references will be cited parenthetically in the text).

55. T. J. Clark discusses prostitution as a problem similar to that of transubstantiation: "It is specifically a matter of bodies turning into what they are usually not, in this case money" (Clark, *Painting of Modern Life*, 102).

56. Horses and women come together for him as they do for Freud's little Hans, who is as afraid of seeing the horse's/woman's genitals as of discovering their absence. "Perhaps you saw something of Mummy's that was black, and it frightened you?" asks his father, trying to understand Hans's fear of a black horse. "Perhaps it was black hair near her widdler, when you were curious and looked." "But I didn't see her widdler," Hans replies, "defending himself," as his father explains. "Analysis of a Phobia," in Sigmund Freud, *The Complete Psychological Works*, trans. James Strachey, vol. 10 (London: Hogarth Press, 1955), 67.

57. Gustave Flaubert, *Madame Bovary* (Paris: Gallimard, 1972).

58. See Floyd Zulli, "Edmond de Goncourt's American Equestrienne," *French American Review* 3 (1979): 53–56.

59. The novel evokes the moment in circus history, at the beginning of the Third Republic, when equestrian spectacles were beginning to share space with acrobatics.

60. Edmond Goncourt, *Les Frères Zemganno* (Geneva: Éditions Slatkine, 1996), 193–94.

61. The Goncourts lamented the disappearance of those noble women of the eighteenth century whose role was primarily to decorate interiors with various "feminine" objects and furnishings. See Deborah Silverman, *Art Nouveau in Fin-de-Siècle France* (Berkeley: University of California Press, 1989), chap. 1.

62. Edmond Goncourt and Jules Goncourt, *Journal*, ed. Robert Ricatte, vol. 9 (Monaco: Fasquelle and Flammarion, 1956), 62.

63. Goncourt and Goncourt, 112.

64. In the story titled "Mathilde," a young woman of that name informs her lover that he is handsome only on horseback and that otherwise he disgusts her. *Les amazones de Paris* (Paris: E. Dentu, 1866), 111–16.

65. Goncourt, *Frères Zemganno*, 199.

66. Goncourt, 203.

67. As Deborah Silverman has demonstrated, neurasthenia was, for the Goncourts, a disease of artists, which gave evidence of the extreme refinement of their nervous systems. Silverman, *Art Nouveau*, 37.

68. This "adaptability" was also part of the discourse on Jews in the nineteenth century. For instance, Beaulieu writes that the Jew "adapts and assimilates himself to everything. This is his ruling faculty, as Mr. Taine would say." Anatole-Leroy Beaulieu, *Israel among the Nations: A Study of the Jews and Antisemitism*, trans. Frances Hellman (New York: Putnam, 1895), 178–79.

69. Pierre de Coubertin, "Equitation and Life," in *Essais de psychologies sportive* (Lausanne: Librairie Payot, 1913), 21.

70. Baron De Vaux, *Les écoles de cavalerie* (Paris: Rothschild, 1896), 13.

71. De Vaux, 6–7.

72. De Vaux, 8.

73. Pierre de Coubertin, "Spurs," in *Essais*, 79.

74. Vicomte de Hédouville, preface, *La femme à cheval* (Paris: Ollendoff, 1884).

75. Catulle Mendès, "Lettre," in Baron de Vaux, *Les femmes de sport* (Paris: Marpon et Flammarion, 1885), 111.

76. Gautier, *Mademoiselle de Maupin*, 282.

77. Octave Uzanne, *La femme à Paris, nos contemporaines* (Paris: Ancienne Maison Quantin, 1894), 197.

78. Mendès, "Lettre," 111.

79. Monsieur le Comte de Montigny, *Équitation des dames*, 2nd ed. (Paris: Librairie nouvelle, 1858), 4, 235. See also P. Vaucottes, who writes to his audience of amazons, "There is nothing left for you, Mesdames, but to bring back that old French gallantry that has been lost in this fin-de-siècle." *La femme à cheval, conseils pratiques* (Falaise: L. Régnault Trolonge, 1893), 43.

80. Baron de Vaux, *Les femmes de sport* (Paris: Marpon et Flammarion, 1885).

81. Uzanne, *Femme à Paris*, 201.

82. While the discourse connecting riding and impotence was primarily directed at men, women were warned that riding could cause abortions. It was also feared, as Maupassant's story suggests, that a woman's passion for her horse might deter her from her passion for men or desire for motherhood.

83. Aristide Fabre, *Amazones d'hier et d'aujourd'hui: Série de découpages* (Paris: Hachette, 1905).

CHAPTER SIX

1. *Buffalo Bill Cody's Wild West and Congress of the Rough Riders of the World*, advertising poster by Courier Litho Company (1896).

2. Robert Nye, *Masculinity and Male Codes of Honor in Modern France* (New York: Oxford University Press, 1993), 8.

3. Guy de Maupassant, "À cheval," in *Contes et nouvelles*, vol. 1 (Paris: Gallimard, 1974), 704 (future references will be cited parenthetically in the text).

4. "From the beginning, the vulture has eaten the dove; the wolf has eaten the lamb; the lion has devoured the sharp-horned buffalo; man has slain the lion with arrow, sword and gun. But the Horla will use man as we have used the horse and the ox: he will make us his chattel, his slave and his food by nothing more than the power of its will (Guy de Maupassant, "Le Horla," in *A Day in the Country and Other Stories*, trans. David Coward (New York: Oxford University Press, 1990), 297.

5. A homonym for the words *hors là*, which could translate as "out of here (or there)," the title refers to an unidentified and irrational force of either supernatural or psychological origin.

6. On the anxieties surrounding the woman rider, see my "Purebreds and Amazones: Saying Things with Horses in Nineteenth-Century France," *Differences* 11 (Spring 1999): 1–37, and chapter 5.

7. Eugen Weber, "Gymnastics and Sport in Fin-de-Siècle France," *American Historical Review* 76 (February 1971): 77–78.

8. On the centaur ideal in eighteenth-century England, see Monica Mattfeld, *Becoming Centaur: Eighteenth-Century Masculinity and English Horsemanship* (University Park: Pennsylvania State University Press, 2017).

9. Stendhal, *Le rouge et le noir* (Paris: Éditions Gallimard, 1972), 124; my translation. Further references to this edition will be cited parenthetically in the text.

10. Stendhal, 112.

11. Maya Longstaffe, "The Hero's Fall from Grace: From Lucien Leuwen on a High Horse to Hector de Gribelin à Cheval," *French Review* 68, no. 2 (1994): 239–50.

12. Longstaffe, 289.

13. Stendhal, "*Le rose et le vert*," in *Romans et nouvelles*, vol. 2 (Paris: Bibliothèque de la Pleiade, 1952), 1075–75.

14. Anne Martin-Fugier, *La vie élégante, ou La formation du Tout-Paris, 1815–1848* (Paris: Fayard, 1990), 332.

15. Stendhal, *Rose et le vert*, 1070.

16. Stendhal, 1070.

17. See Charles O'Keefe, "Horses, Movement, and the Paradox of Security in *La Chartreuse de Parme*," *French Review* 63 (December 1989): 250–59.

18. D. A. Miller, "Body Building and Textual Liberation," in *A New History of French Literature*, ed. Denis Holier (Cambridge, MA: Harvard University Press, 683).

19. J. C. Flugel, *The Psychology of Clothes* (London: Institute of Psycho-Analysis, 1930), 118.

20. See Abigail Solomon-Godeau, *Male Trouble: A Crisis in Representation* (London: Thames and Hudson, 1997).

21. Albert Cler, *La comédie à cheval, ou Manies et travers du monde équestre* (Paris: Ernest Boudin, 1842), 56. On the rise of the *amazone*, see also chapter 5.

22. Charles Baudelaire. "A Thorough-bred," in *Paris Spleen*, trans. Louise Varèse (New York: New Directions, 1970), 82.

23. Martin-Fugier, *Vie élégante*, 340.

24. Thorstein Veblen, *The Theory of the Leisure Class* (Boston: Houghton Mifflin, 1973), 142–43.

25. Thétard, *Merveilleuse histoire du cirque*, 14.

26. Thétard, 184.

27. Thétard, 184.

28. Ernest Molier, *Cirque Molier, 1880–1904* (Paris: Dupont, 1905), 18.

29. Nye, *Masculinity*, 9.

30. Molier, *Cirque Molier*, 185–92. The following excerpts from the press are taken from these pages in Molier.

31. Cited in Molier, 191.

32. Molier, chap. 4.

33. Tamar Garb, *Bodies of Modernity* (London: Thames and Hudson, 1998), 83.

34. Katharine Lochnan, ed., "Introduction," in *Seductive Surfaces: The Art of Tissot* (New Haven, CT: Yale University Press, 1999), xii.

35. Garb, *Bodies of Modernity*, 100.

36. I borrow the term "(be)hindsight" from Lee Edelman, "Seeing Things: Representation, the Scene of Surveillance, and the Spectacle of Gay Male Sex," in *Inside/Out: Lesbian Theories, Gay Theories*, ed. Diana Fuss (New York: Routledge, 1991), 103.

37. Baron De Vaux, *L'équitation en France: Les écoles de cavalerie* (Paris: Rothschild, 1896).

38. Peter Stallybrass and Allon White, *The Politics and Poetics of Transgression* (Ithaca, NY: Cornell University Press, 1986), 5.

39. Marcus Verhagen, "The Poster in Fin-de-Siècle Paris: That Mobile and Degenerate Art," in *Cinema and the Invention of Modern Life*, ed. Leo Charney and Vanessa Schwartz (Berkeley: University of California Press, 1995), 129n50.

40. Daniel Lesueur, *Névrosée* (Paris: Alphonse Lemerre, 1892). Subsequent citations will be noted parenthetically in the text. Translations are my own.

41. According to sports enthusiast Pierre de Coubertin, "a man who likes to put on breeches, boots, and spurs only to look at himself in the mirror would be a sick man, and

that's all." See his "La psychologie du costume sportif," in *Essais de psychologie sportive* (Lausanne: Librairie Payot, 1913), 81.

42. Stallybrass and White, 182–83.

43. "It will be remarked that these recognitions are often made by women and children—that is to say, by precisely the most impressionable persons," he writes in Gustave Le Bon, *The Crowd: A Study of the Popular Mind* (Marietta, GA: Larlin, 1982), 29. And, not surprisingly, they are more like *le peuple* and like animals. Just as individuals in crowds are said to become more like animals, they also become more like women. "Crowds are everywhere distinguished by feminine characteristics," he writes, adding moreover that "Latin crowds are the most feminine of all" (20).

44. Gustave Le Bon, "La psychologie des femmes et les effets de leur éducation actuelle," *Revue scientifique* 46 (October 11, 1890): 452.

45. Robert Nye, "Degeneration, Neurasthenia and the Culture of Sport in Belle Époque France," in "Decadence," special issue, *Journal of Contemporary History* 7 (January 1981): 51–68, 60.

46. De Vaux, *Écoles de cavalerie,* 6–8.

47. Pierre de Coubertin, "L'homme et l'animal," in *Essais de psychologies sportive* (Lausanne: Librairie Payot, 1913), 87.

48. Georges Rouhet Edmond Desbonnet, *L'art de créer le pur-sang humain* (Paris: Berger-Levrault, 1908), lxvii. Future page references will be included in the text.

49. Anson Rabinbach, *The Human Motor* (Berkeley: University of California Press, 1990), 64–68.

50. Rouhet and Desbonnet, lxxii.

51. Rouhet and Desbonnet, lxxv.

52. On the use of classical statuary in the photography of *La culture physique,* see Garb, *Bodies of Modernity,* chap. 2.

53. Coubertin, "Homme et l'animal," 89.

54. Coubertin, "Le sport peut-il enrayer la névrose universelle?" in *Essais,* 164.

55. Coubertin, "Équitation et la vie," in *Essais,* 22.

56. Coubertin, "Remèdes sportifs pour les neurasthéniques," in *Essais,* 245.

57. Pierre Bourdieu, "Sport and Social Class," *Information sur les sciences* 17 (June 1978): 824.

58. Pierre de Coubertin, *Olympisme: Selected Writings,* ed. Norgert Muller (Lausanne: Comité international olympique, 2000), 178.

59. Gustave Le Bon, *L'équitation actuelle et ses principes,* 5th ed. (1922; repr. Paris: Éditions Jean-Michel Place, 1990), 127.

60. Catherine Rouvier, *Les idées politiques de Gustave Le Bon* (Paris: PUF, 1986), 228.

61. "La psychologie des femmes et les effets de leur éducation actuelle," *Revue scientifique* 46 (October 11, 1890): 449–60, 452.

62. Le Bon, "Psychologie des femmes," 460.

63. Editorial in *French Woman,* no. 1, cited in Françoise Labridy-Poncelet, "Imaginaries féminins et pratiques sportives," in *Les athlètes de la république,* ed. Pierre Arnaud (Paris: Harmatton, 1997), 317.

64. Pierre de Coubertin, "Les femmes aux Jeux Olympiques," *Revue Olympique,* July

1912; reprinted in *Olympisme: Selected Writings*, ed. Norbert Muller (Lausanne: Comité international olympique, 2000), 711–13.

65. John Berger, *Ways of Seeing* (New York: Penguin, 1972), 47.

CHAPTER SEVEN

1. On the Idéologues, see chapter 2.

2. On research into reflex as a precursor to ideas of the unconscious, see Marcel Gauchet, *L'inconscient cérébral* (Paris: Éditions du Seuil, 1992).

3. Gauchet, 111.

4. Jean-Joseph Menuret de Chambaud, "Oeconomie animale," in *Encyclopédie*, ed. Denis Diderot and Jean le Rond d'Alembert, 11:360–66, https://artflsrv03-uchicago-edu.ezproxy.wesleyan.edu/philologic4/encyclopedie1117/navigate/11/1905/.

5. See Philippe Huneman, "Animal Economy: Anthropology and the Rise of Psychiatry from the *Encyclopédie* to the Alienists," in *Anthropology and the Enlightenment*, ed. Larry Wolff and Marco Cipolloni (Stanford, CA: Stanford University Press, 2007), 265.

6. See, for instance, Teresa Brennan, *The Transmission of Affect* (Ithaca, NY: Cornell University Press, 2004); Brian Massumi, *The Politics of Affect* (Cambridge: Polity, 2015); Melissa Gregg and Gregory Seigworth, *The Affect Theory Reader* (Durham, NC: Duke University Press, 2010).

7. Brennan, *Transmission of Affect*, 17; cited in Robert Nye, *The Origins of Crowd Psychology: Gustave Le Bon and the Crisis of Mass Democracy in the Third Republic* (London: Sage, 1975), 92.

8. On the two branches of psychology see Jan Goldstein, *Console and Classify: The French Psychiatric Profession in the Nineteenth Century* (Cambridge: Cambridge University Press, 1987), 242.

9. Goldstein, 201.

10. Gustave Flaubert, *Madame Bovary* (Paris: Folio, 1976), chap. 6.

11. Brady Brower, *Unruly Spirits: The Science of Psychic Phenomena in Modern France* (Urbana: University of Illinois Press, 2011), xxii–xxiii.

12. Claude Bernard, *Introduction to Experimental Medicine* (1865); cited in Brower, xxiii.

13. Brower, 21. See also Jacqueline Carroy, "Magnétisme, hypnose et philosophie," in *Importance de l'hypnose*, ed. Isabelle Stengers (Paris: Empêcheurs de penser en rond, 1993), 169–92.

14. On magnetizing a horse, see Adam Crabtree, *From Mesmer to Freud: Magnetic Sleep and the Roots of Psychological Healing* (New Haven, CT: Yale University Press, 1993), 68, and Robert Darnton, *Mesmerism and the End of the Enlightenment in France* (Cambridge, MA: Harvard University Press, 1968), 68. See also *L'Hermès: Journal du magnétisme animale*, vol. 4 (Paris: Levi, 1829), 163, which tells of a *cheval fougueux* who was magnetized in 1826 so he could be shod. After being given a few "passes," the horse became soft and stood calmly for shoeing, to the great surprise of the assistants.

15. Jean-Didier Vincent, "Animalité de la pensée et subjectivité animale," in Stengers, *Importance de l'hypnose*, 153, 152.

16. Vincent, 152.

17. François Roustang, *Influence* (Paris: Éditions de Minuit, 1990), 68–69.

18. Darnton, *Mesmerism*, 40.

19. Darnton, 119.

20. George Boas, *French Philosophies of the Romantic Period* (Baltimore: Johns Hopkins University Press, 1925), 26.

21. Boas, 26; Goldstein, *Console and Classify*, 246.

22. Boas, 25–26.

23. According to Henri Ellenberger, "the influence of magnetism was much stronger among groups of spiritualistic, mystical, and esoteric philosophers, as well as in Romantic circles." Ellenberger, *The Discovery of the Unconscious* (New York: Basic Books, 1970), 161.

24. Honoré de Balzac, *Ursule Mirouët* (Paris: Flammarion, 1928).

25. On the rather vague notion of *soi pour soi* developed especially by Geoffroy Saint-Hilaire, see Toby Appel, "The Cuvier-Geoffroy Debate and the Structure of Nineteenth-Century Zoology" (PhD diss., Princeton University, 1975), 182–83.

26. Christopher Rivers, *Face Value: Physiognomical Thought and the Legible Body in Marivaux, Lavater, Balzac, Gautier and Zola* (Madison: University of Wisconsin Press, 1994), 110–11.

27. Gretchen Besser, *Balzac's Concept of Genius* (Geneva: Librairie Droz, 1969), 137.

28. George Frederic Parsons, Introduction, in Balzac, *Louis Lambert* (Boston: Roberts Brothers, 1890), clv.

29. Edgar Allen Poe, *The Philosophy of Animal Magnetism* (Philadelphia: Patterson and White, 1928), 63, 99, 112.

30. On this see Ceri Crossley, *Consumable Metaphors: Attitudes towards Animals and Vegetarianism in Nineteenth-Century France* (New York: Peter Lang, 2005), 28–29.

31. Susanna Barrows, *Distorting Mirrors: Visions of the Crowd in Late Nineteenth-Century France* (New Haven, CT: Yale University Press, 1981), 77.

32. Barrows, 78, 84.

33. Émile Zola, *Germinal*, trans. Roger Pearson (New York: Penguin Books, 2004), 15, 45. Future references will be given parenthetically in the text.

34. This idea that different individuals will represent different lines of heredity rather than mixing them will be even more pronounced in Le Bon.

35. Barrows, *Distorting Mirrors*, 78.

36. Gleaning from the writings of veterinarians and miners of the period, Éric Baratay similarly writes that it is possible to "mettre l'accent sur des fortes différences individuelles entre les chevaux, des différences dans la psychologie et la façon de ressentir le même environnement." *Le point de vue animal: Une autre version de l'histoire* (Paris: Seuil, 2012), 107–8.

37. Cited in Naomi Schor, *Zola's Crowds* (Baltimore: Johns Hopkins University Press, 1978), 43.

38. See Barrows, *Distorting Mirrors*, 111.

39. What purpose or value this pity for animals will have is unclear. It would be almost another hundred years before the last horse descended into a mine (see Baratay,

Point de vue animal, 33–36). For a fictionalized account of the ineffectiveness of the Humane Society in this regard, see Thalia Field, *Experimental Animals: A Reality Fiction* (New York: Solid Objects, 2016).

40. "We oppose epidemic to filiation, contagion to heredity, peopling by contagion to sexual reproduction, sexual production. Bands, human or animal, proliferate by contagion, epidemics, battlefields, and catastrophes." Gilles Deleuze and Félix Guattari, *A Thousand Plateaus: Capitalism and Schizophrenia*, trans. Brian Massumi (Minneapolis: University of Minnesota Press, 1988), 241.

41. Letter to Georges Sand, September 8, 1871, in *The Letters of Gustave Flaubert, 1857–1880*, trans. Francis Steegmuller (Cambridge, MA: Harvard University Press, 1982), 180.

42. Pierre Hachet-Souplet, *La genèse des instincts: Étude experimentale* (Paris: Flammarion, 1912), 3.

43. Laura Otis, *Organic Memory: History and the Body in the Late Nineteenth and Early Twentieth Centuries* (Lincoln: University of Nebraska Press, 1994), 53.

44. Gustave Le Bon, *The Crowd: A Study of the Popular Mind* (Marietta, GA: Larlin, 1982), xx.

45. On Le Bon's notion of the *race historique*, see Catherine Rouvier, *Les idées politiques de Gustave Le Bon* (Paris: PUF, 1986), 68–69.

46. Gustave Le Bon, Preface, in *L'équitation actuelle et ses principes* (Paris: Éditions Jean-Michel Place, 1990), xvi.

47. Le Bon, 121.

48. Preface, in Le Bon, *L'équitation actuelle et ses principes*, 4th ed. (Paris: Flammarion, 1923), ix.

49. Friedrich Nietzsche, *"Twilight of the Idols" and "The Anti-Christ,"* trans. R. J. Hollingdale (New York: Penguin, 1990), 87.

50. Nietzsche, 102, 110.

51. Nietzsche, 87.

52. Roland Barthes, *Camera Lucida*, trans. Richard Howard (New York: Farrar, Straus and Giroux, 1981), 117.

53. Nietzsche, *Twilight of the Idols*, 87.

54. Vincianne Despret, "The Body We Care For: Figures of Anthropo-zoo-genesis," *Body and Society* 10, no. 2–3 (2004): 111–34. See also Paul Patton, "Language, Power and the Training of Horses," in *Zoontologies*, ed. Cary Wolfe (Minneapolis: University of Minnesota Press, 2003).

55. Quoted in Vicki Hearne, *Adam's Task: Calling Animals by Name* (Pleasantville, NY: Common Reader Editions, 2000), 115.

56. Vincent, "Animalité de la pensée," 152.

57. Frans de Waal, *The Bonobo and the Atheist* (New York: Norton, 2013), 132. See also Kari Weil, "Empathy," in *The Edinburgh Companion to Animal Studies*, ed. Lynn Turner, Ron Broglio, and Undine Sellbach (Edinburgh: Edinburgh University Press, 2018), 126–39.

58. Ruth Leys, "The Turn to Affect: A Critique," *Critical Inquiry* 37 (Spring 2011): 470. See also Lisa Blackman, *Immaterial Bodies: Affect, Embodiment, Mediation* (London: Sage, 2012).

59. Donna Haraway, *When Species Meet* (Minneapolis: University of Minnesota Press, 2008), 16–17.

60. I discuss Deleuze's discounting of the past in Kari Weil, *Thinking Animals: Why Animal Studies Now?* (New York: Columbia University Press, 2012), chap. 6.

61. Hearne, *Adam's Task*, 42.

62. Judith Butler, *Senses of the Subject* (New York: Fordham University Press, 2015), 15.

63. "Entretien avec Dominique Lestel," in *Libérer les animaux, Critique*, no. 747–48 (August-September 2009): 809.

64. Lestel, 810.

65. On this point see my account of Gary Francione in *Thinking Animals*, chap. 8.

66. On the possibility of rendering domestic relations just from a political perspective, see Sue Donaldson and Will Kymlicka, *Zoopolis: A Political Theory of Animal Rights* (London: Oxford University Press, 2013), chap. 4.

AFTERWORD

1. Peter Schjeldahl, "Delacroix's High Performance," *New Yorker*, October 1, 2018, https://www.newyorker.com/magazine/2018/10/01/delacroixs-high-performance.

INDEX

Page numbers followed by *f* refer to figures.